POWERPOINT™ 4

FOR WINDOWS®

FOR

DUMMIES®

POWERPOINT™ 4
FOR WINDOWS®
FOR
DUMMIES®

by Doug Lowe

IDG Books Worldwide, Inc.
An International Data Group Company

Foster City, CA ♦ Chicago, IL ♦ Indianapolis, IN ♦ Braintree, MA ♦ Southlake, TX

PowerPoint™ 4 For Windows® For Dummies®

Published by
IDG Books Worldwide, Inc.
An International Data Group Company
919 E. Hillsdale Blvd.
Suite 400
Foster City, CA 94404

Library of Congress Catalog Card No.: 94-75724

ISBN: 1-56884-161-2

Printed in the United States of America

10 9 8 7 6

1B/RQ/QU/ZW/IN

Distributed in the United States by IDG Books Worldwide, Inc.

Distributed by Macmillan Canada for Canada; by Computer and Technical Books for the Caribbean Basin; by Contemporanea de Ediciones for Venezuela; by Distribuidora Cuspide for Argentina; by CITEC for Brazil; by Ediciones ZETA S.C.R. Ltda. for Peru; by Editorial Limusa SA for Mexico; by Transworld Publishers Limited in the United Kingdom and Europe; by Al-Maiman Publishers & Distributors for Saudi Arabia; by Simron Pty. Ltd. for South Africa; by IDG Communications (HK) Ltd. for Hong Kong; by Toppan Company Ltd. for Japan; by Addison Wesley Publishing Company for Korea; by Longman Singapore Publishers Ltd. for Singapore, Malaysia, Thailand, and Indonesia; by Unalis Corporation for Taiwan; by WS Computer Publishing Company, Inc. for the Philippines; by WoodsLane Pty. Ltd. for Australia; by WoodsLane Enterprises Ltd. for New Zealand.

For general information on IDG Books Worldwide's books in the U.S., please call our Consumer Customer Service department at 800-762-2974. For reseller information, including discounts and premium sales, please call our Reseller Customer Service department at 800-434-3422.

For information on where to purchase IDG Books Worldwide's books outside the U.S., contact IDG Books Worldwide at 415-655-3021 or fax 415-655-3295.

For information on translations, contact Marc Jeffrey Mikulich, Director, Foreign & Subsidiary Rights, at IDG Books Worldwide, 415-655-3018 or fax 415-655-3295.

For sales inquiries and special prices for bulk quantities, write to the address above or call IDG Books Worldwide at 415-655-3200.

For information on using IDG Books Worldwide's books in the classroom, or ordering examination copies, contact the Education Office at 800-434-2086 or fax 817-251-8174.

For authorization to photocopy items for corporate, personal, or educational use, please contact Copyright Clearance Center, 222 Rosewood Drive, Danvers, MA 01923, or fax 508-750-4470.

About the Author

Doug Lowe has written more than 15 computer books (including IDG's *Networking For Dummies*) and knows how to present technobabble in a style that is both entertaining and enlightening. He is a contributing editor to *DOS Resource Guide* magazine.

Welcome to the world of IDG Books Worldwide.

IDG Books Worldwide, Inc., is a subsidiary of International Data Group, the world's largest publisher of computer-related information and the leading global provider of information services on information technology. IDG was founded more than 25 years ago and now employs more than 7,700 people worldwide. IDG publishes more than 250 computer publications in 67 countries (see listing below). More than 70 million people read one or more IDG publications each month.

Launched in 1990, IDG Books Worldwide is today the #1 publisher of best-selling computer books in the United States. We are proud to have received 8 awards from the Computer Press Association in recognition of editorial excellence and three from Computer Currents' First Annual Readers' Choice Awards, and our best-selling *...For Dummies®* series has more than 19 million copies in print with translations in 28 languages. IDG Books Worldwide, through a joint venture with IDG's Hi-Tech Beijing, became the first U.S. publisher to publish a computer book in the People's Republic of China. In record time, IDG Books Worldwide has become the first choice for millions of readers around the world who want to learn how to better manage their businesses.

Our mission is simple: Every one of our books is designed to bring extra value and skill-building instructions to the reader. Our books are written by experts who understand and care about our readers. The knowledge base of our editorial staff comes from years of experience in publishing, education, and journalism — experience which we use to produce books for the '90s. In short, we care about books, so we attract the best people. We devote special attention to details such as audience, interior design, use of icons, and illustrations. And because we use an efficient process of authoring, editing, and desktop publishing our books electronically, we can spend more time ensuring superior content and spend less time on the technicalities of making books.

You can count on our commitment to deliver high-quality books at competitive prices on topics you want to read about. At IDG Books Worldwide, we continue in the IDG tradition of delivering quality for more than 25 years. You'll find no better book on a subject than one from IDG Books Worldwide.

John J. Kilcullen

John Kilcullen
President and CEO
IDG Books Worldwide, Inc.

IDG Books Worldwide, Inc., is a subsidiary of International Data Group, the world's largest publisher of computer-related information and the leading global provider of information services on information technology. International Data Group publishes over 250 computer publications in 67 countries. Seventy million people read one or more International Data Group publications each month. International Data Group's publications include: **ARGENTINA:** Computerworld Argentina, GamePro, Infoworld, PC World Argentina; **AUSTRALIA:** Australian Macworld, Client/Server Journal, Computer Living, Computerworld, Digital News, Network World, PC World, Publishing Essentials, Reseller; **AUSTRIA:** Computerwelt, PC TEST; **BELARUS:** PC World Belarus; **BELGIUM:** Data News; **BRAZIL:** Annuário de Informática, Computerworld Brazil, Connections, Super Game Power, Macworld, PC World Brazil, Publish Brazil, SUPERGAME; **BULGARIA:** Computerworld Bulgaria, Networkworld/Bulgaria, PC & MacWorld Bulgaria; **CANADA:** CIO Canada, ComputerWorld Canada, InfoCanada, Network World Canada, Reseller World; **CHILE:** Computerworld Chile, GamePro, PC World Chile; **COLUMBIA:** Computerworld Colombia, GamePro, PC World Colombia; **COSTA RICA:** PC World Costa Rica/Nicaragua; **THE CZECH AND SLOVAK REPUBLICS:** Computerworld Czechoslovakia, Elektronika Czechoslovakia, PC World Czechoslovakia; **DENMARK:** Communications World, Computerworld Danmark, Macworld Danmark, PC World Danmark, PC World Danmark Supplements, TECH World; **DOMINICAN REPUBLIC:** PC World Republica Dominicana; **ECUADOR:** PC World Ecuador, GamePro; **EGYPT:** Computerworld Middle East, PC World Middle East; **EL SALVADOR:** PC World Centro America; **FINLAND:** MikroPC, Tietoverkko, Tietoviikko; **FRANCE:** Distributique, Golden, Info PC, Le Guide du Monde Informatique, Le Monde Informatique, Reseaux & Telecoms; **GERMANY:** Computer Business, Computerwoche, Computerwoche Extra, Computerwoche Focus, Electronic Entertainment, GamePro, I/M Information Management, Macwelt, PC Welt; **GREECE:** GamePro, Macworld & Publish; **GUATEMALA:** PC World Centro America; **HONDURAS:** PC World Centro America; **HONG KONG:** Computerworld Hong Kong, PCWorld Hong Kong, Publish in Asia; **HUNGARY:** ABCD CD-ROM, Computerworld Szamitastechnika, PC & Mac World Hungary, PC-X Magazine; **INDIA:** Computerworld India, PC World India, Publish in Asia; **INDONESIA:** InfoKomputer PC World, Komputek Computerworld, Publish in Asia; **IRELAND:** ComputerScope, PC Live!; **ISRAEL:** PC World 32 BIT, People & Computers; **ITALY:** Computerworld Italia, Computerworld Italia Special Editions, Lotus Italia, Macworld Italia, Networking Italia, PC Shopping, PC World Italia, PC World/Walt Disney; **JAPAN:** Macworld Japan, Nikkei Personal Computing, SunWorld Japan, Windows World Japan; **KENYA:** East African Computer News; **KOREA:** Hi-Tech Information/Computerworld, Macworld Korea, PC World Korea, Macworld; **MACEDONIA:** PC World Macedonia; **MALAYSIA:** Computerworld Malaysia, PC World Malaysia, Publish in Asia; **MEXICO:** Computerworld Mexico, GamePro, Macworld, PC World Mexico; **MYANMAR:** PC World Myanmar; **NETHERLANDS:** Computable, Computer! Totaal, LAN Magazine, Macworld, Net Magazine; **NEW ZEALAND:** Computer Buyer, Computerworld New Zealand, MTB, Network World, PC World New Zealand; **NICARAGUA:** PC World Costa Rica/Nicaragua; **NIGERIA:** PC World Africa; **NORWAY:** Computerworld Norge, Computerworld Privat, CW Rapport Klient/Tjener, CW Rapport Nettverk & Telecom, CW Rapport Offentlig Sektor, IDG's KURSGUIDE, Macworld Norge, Multimedia World, PC World Ekspress, PC World Nettverk, PC World Norge, PC World's Produktguide, Windows Spesial; **PAKISTAN:** Computerworld Pakistan, PC World Pakistan; **PANAMA:** GamePro, PC World Panama; **PARAGUAY:** PC World Paraguay; **P. R. OF CHINA:** China Computerworld, China Infoworld, Computer & Communication, Electronic Product World, Electronics Today, Game Camp, PC World China, Popular Computer Week, Software World, Telecom Product World; **PERU:** Computerworld Peru, GamePro, PC World Profesional Peru, PC World Peru; **POLAND:** Computerworld Poland, Computerworld Special Report, Macworld, Networld, PC World Komputer; **PHILIPPINES:** Computerworld Philippines, PC Digest, Publish in Asia; **PORTUGAL:** Cerebro/PC World, Correio Informático/Computerworld, Mac•In/PC•In Portugal; **PUERTO RICO:** PC World Puerto Rico; **ROMANIA:** Computerworld Romania, PC World Romania, Telecom Romania; **RUSSIA:** Computerworld Rossiya, Network World Russia, PC World Russia; **SINGAPORE:** Computerworld Singapore, PC World Singapore, Publish in Asia; **SLOVENIA:** MONITOR; **SOUTH AFRICA:** Computing S.A., Dealer World, Macworld South Africa, Network World S.A., Software World; **SPAIN:** Computerworld España, COMUNICACIONES WORLD, Dealer World, Macworld España, PC World España; **SWEDEN:** CAP&Design, Computer Sweden, Corporate Computing, MacWorld, Maxi Data, MikroDatorn, Natverk & Kommunikation, PC/Aktiv, PC World, Windows World; **SWITZERLAND:** Computerworld Schweiz, Macworld Schweiz, PCtip; **TAIWAN:** Computerworld Taiwan, Macworld Taiwan, PC World Taiwan, Publish in Asia; **THAILAND:** Thai Computerworld, Publish in Asia; **TURKEY:** Computerworld Monitör, MACWORLD Turkiye, PC WORLD Turkiye; **UKRAINE:** Computerworld Kiev, Computers & Software Magazine, PC World Ukraine; **UNITED KINGDOM:** Acorn User, Amiga Action, Amiga Computing, Amiga, Appletalk, CD Powerplay, CD-ROM Now, Computing, Connexion, GamePro, Lotus Magazine, Macaction, Macworld, Open Computing, Parents and Computers, PC Home, PC Works, The WEB; **UNITED STATES:** Cable in the Classroom, CD Review, CIO Magazine, Computerworld, Computerworld Client/Server Journal, Digital Video Magazine, DOS World, Electronic, InfoWorld, I-Way, Macworld, Maximize, MULTIMEDIA WORLD, Network World, PC World, PUBLISH, SWATPro Magazine, Video Event, WebMaster; **URUGUAY:** PC World Uruguay; **VENEZUELA:** Computerworld Venezuela, GamePro, PC World Venezuela; and **VIETNAM:** PC World Vietnam   10/17/95

Dedication

To Debbie, Rebecca, Sarah, and Bethany

Acknowledgments

Thanks to Kezia Endsley for whipping this book into shape and not yelling at me when I was a day or two late, and to Becky Whitney and Michael Partington for their editorial and technical prowess. Thanks also to the Branch San Mateoan Janna Custer for giving me a chance to write a book about one of my favorite programs, and to Megg Bonar for not changing her phone number. Oops, gotta run, another deadline coming up...

The publisher would like to give special thanks to Patrick J. McGovern, without whom this book would not have been possible.

Credits

Senior Vice President and Publisher
Milissa L. Koloski

Associate Publisher
Diane Graves Steele

Brand Manager
Judith A. Taylor

Editorial Managers
Kristin A. Cocks
Mary Corder

Product Development Manager
Mary Bednarek

Editorial Executive Assistant
Richard Graves

Editorial Assistants
Constance Carlisle
Chris H. Collins
Kevin Spencer

Production Director
Beth Jenkins

Production Assistant
Jacalyn L. Pennywell

Supervisor of Project Coordination
Cindy L. Phipps

Supervisor of Page Layout
Kathie S. Schnorr

Supervisor of Graphics and Design
Shelley Lea

Reprint Coordination
Tony Augsburger
Theresa Sánchez-Baker
Todd Klemme

Blueline Coordinator
Patricia R. Reynolds

Media/Archive Coordination
Leslie Popplewell
Melissa Stauffer
Jason Marcuson

Project Editor
Kezia Endsley

Editor
Rebecca Whitney

Technical Reviewer
Michael Partington

Graphics Coordination
Gina Scott
Angela F. Hunckler
Carla C. Radzikinas

Production Page Layout
Valery Bourke
Mary Breidenbach
Chris Collins
Dominique DeFelice
Sherry Gomoll
Drew R. Moore

Proofreaders
Chuck Hutchinson
Dwight Ramsey

Indexer
Steve Rath

Book Design
University Graphics

Cover Design
Kavish + Kavish

Contents at a Glance

Cartoons at a Glance

By Rich Tennant

page 250

"IT WAS BETWEEN THAT AND NEW CLASSROOM COMPUTERS."

page 6

"Well, a graphics presentation package helps show you the connection between seemingly disparate items, like, oh say, that tie you're wearing, and this bowl of dog vomit."

page 7

"This color scheme is really going to give our presentation style!"

page 309

"It's powerful enough for me."

page 300

"IF YOU THINK WE'VE HAD TOUGH AUDIENCES UP TO NOW, WAIT'LL YOU MEET THIS GUY."

page 277

"There's been some concern, Roy, that, as Director of Finance, you've been spending a little too much time with our new graphics presentation package."

page 239

"AND TO COMPLETE OUR MULTI MEDIA PRESENTATION,..."

page 87

"These kidnappers are clever, Lieutenant... Look at this ransom note, the use of 4-color graphics to highlight the victim's photograph. And the fonts! They must be creating their own... must be over 35 typefaces here..."

page 230

"MAINFRAME INTEGRATION"

page 155

"And, as you can see by slide 9, clowning is up 20%."

Table of Contents

Introduction

● ●

*W*elcome to *PowerPoint 4 For Windows For Dummies,* the book written especially for those who are forced to use PowerPoint at gunpoint and want to learn just enough to save their necks.

Do you ever find yourself in front of an audience, no matter how small, flipping through flip charts or shuffling through a stack of handwritten transparencies? You need PowerPoint! Have you always wanted to take your notebook computer with you to impress a client at lunch, but don't know what to do with it between trips to the salad bar? You need PowerPoint! Are you H. Ross Perot and you just spent $5 million for a 30-minute commercial, and you want to use some flip charts? You *really* need PowerPoint!

Or maybe you're one of those hapless chaps who bought Microsoft Office because it was such a bargain and you needed a Windows word processor and spreadsheet anyway and hey, you're not even sure what PowerPoint is, but it was free. Who can resist a bargain like that?

Either way, you're holding the perfect book right here in your magic-marker-stained hands. Help is here, within these humble pages.

This book talks about PowerPoint in everyday — and often irreverent — terms. No lofty prose here; the whole thing checks in at about the fifth-grade reading level. I have no Pulitzer expectations for this book. My goal is to make an otherwise dull and lifeless subject at least tolerable, if not kind of fun.

About this Book

This isn't the kind of book you pick up and read from start to finish, as though it were a cheap novel. If I ever see you reading it at the beach, I'll kick sand in your face. This book is more like a reference, the kind of book you can pick up, turn to just about any page, and start reading. It has 27 chapters, each one covering a specific aspect of using PowerPoint — such as printing, changing colors, or using clip art. Appendix A tells you how to install PowerPoint on your computer.

Each chapter is divided into self-contained chunks, all related to the major theme of the chapter.

For example, the chapter on using clip art contains nuggets like these:

- ✔ Dropping in some clip art
- ✔ Moving, sizing, and stretching pictures
- ✔ Boxing, shading, and shadowing a picture
- ✔ Editing a clip art picture
- ✔ Adding your own pictures to the ClipArt Gallery
- ✔ Inserting pictures without using the ClipArt Gallery

You don't have to memorize anything in this book. It's a "need-to-know" book: You pick it up when you need to know something. Need to know how to create an organization chart? Pick up the book. Need to know how to override the Slide master? Pick up the book. Otherwise, put it down and get on with your life.

How to Use this Book

This book works like a reference. Start with the topic you want to learn about; look for it in the table of contents or in the index to get going. The table of contents is detailed enough that you should be able to find most of the topics you look for. If not, turn to the index, where you find even more detail.

When you've found your topic in the table of contents or the index, turn to the area of interest and read as much or as little as you need or want. Then close the book and get on with it.

This book is loaded with information, of course, so if you want to take a brief excursion into your topic, you're more than welcome. If you want to know all about Slide masters, read the chapter on templates and masters. If you want to know all about color schemes, read the chapter on color schemes. Read whatever you want. This is *your* book, not mine.

On occasion, this book directs you to use specific keyboard shortcuts to get things done. When you see something like this,

    Ctrl+Z

it means to hold down the Ctrl key while pressing the *Z* key and then release both together. Don't type the plus sign.

Sometimes I tell you to use a menu command, like this:

    File⇨Open

This line means to use the keyboard or mouse to open the File menu and then choose the Open command. (The underlined letters are the keyboard *hot keys* for the command. To use them, first press the Alt key. In the preceding example, you press and release the Alt key, press and release the F key, and then press and release the O key.)

Whenever I describe a message or information you see on-screen, it looks like this:

> *Are you having fun yet?*

Anything you are instructed to type appears in bold like so: Type **b:setup** in the Run dialog box. You type exactly what you see, with or without spaces.

Another nice feature of this book is that, the first time I discuss a certain button you need to click to accomplish the task at hand, the button appears in the margin. This way, you can easily locate it on your screen!

This book rarely directs you elsewhere for information — just about everything you need to know about using PowerPoint is right here. On occasion, I suggest that you turn to *DOS For Dummies* (by Dan Gookin) or *Windows For Dummies* (by Andy Rathbone) for more specific information about wildebeests and dilithium mining techniques — oops — I mean DOS and Windows. Both books are published by IDG Books Worldwide.

What You Don't Need to Read

Much of this book is skippable. I've carefully placed extra-technical information in self-contained sidebars and clearly marked them so that you can give them a wide berth. Don't read this stuff unless you just gots to know. Don't worry; I won't be offended if you don't read every word.

Foolish Assumptions

I make only three assumptions about you:

- ✔ You use a computer.
- ✔ You use Windows 3.1.
- ✔ You use or are thinking about using PowerPoint 4.

Nothing else. I don't assume that you're a computer guru who knows how to change a controller card or configure memory for optimal use. These types of computer chores are best handled by people who *like* computers. Hopefully, you are on speaking terms with such a person. Do your best to stay there.

How this Book Is Organized

Inside this book are chapters arranged in five parts. Each chapter is broken down into sections that cover various aspects of the chapter's main subject. The chapters have a logical sequence, so it makes sense to read them in order if you want. But you don't have to read it that way: You can flip the book open to any page and start reading.

Here's the lowdown on what's in each of the five parts:

Part I: Basic PowerPoint Stuff

In this part, you learn the basics of using PowerPoint. This is a good place to start if you're clueless about what PowerPoint is, let alone how to use it.

Part II: Dressing Up Your Presentations

The five chapters in this part show you how to make presentations that look good. Most important is the chapter about templates and masters, which control the overall look of a presentation. Get the template right and everything else falls into place.

Part III: Pictures, Charts, and Grunts

The six chapters in this part show you how to spice up an otherwise dreary presentation with clip art, graphs, drawings, organization charts, sealing wax, and other fancy stuff. It also shows you how to make your slides grunt like Tim Allen.

Part IV: Working with Files

Unfortunately, you can't live your entire life hiding under the shadow of PowerPoint's menus. Once in a while, you have to peer out into the real world for some routine housekeeping chores. That's what the four chapters in this part are all about.

Part V: The Part of Tens

This wouldn't be a *...For Dummies* book without lists of interesting snippets:
Ten PowerPoint Commandments, Ten Things That Often Go Wrong, Ten
PowerPoint Shortcuts, and more!

There's also a free bonus appendix that shows you how to install PowerPoint.
Sorry, no Ginsu knives.

Icons Used in this Book

As you are reading all this wonderful prose, you'll occasionally see the following
icons. They appear in the margins to draw your attention to important information. They are defined as follows:

Watch out! Some technical drivel is just around the corner. Read it only if you
have your pocket protector firmly attached.

Pay special attention to this icon — it tells you that some particularly useful
tidbit is at hand, perhaps a shortcut or a way of using a command you may not
have considered.

Danger! Danger! Danger! Stand back, Will Robinson!

Did I tell you about the memory course I took?

Pay attention; something interesting is on its way.

Stuff you may already know how to do if you use any of the other programs in
Microsoft Office, specifically Word for Windows 6 or Excel 5.

Where to Go from Here

Yes, you can get there from here. With this book in hand, you're ready to charge full speed into the strange and wonderful world of desktop presentations. Browse through the table of contents and decide where you want to start. Be bold! Be courageous! Be adventurous! Above all else, have fun!

The 5th Wave   **By Rich Tennant**

"Well, a graphics presentation package helps show you the connection between seemingly disparate items, like, oh say, that tie you're wearing, and this bowl of dog vomit."

Part I
Basic PowerPoint Stuff

The 5th Wave
By Rich Tennant

"This color scheme is really going to give our presentation style!"

In this part...

*J*ust a few short years ago, the term *presentation software* meant poster board and marker pens. But now, programs such as Microsoft's PowerPoint enable you to create spectacular presentations on your computer.

The chapters in this part comprise a barebones introduction to PowerPoint. You'll learn exactly what PowerPoint is and how to use it to create simple presentations. More advanced stuff like adding charts or using fancy text fonts is covered in later parts. This part is just the beginning. As a great king once advised, begin at the beginning, and go on 'til you come to the end; then stop.

Chapter 1
PowerPoint 101

This chapter is sort of the Kindergarten of PowerPoint. It takes your hand and walks you around, showing you some really basic stuff like how to start PowerPoint, how to save your work in a file, and how to print. It even explains what PowerPoint is, just in case you're starting at the very beginning. If you get tired midway through this chapter, feel free to have some milk and graham crackers and maybe even take a nap.

What in Sam Hill Is PowerPoint?

PowerPoint is the oddball program that comes with Microsoft Office. Most people buy Microsoft Office because it's a great bargain: you get Microsoft Word and Excel for less than it would cost to buy them separately. As an added bonus, you get Microsoft Mail, PowerPoint, a complete set of Ginsu knives, and a Binford VegaPneumatic Power Slicer and Dicer (always wear eye protection).

You know what Word is — a word processor, like WordPerfect but trendier. Excel is a spreadsheet kind of like Lotus 1-2-3, but with more ambition. But what the heck is PowerPoint? Does anybody know or care?

PowerPoint is a *desktop presentation* program. It's one of the coolest programs I know. If you've ever flipped a flip chart, headed over to an overhead projector, or slipped on a slide, you're going to love PowerPoint. With just a few clicks of the mouse, you can create presentations that bedazzle your audience and instantly sway them to your point of view, even if you're selling real estate on Mars, Ruble futures, or season tickets for the Mets.

PowerPoint is kind of like a word processor, except that it's geared towards producing *presentations* rather than *documents*. In PowerPoint lingo, a presentation consists of a sequence of *slides*. Once you've created the slides, you can print them on plain paper or on transparencies for overhead projection, or you can have them made into glorious 35mm color slides. You can print handouts with two, three, or six slides on each page, notes on the pages to help you bluff your way through your presentation, and a complete outline of your presentation.

Here are a few important features of PowerPoint:

- ✔ PowerPoint is a great time-saver for anyone who makes business presentations, whether you've been asked to speak in front of hundreds of people at a shareholders convention, a group of sales reps at a sales conference, or one-on-one with a potential client.

- ✔ PowerPoint is great also for teachers or conference speakers who want to back up their lectures with slides or overheads.

- ✔ You can use PowerPoint also to create fancy on-computer presentations, where the slides are displayed on-screen one at a time. You can embellish an on-computer presentation with all sorts of jazzy effects like slides, wipes, and dissolves. This process can get a bit theatrical, but it's loads of fun. It is an especially popular feature with insurance reps who own laptop computers.

✔ OK, not everybody buys PowerPoint as part of Microsoft Office. Some people buy it separately. I figured that if you bought PowerPoint by itself, you probably did it on purpose, so it's safe to assume that you already know what PowerPoint is (at least sort of). Heck, you didn't need to read this section anyway. I wrote this little section for the millions of innocent people who bought Microsoft Office just to get Word and Excel and have no idea what to do with PowerPoint other than use it as a bookend.

✔ Who in Sam Hill was Sam Hill?

TECHNICAL STUFF

PowerPoint lingo — you can't escape

Sorry, but if you're going to use PowerPoint, you'll have to get used to its own peculiar lingo. Here's a quick spin through the PowerPoint lexicon:

Presentation: All of the supporting materials you need to present information to an audience. The audience may be small (just one person) or large (63 million people tuned in to watch you in a presidential debate). In PowerPoint, a presentation consists of slides, presenter notes, handouts, and an outline.

Presentation file: A PowerPoint file that contains the presentation materials, the PowerPoint equivalent of a Microsoft Word document file or an Excel spreadsheet file. The three-character extension part of a PowerPoint filename is PPT.

Slide: One page of a PowerPoint presentation. You can set up the slide page to fit the dimensions of an overhead transparency, a 35mm film slide, or the actual computer screen.

Slide master: Sets up elements that appear on all slides, such as a background design, your name, the date, and so on.

Object: An element on a slide. Objects can contain text, clip art pictures, charts, organization charts, or other types of graphics. You cannot place text directly on a slide; instead, a slide must contain at least one text object if you want text to appear on the slide.

Title: Most slides have a text object called the title. The format of the title text is governed by the Slide master.

Body text: Most slides also have a text object called the body text. The body text usually (but not always) consists of a series of main points set off by bullets. The main points can have subpoints that are indented under the main points. (The subpoints can have sub-subpoints and sub-sub-subpoints, but let's not get ridiculous.) The format of body text is also controlled by the Slide master.

View: How you look at your presentation while working in PowerPoint. There are four views: Slide view, Outline view, Notes Pages view, and Slide Sorter view. Each view is best at a particular editing task.

Slide show: Displays slides in sequence on your computer screen. You can use slide show to preview the appearance of your slides before you print them, or you can use it to actually present your slides to your audience.

Starting PowerPoint

Here's the procedure for starting PowerPoint:

1. Get ready.

Light some votive candles. Take two Tylenol. Sit in the Lotus Position facing Redmond, WA and recite the Windows creed three times:

I will use Windows and I will like it. Click click.
I will use Windows and I will like it. Click click.
I will use Windows and I will like it. Click click.

2. Start your engines.

Turn your computer on. Hopefully, you have to flip only one switch to do that. But if your computer, monitor, and printer are plugged in separately, you'll have to turn each one on separately.

3. Start Windows.

If you're lucky, Windows starts right up when you start your computer. If it doesn't, you are greeted with the warm and friendly DOS prompt, which usually looks like C> or C\>. Close your eyes; don't look at it, lest you turn into a pillar of salt. Instead, type **WIN** and press the Enter key:

```
C:\> WIN
```

This command blasts you into the world of Windows, wherein PowerPoint is surely to be found.

4. Find the PowerPoint icon.

Next, you need to find the little picture, called an *icon*, that represents PowerPoint. It's shown in Figure 1-1. If you can't find the PowerPoint icon, it's probably nestled safely in a group window labeled "Microsoft Office." Find the Microsoft Office icon and double-click it and pray that the PowerPoint icon appears.

If you're not sure what I mean by *double-click,* read the following sidebar, "The mouse is your friend."

5. Start PowerPoint.

Having found the PowerPoint icon, double-click it. Then go get a cup of coffee. Unless you have a Binford 486-DX2 66 with 20M of RAM and alloy trim, PowerPoint takes forever to start up.

Figure 1-1:
The
PowerPoint
icon.

The mouse is your friend

Remember that scene in *Star Trek IV* when Scotty, having been zapped back into the 1980s and forced to use a primitive computer (it was a Macintosh), picked up the mouse and talked into it like a microphone? "Computer! Hello computer! Hmmph. How quaint."

You don't get very far with PowerPoint (or any other Windows program) until you learn how to use the mouse. You can try picking it up and talking into it if you want, but you don't get any better results than Scotty did.

Most mice have two or three buttons on top and a ball underneath. When you move the mouse, the ball rolls. The rolling motion is detected by little wheels inside the mouse and sent to your computer, which responds to your mouse movements by moving the mouse cursor on-screen. What will they think of next?

A mouse works best when used with a *mouse pad*, a small (7-inch × 9-inch or so) rubbery pad that gives better traction for the rolling ball on the mouse's rump. You can use the mouse directly on a desk surface, but it doesn't roll as smoothly.

Here's the lowdown on the various acts of mouse dexterity you are asked to perform as you use PowerPoint:

✔ To *move* or *point* the mouse means to move it so that the mouse cursor moves to a desired screen location, without pressing any mouse buttons. Remember to leave the mouse on the mouse pad as you move it; if you pick it up,

the ball doesn't roll and your movement doesn't register.

✔ To *click* means to press and release the left mouse button. Usually, you'll be asked to click something, which means to point to the something, and then click the left button.

✔ To *double-click* means to press and release the left mouse button twice, as quickly as you can.

✔ To *triple-click* means to click the left mouse button *three* times as quickly as you can. Right.

✔ To *right-click* means to click the right mouse button instead of the left.

✔ To *click and drag* something (also called simply *drag*) with the mouse means to point at it, press the left button (or right button, depending on the task), and move the mouse while holding down the button. When you arrive at your destination, you release the mouse button.

✔ To *stay* the mouse means to let go of the mouse and give it the command "Stay!" There is no need to raise your voice; speak in a normal but confident and firm voice. If your mouse starts to walk away, say "No," put it back in its original position, and repeat the command "Stay!" Under no circumstances should you strike your mouse. Remember, there are no bad mice.

What is all this stuff? (Making sense of the PowerPoint screen)

When you start PowerPoint, it greets you with a screen that's so cluttered with stuff you'll soon be ready to consider newsprint and markers as a viable alternative for your presentation. The center of the screen is mercifully blank, but all around the edges and tucked into every corner are little icons and buttons and menus and whatnot. What is all that stuff?

Figure 1-2 provides a road map to the PowerPoint screen. Look this map over briefly to get your bearings. North is up.

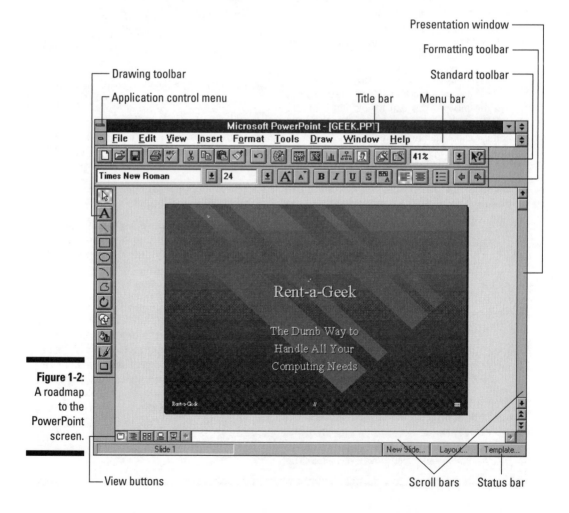

Figure 1-2: A roadmap to the PowerPoint screen.

Five items on the PowerPoint screen are worthy of your attention:

✔ Across the top of the screen, just below the Microsoft PowerPoint title, is the *menu bar*. PowerPoint's deepest and darkest secrets are hidden on the menu bar. Wear a helmet when exploring it.

✔ Just below the menu bar are two of the many *toolbars* PowerPoint offers you in an effort to make its most commonly used features easy to use. Each toolbar consists of a bunch of buttons you can click to perform common functions, provided you can figure out what the buttons stand for. The toolbar on the top is the *Standard toolbar;* immediately beneath it is the *Formatting toolbar.* Down the left side of the screen is the *Drawing toolbar.*

✔ Right smack in the middle of the screen is the *Presentation window.* That's where the presentation you're working on is displayed. Initially, it's completely blank. That's kind of boring, so I took the liberty of retrieving a presentation to make this figure more interesting. What you're looking at in Figure 1-2 is the first slide of a sales presentation for a fictitious computer consulting company named "Rent-a-Geek."

✔ At the bottom of the screen is the *status bar*, which tells you which slide is currently displayed (in this example, *Slide 1*). The status bar includes helpful buttons to create a new slide, change the layout of the slide that's showing in the window, or change the *template,* which governs the overall look of all the slides in a presentation.

✔ The *salad bar* is located ... well, actually there is no salad bar. I lied. There are really only four things worth noticing in Figure 1-2.

✔ You'll never get anything done if you feel that you have to understand every pixel of the PowerPoint screen before you can do anything. Don't worry about the stuff you don't understand; just concentrate on what you need to know to get the job done and worry about the bells and whistles later.

✔ There's lots of stuff crammed into the PowerPoint screen, enough stuff that the program works best if you let it run in *Full Screen* mode. If PowerPoint doesn't take over your entire screen, look for the upward-pointing arrowhead in the top right corner of PowerPoint's window. Click it to *maximize* the PowerPoint screen. PowerPoint overtakes your entire screen and the single upward-pointing arrowhead changes into two smaller arrowheads — one pointing up, the other pointing down.

✔ On the left bottom edge of the Presentation window is a series of View buttons. These buttons enable you to switch among PowerPoint's various *views,* or ways of looking at your presentation. Table 1-1 summarizes what each of these buttons does.

Table 1-1	View Buttons
Button	*What It Does*
▣	Switches to Slide view, which shows the slides as they appear when printed.
▣	Switches to Outline view, which enables you to focus on the content of your presentation rather than its appearance.
▦	Switches to Slide Sorter view, which enables you easily to rearrange the slides in your presentation.
▣	Switches to Notes Pages view, which enables you to add speaker notes so that you can remember what you want to say.
▣	Switches to Slide Show view, which displays your slides in an on-screen presentation.

If you're not sure about the function of any of the billions and billions of buttons that appear on the PowerPoint screen, simply point to the button with the mouse. After a second or so, a short description of the button's function pops up in a little yellow box. Most ingenious. It must have been raining too hard to go outside during recess one day, so the Microsoft programmers who were working on PowerPoint decided to stay indoors and add this nifty little feature.

Don't read this unless you already know WinWord

If you already know how to use Word for Windows, thank your lucky stars because you already know how to use many of PowerPoint's features. Here are a few examples of things you already know how to do:

✔ *Open a file:* Use the File⇨Open command or click the Open button on the Standard toolbar.

✔ *Save a file:* Use the File⇨Save or File⇨Save As command or click the Save button on the Standard toolbar.

✔ *Print a file:* Use the File⇨Print command or click the Print button on the Standard toolbar.

✔ *Cut, Copy, or Paste text:* Use the Ctrl+X, Ctrl+C, or Ctrl+V keyboard combinations.

✔ *Check a presentation for spelling errors:* Use the Tools⇨Spelling command or click the Spelling button on the Standard toolbar.

✔ *Change the format of selected text:* Use the Format⇨Font command or the controls on the Formatting toolbar, which work just as they do in Word 6. The keyboard shortcuts for formatting text — such as Ctrl+B for Bold or Ctrl+I for italic — work the same way too.

This list can go on and on. When in doubt about how to do something, try it the way you would in Word 6 and odds are it will work. On the other hand, you may end up shutting down the power grid for all of San Diego. It just depends.

How much should I tip?

When you start PowerPoint, you'll first see a helpful PowerPoint tip like the one shown in Figure 1-3. You have to click the OK button to dismiss this helpful tipmeister. (It helps if you shove a five-spot its way, too.)

Figure 1-3:
PowerPoint
greets you
each day
with a
helpful (or
annoying,
depending
on your
temperament)
tip.

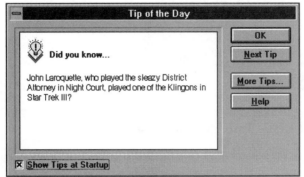

If you're the type who likes to learn a little something every day, you'll appreciate these tips. If this tips serve only as a daily reminder that you don't have a clue about what you're doing, you may want to throw them over a cliff. Fortunately, you can do that (without breaking any laws) by unchecking the check box that reads Show Tips at Startup so that the X goes away. Then click the OK button.

If you disable the tips and then later decide you want to see them again, don't fret, you can call them up by using the Help⇨Tip of the Day command. PowerPoint displays a different tip each day. If you don't want to wait all year to see all the tips, you can click the Next Tip button to look ahead. This is a great way to avoid doing real work.

Help me get started, wizard!

The next thing you'll see as a result of PowerPoint's ongoing efforts to make you realize you need to get a life is the innocent-looking dialog box shown in Figure 1-4.

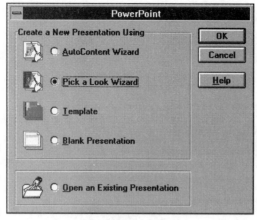

Figure 1-4:
Choose your
weapon.

PowerPoint gives you five options to choose from:

✔ *AutoContent Wizard:* This option practically builds a whole presentation for you by asking you basic questions about what you want to say. It is designed for true beginners who not only know nothing about PowerPoint but also know nothing about giving presentations. It's pretty limited but can help get you going.

The marketing folks at Microsoft want you to believe that the AutoContent writes your presentation for you, as if you just click the button and then go play a round of golf while PowerPoint does your research, organizes your thoughts, writes your text, and throws in a few good lawyer jokes to boot. Sorry. All the AutoContent Wizard does is create an outline for several common types of presentations. It doesn't do your thinking for you.

✔ *Pick-a-Look Wizard*: This option asks you some questions about how you want your presentation to look and then automatically sets up the appearance of your slides. This method is usually the most efficient to use when you need to create a new presentation. It enables you to choose from several slide styles, asks whether you want to create speaker notes, handouts, and outline pages, and asks for information you want to appear on each page, such as your name or your company's name, the date, and the slide number. Then it whizzes off and creates a presentation according to the formats you picked. The new presentation includes one slide to serve as a title slide. To finish the presentation, all you have to do is create additional slides and type the text for each new slide.

✔ *Template:* This option enables you to pick from one of the 150 predefined *templates* supplied with PowerPoint. The template you use governs the basic appearance of each slide in your presentation ... things like the background color, text font, and so on. The Pick-a-Look Wizard picks a template for you but does a little more formatting work than the Template option.

✔ *Blank Presentation:* This option is useful in two situations: (1) you're a computer whiz who is insulted by the shortcuts provided by the Pick-a-Look Wizard or Template options, or (2) you're an incredibly boring person and you *want* your presentations to have a blank sort of look to them.

✔ *Open an Existing Presentation:* You pick this option if you want to work a little more on that presentation you didn't quite finish yesterday, or if the presentation you want to create is so similar to the one you gave last month that there's no point in starting all over again.

To choose one of these options, click the appropriate check box; then click the OK button. You can bail out of this start-up dialog box altogether by clicking the Cancel button or pressing the Escape key. Doing so leaves you with a blank screen but enables you to use the menus or toolbars to create a new presentation or open an existing one.

"Click to add stuff"

If you use the Pick-a-Look Wizard to create a new presentation and immediately click the Finish button in the dialog box that follows, your presentation starts off with just one slide, a barebones title slide that looks something like Figure 1-5. PowerPoint sets up this slide with areas — called *placeholders* — where you can type a title and a subtitle. Unless the actual title of your presentation is "Click to add title" (which is unlikely, but I suppose possible), you'll want to change the title and subtitle before you continue.

Whenever you move the mouse cursor over a place where you can type text, the cursor changes from an arrow to what's lovingly called the *I-beam,* which you can use to support bridges or build aircraft carriers. Seriously, when the mouse cursor changes to an I-beam, you can click the mouse button and start typing text.

Here are a few important things to keep in mind when you begin adding your title:

✔ You can't capriciously type text anywhere you please on a PowerPoint slide. Text must be confined to *text objects* — rectangular areas of the slide designed specially for holding text. You'll learn more than you can possibly want to know about text objects in Chapter 2, so don't lose sleep over them tonight. The title slide created by the Pick-a-Look Wizard includes two text objects: one for the title, the other for the subtitle.

✔ When you click the mouse button when the cursor is an I-beam, a box appears around the text and an *insertion pointer* appears right at the spot where you clicked. PowerPoint then becomes like a word processor. Any characters you type at the keyboard are inserted into the text at the insertion pointer. You can use the Del or Backspace keys to demolish text, and you can use the arrow keys to move the insertion pointer around in the text object. If you press the Enter key, a new line of text begins within the text object.

✔ If you start typing without clicking anywhere, the text you type is entered into the title text object.

✔ When you're done typing text, press the Esc key or click the mouse anywhere outside of the text object.

In Chapter 2, you find many details about playing with text objects. So hold your horses. You've more important things to attend to first.

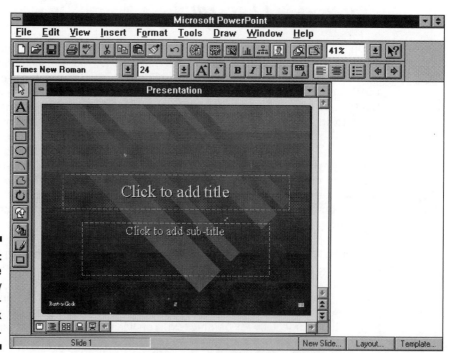

Figure 1-5:
A title slide created by the Pick-a-Look Wizard.

I Can't See the Whole Slide!

PowerPoint has an annoying habit of displaying your presentation in a small window sandwiched in among all its toolbars. When you first create a presentation, this window may not be as big as it can be. PowerPoint compensates by displaying your slides in miniature view or by lopping off the part of each slide that doesn't fit in the window.

To maximize this subwindow, click the upward-pointing arrow at the top right corner. The subwindow expands to fill all of the available space in the larger PowerPoint application window. You now have much more room to work and can see the whole slide.

There's really no reason to work on a presentation without first maximizing its window unless you plan on working with more than one presentation at a time. That's an advanced topic that you don't get to until Chapter 18, though. Certainly not something you want to mess with here.

If you still can't see all of each slide after maximizing the Presentation window, you have the zoom set too high. Reduce the zoom setting using the View⇨Zoom command or the Zoom control on the Standard toolbar. Usually, a zoom setting of 50 percent enables you to see the entire slide and still be able to read the text.

If for some reason you want to work with the zoom set so high that the entire slide doesn't fit in the window, PowerPoint calls up the scroll bars at the right and the bottom of the window. You can use these scroll bars to scoot the slide around so you can see the *zoomed* (magnified) parts that don't fit in the window.

50 Ways to Add a New Slide

Your audience will be pretty disappointed if the only slide you show them is the title slide that was generated by the Pick-a-Look wizard. To save your job, you'll probably want to add more slides to your presentation, maybe some slides that actually *say* something.

You're in luck! PowerPoint gives you about 50 ways to add new slides to your presentation. You learn only three of them here:

New Slide...

    ✔ Click the New Slide button on the status bar (shown in the margin).

    ✔ Choose the Insert⇨New Slide command.

    ✔ Press Ctrl+M.

In all three cases, PowerPoint displays the New Slide dialog box shown in Figure 1-6. This dialog enables you to pick from 21 different types of slide layouts. Just click the mouse on the one you want to use and click OK. PowerPoint inserts the new slide into your presentation immediately *after* the slide currently shown on-screen.

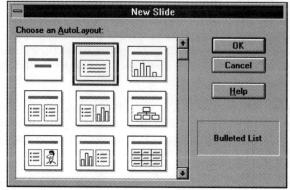

Figure 1-6:
The New
Slide dialog
box.

If the slide layout you want to use doesn't appear in the New Slide dialog box, use the scroll bar that's next to the slide layouts to display additional layouts. If you still can't find the layout you want, pick the layout that's closest to what you want and then adjust it later.

Notice that each slide layout has a name. The one that's highlighted in Figure 1-6 is called *Bulleted List.* The layout name tells you which types of objects are included in the layout. For example, *Bulleted List* includes a text object that contains a bulleted list. *Text & Clip Art* layout includes two objects: one for text, the other for a picture from the PowerPoint clip art gallery. You'll probably use the *Bulleted List* layout most. It's the best format for presenting a topic along with several supporting points. For example, Figure 1-7 shows a bulleted list slide that may be included in the Rent-a-Geek presentation; the bullet items in this slide explain why computer consultants from Rent-a-Geek are better than other consultants.

One of the layouts available in the AutoLayout section of the New Slide dialog box is named *Blank Slide.* This layout doesn't include any objects; it's a blank slate you can use to create a slide that doesn't fit any of the predefined layouts. All of the slide layouts except *Blank Slide* include a single line text object that serves as a title for the slide. This title is formatted consistently from slide to slide to give your presentation a professional look.

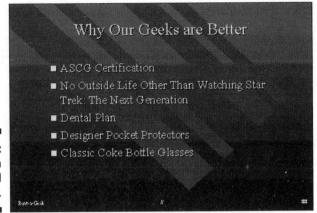

Figure 1-7:
A slide with
a bulleted
list.

Moving from Slide to Slide

Once you've created more than one slide, you need a way to move the PowerPoint display from slide to slide. There are two ways to do that:

- Click one of the double-headed arrows at the bottom of the vertical scroll bar.
- Use the PageUp and PageDown keys on your keyboard.

Outline That for Me!

So far, you've been working with PowerPoint in *Slide view*, the view mode that shows your presentation's slides one at a time exactly as they appear when you print them. Slide view is useful for tinkering with each slide's appearance, but it's not exactly the most efficient way to dump a bunch of text into PowerPoint to make a whole series of slides. To do that, you need to switch PowerPoint to *Outline view*.

Figure 1-8 shows the Rent-a-Geek presentation as displayed in Outline view. Gone are the glamorous graphics, the fancy fonts, the cheery colors. Instead, all you get is the text that shows up on each slide, in that most boring of all formats: the good old-fashioned outline. It's not pretty, but it frees you from the tyranny of appearances and enables you to concentrate on your presentation's content, which is what you should be concentrating on. (Unless your audience is so gullible that they'd buy the Brooklyn Bridge if your slides were dazzling enough.)

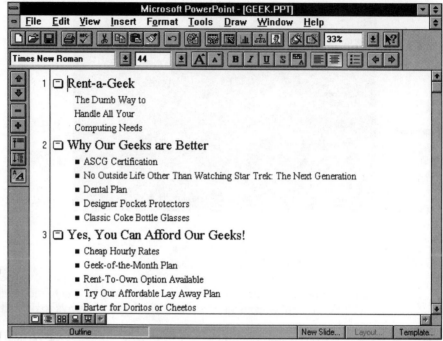

Figure 1-8:
Outline
view.

There are three ways to flip PowerPoint to Outline view:

▶ Click the Outline View button on the status bar.

▶ Choose the View⇨Outline command.

▶ Press Ctrl+Alt+O.

Once in Outline view, you can zip back to Slide view using any of these procedures:

▶ Click the Slide View button on the status bar.

▶ Choose the View⇨Slides command.

▶ Press Ctrl+Alt+N.

Yes, I know it sort of makes sense that Ctrl+Alt+O stands for Outline view but using Ctrl+Alt+N to switch to Slide view makes no sense at all. Don't blame me; the programmers at Microsoft must have consumed too much Jolt Cola that day. (Maybe the N stands for Normal view, because Slide view is the view you normally work in. Who knows.)

A few hints on using Outline view:

 Once in Outline view, press the Enter key to create a new line. Then use the Tab key at the beginning of a line to indent the line or use the Shift+Tab key to reduce the line's indent.

✔ There are loads of other tricks to learn about working in Outline view. If you're totally confused but think Outline view sounds like the greatest thing since sliced bread, you can find more about it in Chapter 3.

Print That Puppy

Once you've finished your masterpiece, you'll probably want to print it. Here's the procedure for printing all of the slides in your presentation:

1. **Make sure your printer is turned on and ready to print.**

   Make sure the *select* or *on-line* light is on. If it isn't, press the *select* or *on-line* button to make it so. Check the paper while you're at it.

2. **Click the Print button on the Standard toolbar.**

   Or if you prefer, use the File➪Print command or press Ctrl+P or Ctrl+Shift+F12. Whichever way you do it, the Print dialog box appears. It has myriad options you can fiddle with to print your presentation just so, but you can leave them alone if you want to print all of the slides in your presentation.

3. **Click the OK button or press the Enter key.**

   Make sure you say "Engage" in a knowing manner, pointing at your printer as you do so. The main idea is to fool your printer into thinking that you know what you are doing.

Printed pages should soon appear on your printer. Check them to make sure they look the way you want. Depending on how complex your slides are and how fast your printer is, your slides may pop right out of your printer before you can say "I love this program," or you may be able to take a family vacation to Disneyland while your slides print.

 If you are using overhead transparencies, you can load them directly into your laser printer provided that you get transparencies that are designed for laser printers — ordinary transparencies may melt and leave gooey stuff all over your laser printer's guts and possibly spread radioactive dust throughout the entire tri-state area. Bad idea. Laser transparencies are expensive, though, so it's a good idea to print a proof on plain paper before printing on the transparencies.

Tune in to Chapter 6 if you want to more know about printing. If you want your output printed on 35mm slides, check out Chapter 12.

Save Your Work

Now that you've spent hours creating the best presentation since God gave Moses the 10 commandments, you can just turn your computer off, right? Wrong-o! All of your precious work is held in your computer's fleeting RAM memory until you save your work to a disk file. Turn off your computer before you save your work and Poof! your work vanishes as if David Copperfield were in town.

Like everything else in PowerPoint, there are four ways to save a document:

- ✔ Click the Save button on the Standard toolbar.
- ✔ Choose the File⇨Save command.
- ✔ Press Ctrl+S.
- ✔ Press Shift+F12.

If you haven't yet saved the file to disk, the magical Save As dialog box appears, on which you can type the name you want to use for the file. Click the OK button to save the file. After you've saved the file, subsequent saves update the disk file with any changes you made to the presentation since the last time you saved it.

Some notes to keep in mind when saving files:

- ✔ Use your noggin when assigning a name to a new file. The filename is how you'll recognize the file later on, so pick a meaningful name that suggests the file's contents.
- ✔ When you save a document, PowerPoint displays a bar graph at the bottom on the screen to prove that it's really doing something. See how PowerPoint saves. Save, PowerPoint, save!
- ✔ After you save a file for the first time, the name in the presentation window's title area changes from *Presentation* to the name of your file. Still more proof that the file has been saved.
- ✔ Don't work on your file for hours at a time without saving it. I've learned the hard way to save my work every few minutes. After all, the earth may be hit by a giant asteroid any time now. Get into the habit of pressing Ctrl+S every few minutes, especially after making a significant change to a presentation, like adding a covey of new slides or making a gaggle of complicated formatting changes.

> ✔ If you're not sure about how to make up a filename, consult the following sidebar, "I wish I didn't have to tell you about DOS filenames." If you try to use a filename that doesn't conform to DOS rules, you'll receive an electrical jolt of approximately 300,000 volts through the mouse. (Not really ... just a mild message muttering something about the filename not being valid. I voted for the electrical shock, but no one at Microsoft listens to me.)

I wish I didn't have to tell you about DOS filenames

DOS is very strict about the names you can use for files. Obey the following restrictions, and you will be a happy PowerPoint user all the days of your life:

✔ No more than eight characters per filename, please.

✔ You can use letters *and* numbers. Avoid special characters like #, $, and %; some of them are allowed, but others aren't. I never can remember which is which, so I just avoid them all.

✔ Did you know that when cartoonists use a bunch of those special characters in place of swearing, it is called a *maledictory?* DOS considers these characters profane. That's why you can't use them in filenames.

✔ DOS enables you to add a three-character *extension* to the end of the filename. The extension is separated from the rest of the filename by a period, but the period isn't a part of the filename itself ... it's just a separator. PowerPoint automatically adds the extension PPT to your presentation files, so you needn't mess with extensions or periods.

Here are some acceptable filenames for PowerPoint presentation files, complete with the PPT extension:

SALES.PPT A perfectly acceptable filename, although it's pretty generic. If you give only one sales presentation in your lifetime, it will suffice. Other-

wise, a more specific filename is in order.

BRODART.PPT Ah, now this one is better. Here the filename indicates the client to whom the presentation is to be given. But you're still stuck if you need to make more than one presentation to this client.

BROD001.PPT Even better. See how you can freely mix letters and numbers?

27.PPT No problem. You can use numbers by themselves.

3BQ4-72C.PPT Still not a problem. The hyphen is one of those allowable special characters. The only problem with this filename is that you have to work for a government procurement office to know what it stands for.

Here are some filenames that don't work:

MY CLASS.PPT Nope. No spaces allowed in the middle of filenames.

34+35.PPT Nope. The hyphen or minus sign is OK, but the plus sign isn't. Best to avoid them all.

ECONOMICS.PPT Nope. One too many letters. Sorry.

TRY.THIS.ONE Nope. Too many periods.

$@#&!.*#! Nope. Profane filename. Makes DOS blush.

When you save a file for the first time, you may get a dialog box asking you for a title, author, and other useful information about the presentation. Type away; then click OK or press Enter to save the file. If you try to save a file using a filename you've already used for another presentation, PowerPoint asks whether you're sure you want to replace the existing disk file. Assuming you made a mistake and didn't really mean to assign a filename that's already in use, click <u>N</u>o and save the file under a different name. For more information on filenames, consult Chapter 20, "Managing Your Files."

Retrieving a Presentation from Disk

Having saved your presentation to a disk file, you'll probably want to retrieve it later to make additional changes or print it. As you may guess, there are about 40 ways to do that. Here are the four most common:

- ✔ Click the Open button on the Standard toolbar.
- ✔ Use the <u>File</u>⇨<u>O</u>pen command.
- ✔ Press Ctrl+O.
- ✔ Press Ctrl+F12.

All four pop up the Open dialog box, which gives you a list of files to choose from. Click the file you want; then click the OK button or press the Enter key. The file is read from disk into your computer's RAM where you can work on it.

The Open dialog box has controls that enable you to rummage through the various directories on your hard disk in search of your files. If you know how to open a file in any Windows application, you know how to do it in PowerPoint because the Open dialog box is pretty much the same in any Windows program. If you seem to have lost a file, rummage around in different directories to see whether you can find it. It may be that you accidentally saved the file in the wrong directory. Also, check the spelling of the filename. Maybe your fingers weren't on the home row when you typed the filename, so instead of BRODART.PPT, you saved the file as NTPFSTY.PPT. I hate it when that happens.

The fastest way to open a file from the Open dialog box is to double-click the file you want to open. Point to the file and click the mouse twice as fast as you can. This spares you from having to click the file once and then clicking the OK button. It also exercises the fast-twitch muscles in your index finger.

PowerPoint keeps track of the last few files you've opened and displays them on the <u>File</u> menu. To open a file you've recently opened, click the <u>File</u> menu and inspect the list of files at the bottom of the menu. If the file you want is in the list, click it to open it.

Closing a Presentation

Having finished your presentation and printed it just right, it's time to close it. Closing a presentation is kind of like gathering up your papers, putting them neatly in a file folder, and returning the folder to its proper file drawer. The presentation disappears from your computer screen. Don't worry: It's tucked safely away on your hard disk where you can get to it later if you need to.

To close a file, use the File⇨Close command. You also can use the keyboard shortcut Ctrl+W, but you'd have to have a mind like a steel trap to remember that Ctrl+W stands for Close.

Yet another way to close a file is to double-click the control box in the upper left corner of the Presentation window. Note that if you've maximized the presentation window, the control box is just to the left of the menu bar.

You don't have to close a file before exiting PowerPoint. If you exit PowerPoint without closing a file, PowerPoint graciously closes the file for you. The only reason you may want to close a file is when you want to work on a different file and you don't want to keep both files open at the same time.

If you've made changes since the last time you saved the file, PowerPoint offers to save the changes for you. Click Yes to save the file before closing or click No to abandon any changes you've made to the file.

If you close all the open PowerPoint presentations, you may discover that most of PowerPoint's commands have been rendered useless (they are *grayed* on the menu). Fear not. Open a presentation or create a new one and the commands return to life.

Help Is on the Way!

Lost within the dark woods of PowerPoint and don't know how to get out? Fret not, for PowerPoint has an excellent Help system that can answer all of your questions, provided of course you know what your questions are.

PowerPoint's Help system is similar to the Help system found in other Windows programs, so if you know how to use another program's Help system, you'll have no trouble figuring out PowerPoint's.

Several ways to get help

When lost at sea, the universal help signal is S.O.S. When you're lost in PowerPoint, the universal help signal is F1. Press F1 at any time and help is on its way. If you press F1 when you're in the middle of something, odds are PowerPoint comes through with help on doing just the task you were trying to accomplish. This slick little bit of wizardry is called *context-sensitive help*.

If you click Help on the menu bar, you get a whole menu of help stuff, most of which is only moderately helpful. Help⇨Contents shows a list of broad help categories you can pick from. It's useful when you're not sure what you're looking for. Help⇨Index gives you an A to Z index of all help topics. And Help⇨Search for Help On enables you to search the index by typing a portion of the word you want to look up. For example, type **sh** and you'll see entries for Shade, Shadow, Shadow Offset, and a bunch of other stuff that starts with *sh*.

You also can call up help on just about any PowerPoint dialog box by clicking the Help button that appears in the dialog box.

You also can use the Help button on the Standard toolbar. Frankly, it's a little weird. Click it and the cursor becomes an arrow with a question-mark grafted on to its back. Point it at just about anything on-screen and click to get help about that thing.

Cue cards

PowerPoint also includes a handy *cue card* feature that displays on-screen instructions for common tasks. Here's the procedure for using cue cards:

1. **Choose the Help⇨Cue Cards command.**

   The PowerPoint Cue Cards dialog box, shown in Figure 1-9, appears.

2. **Find the procedure you want help with and click the arrow button to call up that cue card.**

3. **Study the cue card, paying special attention to the numbered steps. Do what the steps say.**

4. **The cue card may offer you choices. Click the arrow button for the choice you wish to take.**

5. **If the instructions don't fit on one page, the cue card offers you a Next button. Click it to see additional instructions.**

Control box

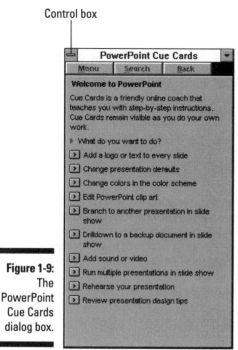

Figure 1-9:
The
PowerPoint
Cue Cards
dialog box.

The Cue Card dialog box remains on-screen as you work. If it is covering up your work, move it by clicking its title bar and dragging it to a new location. The Cue Card is handy for the specific tasks it addresses, but otherwise it simply gets in the way. To get rid of the Cue Cards dialog box, double-click its control box.

Exiting PowerPoint

Had enough excitement for one day? Use any of these techniques to shut PowerPoint down:

- ✔ Choose the File➪Exit command.
- ✔ Double-click the control box at the top left corner of the PowerPoint window.
- ✔ Press Alt+F4.

Bammo! PowerPoint is history.

There are a few things you should know about exiting from PowerPoint (or from any application):

✔ PowerPoint doesn't enable you to abandon ship without first considering to save your work. If you've made changes to any presentation files and haven't saved them, PowerPoint offers to save the files for you. Lean over and plant a fat kiss right in the middle of your monitor — PowerPoint just saved you your job.

✔ Never never never ever never turn off your computer while PowerPoint or any other program is running. You may as well pour acid into the keyboard or run over the motherboard with a truck. Always exit PowerPoint and any other program that's running before you turn off your computer.

✔ In fact, you'd best get clean out of Windows before shutting down your computer. Exit all of your programs the same way you exited PowerPoint. Then, when Windows is the only thing left, exit it the same way. Only when you see the happy DOS prompt (C>) can you safely turn off your computer.

Chapter 2
Editing Slides

* *

In This Chapter

▶ Moving around in a presentation

▶ Working with objects

▶ Editing text

▶ Undoing a mistake

▶ Deleting slides

▶ Finding and replacing text

▶ Rearranging slides

* *

*I*f you're like Mary Poppins ("Practically Perfect in Every Way"), you can skip this chapter. Perfect people never make mistakes, so everything they type in PowerPoint comes out right the first time. They never have to press Backspace to erase something they typed wrong by mistake, go back and insert a line to make a point they left out, or rearrange their slides because they didn't add them in the right order to begin with.

If you're more like Jane ("Rather Inclined to Giggle; Doesn't Put Things Away") or Michael ("Extremely Stubborn and Suspicious"), you probably make mistakes along the way. This chapter shows you how to go back and correct them.

Reviewing your work and correcting it if necessary is called *editing*. It's not a fun job, but it has to be done. A spoonful of sugar usually helps.

This chapter focuses mostly on editing text objects. Many of the techniques apply to editing other types of objects, such as clip art pictures or drawn shapes. For more information about editing other object breeds, see Part III, "Pictures, Charts, and Grunts."

Moving from Slide to Slide

The most common way to move around in a PowerPoint presentation is to press the PageUp and PageDown keys on your keyboard, as shown in this list:

PageDown   Moves forward to the next slide in your presentation.

PageUp   Moves backward to the preceding slide in your presentation.

Alternatively, you can move forward or backward through your presentation by clicking the double-headed arrows at the bottom of the vertical scroll bar on the right edge of the Presentation window. You also can use the vertical scroll bar on the right edge of the Presentation window to move forward or backward through your presentation.

Another way to move quickly from slide to slide is to click the scroll box within the vertical scroll bar on the right side of the window and drag it up or down by holding down the left mouse button. As you drag the box, a little text box pops up next to the slide bar to tell you which slide will be displayed if you release the button at that position.

Dragging the scroll box to move from slide to slide is just one example of the many Windows tasks that are much harder to explain than to actually do. After you read this, you probably will say to yourself, "Huh?" But after you try it, you'll say, "Oh, I get it! Why didn't he just say so?"

Working with Objects

In the beginning, the User created a slide. And the slide was formless and void, without meaning or content. And the User said, "Let there be a Text Object." And there was a Text Object. And there was evening and there was morning, one day. Then the User said, "Let there be a Picture Object." And there was a Picture Object. And there was evening and there was morning, a second day. This continued for forty days and forty nights, until there were forty objects on the slide, each after its own kind. And the User was laughed out of the auditorium by the audience who could read the slide not.

This charming little parable is presented solely to make the point that PowerPoint slides are nothing without objects. Objects are the lifeblood of PowerPoint that give meaning and content to otherwise formless and void slides.

Most slide objects are simple text objects, which you don't have to worry much about. If you're interested, read the following sidebar about other types of objects. Otherwise, just plow ahead.

I object to this meaningless dribble about PowerPoint objects

I don't really want to do this to you, but I feel compelled to point out that you can use several distinct types of objects on a PowerPoint slide. They're shown in this list:

✔ *Text object:* The first and most common type of object. Most of the objects you create are probably text objects. Text objects contain, uh, text.

✔ *Shape objects:* Contain shapes such as rectangles, circles, and arrowheads. Odd as it may seem, shape objects can also contain text. To confuse the issue even more, PowerPoint uses the term *text object* to refer to both text objects and shape objects.

✔ *Line objects:* Lines and free-form drawing objects made up of line segments. Unlike shapes, lines cannot contain text.

✔ *Embedded objects:* Beasties created by some other program. Embedded objects can be clip art pictures, organization charts, graphs, or other types of ornaments. PowerPoint comes with a handful of programs for creating embedded objects, and it can also work with Microsoft Word and Excel to create embedded tables and spreadsheets in a slide.

Forget about everything except text objects for now. All these other types of objects are covered in later chapters.

When you add a new slide to your presentation, the slide layout you choose determines which objects are initially placed on the new slide. You can add more objects to the slide later, or you can delete objects or move them around or resize them if you want. Most of the time, though, you will be content to leave the objects where they are.

Each object occupies a rectangular region on the slide. The contents of the object may or may not visually fill the rectangular region, but you can see the outline of the object when you select it (see the section "Selecting objects," later in this chapter).

Objects can overlap. Usually, you don't want them to, but sometimes doing so creates a jazzy effect. You may lay some text over the top of some clip art, for example.

Selecting objects

Before you can edit anything on a slide, you have to *select* the object that contains whatever it is you want to edit. For example, you cannot start typing away to edit text on-screen. Instead, you must first select the text object that contains the text you want to edit. Likewise, you must select other types of objects before you can edit their contents.

Here are some guidelines to keep in mind when selecting objects:

✔ Before you can select anything, make sure that the cursor is shaped like an arrow. If it isn't, click the arrow button on the Drawing toolbar. (This button is officially called the *selection button*, but it sure looks like an arrow to me.)

✔ To select a text object so that you can edit its text, move the arrow pointer over the text you want to edit and click the left button. A rectangular box appears around the object, and the background behind the text changes to a solid color to make the text easier to read. A text cursor appears so that you can start typing away.

✔ Other types of objects work a little differently. Click an object and the object is selected. The rectangular box appears around the object to let you know that you have hooked it. After you have hooked the object, you can drag it around the screen or change its size, but you cannot edit it. To edit a nontext object, you must double-click it. (It's not necessary to first select the object. Just point to it with the arrow pointer and double-click.)

✔ Another way to select an object — or more than one object — is to use the arrow pointer to drag a rectangle around the objects you want to select. Point to a location above and to the left of the object or objects you want to select, click and drag the mouse down and to the right until the rectangle surrounds the objects. When you release the button, all the objects within the rectangle are selected.

✔ You can also press the Tab key to select objects. Press Tab once to select the first object on the slide. Press Tab again to select the next object. Keep pressing Tab until the object you want is selected.

Pressing Tab to select objects is handy when you cannot easily point to the object you want to select. This problem can happen if the object you want is buried underneath another object or if the object is empty or otherwise invisible and you're not sure of its location.

Resizing or moving an object

When you select an object, an outline box appears around it, as shown in Figure 2-1. If you look closely at the box, you can see that it has love handles, one on each corner and one in the middle of each edge. You can use these love handles to adjust the size of an object. And you can grab the box between the love handles to move the object around on the slide.

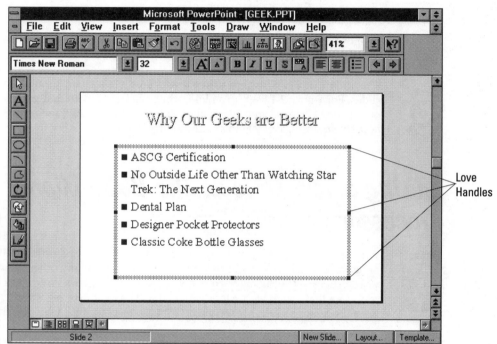

Figure 2-1: PowerPoint's love handles enable you to adjust an object's size.

To change the size of an object, click it to select it and then grab one of the love handles by clicking it with the arrow pointer. Hold down the mouse button and move the mouse to change the object's size.

The love handles on a text object don't appear unless you click directly on the text object's outline box.

Why so many handles? To give you different ways to change the object's size. The handles at the corners allow you to change both the height and width of the object. The handles on the top and bottom edge allow you to change just the object's height, and the handles on the right and left edges change just the width.

Changing a text object's size does not change the size of the text in the object; it changes only the size of the "frame" that contains the text. Changing the width of a text object is equivalent to changing margins in a word processor: it makes the text lines wider or narrower. To change the size of the text within a text object, you must change the point size. Chapter 7 has the exciting details.

If you hold down the Ctrl key while you drag one of the love handles, the object stays centered at its current position on the slide. Try it and you'll see what I mean. Also, try holding down the Shift key as you drag an object using one of the corner love handles. This maintains the object's proportions as you resize it.

To move an object, click anywhere on the outline box except on a love handle; then drag the object to its new locale.

The outline box can be hard to see if you have a fancy background on your slides. For Figure 2-1 I set up a plain, white background so that you can see the outline box better. If you select an object and have trouble seeing the outline box, try squinting or cleaning your monitor screen.

Editing a Text Object: The Baby Word Processor

When you select a text object for editing, PowerPoint transforms itself into a baby word processor. If you're familiar with just about any other Windows word processor, including Microsoft Word or even Windows Write (the free word processor that comes with Windows), you will have no trouble working in baby word processor mode. This section presents some of the highlights, just in case.

PowerPoint automatically splits lines between words so that you don't have to press the Enter key at the end of every line. Press Enter only when you want to begin a new paragraph.

Text in a PowerPoint presentation is usually formatted with a *bullet character* at the beginning of each paragraph. The default bullet character is usually a simple square box, but you can change it to just about any shape you can imagine (see Chapter 7). The point to remember here is that the bullet character is a part of the paragraph format, not a character you have to type in your text.

Most word processors enable you to switch between *insert mode* and *typeover mode* by pressing the Insert key on the right side of your keyboard. In insert mode, characters you type are inserted at the cursor location; in typeover mode, each character you type replaces the character at the cursor location. PowerPoint always works in insert mode, so any text you type is inserted at the cursor location. Pressing the Insert key has no effect on the way text is typed.

Using the arrow keys

You can move around within a text object by pressing the *arrow keys*. I looked
at my computer's keyboard and saw that 13 of the keys have arrows on them —
16, if you count the greater-than (>) and less-than (<) signs and the ubiquitous
caret (^), which look sort of like arrows. So I have included Figure 2-2, which
shows you the arrow keys I'm talking about.

Figure 2-2:
The arrow
keys I'm
talking
about.

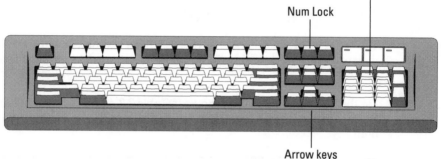

The arrow keys are sometimes called the *cursor keys* because they move the
cursor around the screen. Each key moves the cursor in the direction in which
the arrow points, as shown in Table 2-1.

Table 2-1	The Arrow Keys
Keystroke	*Where the Cursor Moves*
↑	Up one line
↓	Down one line
←	One character to the left
→	One character to the right

The arrow keys are duplicated on the 2, 4, 6, and 8 numeric keys on the right
side of the keyboard. The function of these keys alternates between numeric
keys and cursor-control keys, depending on whether you have pressed the Num
Lock key. When you press Num Lock once, the Num Lock light comes on,
indicating that the numeric keys will create numerals when you press them.
When you press Num Lock again, the Num Lock light goes off, which indicates
that these keys control the cursor.

Sometimes the mouse is the fastest way to get somewhere. Point at the exact spot in the text where you want the cursor to appear and click the left button. The cursor magically jumps to that spot.

The left-arrow key looks just like the Backspace key. This evil plot is designed to fool computer novices into fearing that the arrow keys will erase text, just as the Backspace key does. Not so! Pay no attention to those fearmongers! The arrow keys are completely docile. All they do is move the cursor around; they do not destroy text.

Moving around faster

The arrow keys can get you anywhere within a text object, but sometimes they're as slow as molasses. Table 2-2 shows a few tricks for moving around faster.

For the Ctrl-key combinations listed in Table 2-2, first press and hold the Ctrl key and then press the arrow key, the End key, or the Home key. Then release both keys.

Table 2-2	Keyboard Tricks for Moving Around Faster
Keystroke	*Where the Cursor Moves*
Ctrl+↑	Up one paragraph
Ctrl+↓	Down one paragraph
Ctrl+←	Left one word
Ctrl+→	Right one word
End	To end of line
Home	To beginning of line
Ctrl+End	To end of text object
Ctrl+Home	To beginning of text object

Your keyboard has two Ctrl keys, a lefty and a righty. Either one works. I usually press the one on the left with my little finger and press the arrow key with my right hand. Whatever feels good is OK by me.

As long as the Ctrl key is pressed, you can press any of the arrow keys repeatedly. To move three words to the right, for example, hold down the Ctrl key and press the right-arrow key three times. Then release the Ctrl key. If the cursor is in the middle of a word, pressing Ctrl+← moves the cursor to the beginning of that word. Pressing it again moves the cursor to the beginning of the preceding word.

Deleting text

You delete text by pressing the Del or Backspace keys, which work as shown in Table 2-3.

Table 2-3	Deleting Text
Keystroke	*What It Deletes*
Del	The character immediately to the right of the cursor
Backspace	The character immediately to the left of the cursor
Ctrl+Del	Characters from the cursor all the way to the end of the current word
Ctrl+Backspace	Characters from the cursor all the way to the beginning of the current word

You can press Ctrl+Del to delete an entire word by first pressing Ctrl+→ or Ctrl+← to move the cursor to the beginning of the word you want to delete. Then press Ctrl+Del.

If you first select a block of text, the Del and Backspace keys delete the entire selection. If you don't have a clue about what I'm talking about, skip ahead to the following section, "Marking text for surgery."

Another way to delete a word is to double-click anywhere in the middle of the word and then press the Del key. The double-click marks the entire word and then the Del key deletes the marked word.

You can also use the Edit⇨Clear command to delete text permanently. The Del key is simply a keyboard shortcut for the Edit⇨Clear command.

Marking text for surgery

Some text-editing operations — such as amputations and transplants — require that you first mark the text on which you want to operate. This list shows you the methods for doing so:

✔ When you use the keyboard, hold down the Shift key while you press any of the cursor-movement keys to move the cursor.

✔ When you use the mouse, point to the beginning of the text you want to mark and then click and drag the mouse over the text. Release the button when you reach the end of the text you want to mark.

PowerPoint's Automatic Word Select option tries to guess when you intend to select an entire word. If you use the mouse to mark a block of text, you will notice that the selected text jumps to include entire words as you move the mouse. If you don't like this feature, you can disable it by using the Tools⇨Options command (uncheck the Automatic Word Selection check box).

✔ To mark a single word, point the cursor anywhere in the word and double-click.

✔ To mark an entire paragraph, point anywhere in the paragraph and triple-click. Click-click-click.

✔ To delete the entire block of text you have marked, press the Del key or the Backspace key.

✔ To replace an entire block of text, mark it and then begin typing. The marked block vanishes and is replaced by the text you are typing.

✔ You can use the Cut, Copy, and Paste commands from the Edit menu with marked text blocks. These commands are described in the following section.

Using Cut, Copy, and Paste

Like any good Windows program, PowerPoint uses the standard Cut, Copy, and Paste commands. These commands work on the *current selection*. When you're editing a text object, the current selection is the block of text you have marked. But if you select an entire object, the current selection is the object itself. In other words, you can use the Cut, Copy, and Paste commands with bits of text or with entire objects.

Cut, Copy, and Paste all work with one of the greatest mysteries of Windows, the Clipboard. The *Clipboard* is where Windows stashes stuff so that you can get to it later. The Cut and Copy commands add stuff to the Clipboard, which you can later retrieve by using the Paste command. After you have placed something on the Clipboard, it stays there until you replace it with something else by using another Cut or Copy command or until you exit from Windows.

The keyboard shortcuts for Cut, Copy, and Paste are the same as they are for other Windows programs: Ctrl+X for Cut, Ctrl+C for Copy, and Ctrl+V for Paste.

The Copy and Paste commands are often used together to duplicate information. If you want to repeat an entire sentence, for example, you first copy the sentence to the Clipboard and then place the cursor where you want the sentence duplicated and use the Paste command.

The Cut and Paste commands are used together to move stuff from one location to another. To move a sentence to a new location, for example, select the sentence and cut it to the Clipboard. Then place the cursor where you want the sentence moved and use the Paste command.

Cutting or copying a text block

When you cut a block of text, the text is removed from the slide and placed on the Clipboard, where you can retrieve it later if you want. Copying a text block stores the text in the Clipboard but doesn't remove it from the slide.

To cut a block, first mark the block you want to cut by using the keyboard or the mouse. Then conjure up the Cut command by using any of these three methods:

- ✔ Use the Edit⇨Cut command from the menu bar.
- ✔ Click the Cut button on the Standard toolbar (shown in the margin).
- ✔ Press Ctrl+X.

Using any method causes the text to vanish from your screen. Don't worry, though. It's safely nestled away in the Clipboard.

To copy a block, mark the block and invoke the Copy command, by using one of these methods:

- ✔ Use the Edit⇨Copy command.
- ✔ Click the Copy button on the Standard toolbar (shown in the margin).
- ✔ Press Ctrl+C.

The text is copied to the Clipboard, but this time it doesn't vanish from the screen. To retrieve the text from the Clipboard, use the Paste command, described in the following section.

Every time you cut or copy text to the Clipboard, the previous contents of the Clipboard are lost. If you want to move several blocks of text, move them one at a time: cut-paste, cut-paste, cut-paste, not cut-cut-cut, paste-paste-paste. The latter method pastes the results of the third cut three times; the first two cuts are lost.

Pasting text

To paste text from the Clipboard, first move the cursor to the location at which you want the text to be inserted. Then invoke the Paste command, by using whichever of the following techniques suits your fancy:

- ✔ Choose the Edit➪Paste command from the menu bar.
- ✔ Click the Paste button on the Standard toolbar.
- ✔ Press Ctrl+V.

Cutting, copying, and pasting entire objects

The use of Cut, Copy, and Paste isn't limited to text blocks; they work with entire objects also. Just select the object, copy or cut it to the Clipboard, move to a new location, and paste the object from the Clipboard.

To move an object from one slide to another, select the object and cut it to the Clipboard. Then move to the slide where you want the object to appear and paste the object from the Clipboard.

To duplicate an object on several slides, select the object and copy it to the Clipboard. Then move to the slide you want the object duplicated on and paste it.

You can duplicate an object on the same slide by selecting the object, copying it to the Clipboard, and then pasting it. The only glitch is that the pasted object appears exactly on top of the original object, so you cannot tell that you now have two copies of the object on the slide. Never fear! Just grab the newly pasted object with the mouse and move it to another location on the slide. Moving the object uncovers the original so that you can see both objects.

An easier way to duplicate an object is to use the Edit➪Duplicate command. It combines the function of Copy and Paste but doesn't disturb the Clipboard. The duplicate copy is offset slightly from the original so that you can tell them apart. (The keyboard shortcut for the Edit➪Duplicate command is Ctrl+D.)

If you want to blow away an entire object permanently, select it and press the Del key or use the Edit➪Clear command. This step removes the object from the slide but does *not* copy it to the Clipboard. It is gone forever. (Well, sort of — you can still get it back by using the Undo command, but only if you act fast. See the section "Oops! I Didn't Mean It!" later in this chapter.)

To include the same object on each of your slides, you can use a better way than copying and pasting: add the object to the *master slide*, which governs the format of all the slides in a presentation (see Chapter 8).

Oops! I Didn't Mean It (or the Marvelous Undo Command)

Made a mistake? Don't panic. Use the Undo command. Undo is your safety net. If you mess up, Undo can save the day.

There are three ways to undo a mistake:

> ✔ Use the Edit➪Undo command from the menu bar.
>
> ✔ Click the Undo button on the Standard toolbar.
>
> ✔ Press Ctrl+Z.

Undo reverses whatever you did last. If you deleted text, Undo adds it back in. If you typed text, Undo deletes it. If you moved an object, Undo puts it back where it was. You get the idea.

Undo remembers only your most recent action. If you make a mistake, feel free to curse, kick something, or fall on the floor in a screaming tantrum if you must, but *don't do anything else on your computer!* If you use Undo immediately, you can zap your presentation back to its previous condition.

After you undo something, the Undo command becomes your "last action." If you use Undo again, whatever was undone gets redone. What was, has been, and will be again. Something like that, anyway.

Deleting a Slide

Want to delete an entire slide? No problem. Move to the slide you want to delete and use the Edit➪Delete Slide command. Zowie! The slide is history.

No keyboard shortcut for deleting a slide exists, nor does the Standard toolbar have a button for it. Sorry — you have to use the menu for this one.

You can also delete a slide in Outline or Slide Sorter view. Outline view is covered in Chapter 3 and Slide Sorter view is covered at the end of this chapter.

Remembering those confounded Ctrl+key combinations

Quick — memorize these four keyboard short-cuts:

Ctrl+Z Undo

Ctrl+X Cut

Ctrl+C Copy

Ctrl+V Paste

Do these Ctrl-key combinations make any sense to you? If not, the following two memory tricks can help you tuck these four key combinations into your frontal lobe for easy access:

✔ Notice that all four keys flank each other on the keyboard. They're the first four keys on the bottom row, just above the spacebar.

✔ At first glance, there's no mnemonic trick for remembering these combinations. Ctrl+C makes sense if you remember C for Copy, but what about the others? Try these tips:

Ctrl+Z "Zap," as in "Zap the last thing I did. It was a mistake!"

Ctrl+X How do you mark something you want deleted? By crossing it out — drawing an X through it.

Ctrl+C Easy. C is for Copy.

Ctrl+V The standard editing symbol for inserting text is a caret (^), which is an up side-down V.

It pays to memorize these key combinations because they work in just about every Windows program. I hope that they help you.

Finding Text

You know that buried somewhere in that 60-slide presentation is a slide that lists the options available on the Vertical Snarfblat, but where is it? This sounds like a job for PowerPoint's Find command!

The Find command can find text buried in any text object on any slide. These steps show you the procedure for using it:

1. Move to the first slide in the presentation.

This step is optional, but if you don't do it, Find begins looking from the current slide. It's best to start from the beginning, I say.

2. Think of what you want to find.

Snarfblat will do in this example.

3. Summon the Edit⇨Find command.

The keyboard shortcut is Ctrl+F. Figure 2-3 shows the Find dialog box, which contains the secrets of the Find command.

Figure 2-3:
The Find
dialog box.

4. Type the text you want to find.

It shows up in the Find What box.

5. Press the Enter key.

Or click the Find Next button. Either way, the search begins.

If the text you type is located anywhere in the presentation, the Find command zips you to the slide that contains the text and highlights the text. You can then edit the text object or search for the next occurrence of the text within your presentation. If you edit the text, the Find dialog box stays on-screen to make it easy to continue your quest.

Here are some facts to keep in mind when using the Find command:

✔ To find the next occurrence of the same text, press Enter or click the Find Next button again.

✔ To edit the text you found, click the text object. The Find dialog box remains on-screen. To continue searching, click the Find Next button again.

✔ If you see the following message:

End of presentation. Continue searching from beginning?

it means that PowerPoint has reached the end of your presentation and wants to resume the search at the beginning. Click the Continue button here for a thorough search. Don't worry — PowerPoint asks this question only once. It doesn't send you into an endless loop, searching your presentation over and over again.

✔ The message *Text not found.* means that PowerPoint has given up. The text you typed just isn't anywhere in the presentation. Maybe you spelled it wrong or maybe you didn't have a slide about Vertical Snarfblat options after all.

✔ If the right mix of upper- and lowercase letters is important to you, check the Match Case box before beginning the search. This option is handy when you have, for example, a presentation about Mr. Smith the Blacksmith.

✔ Speaking of Mr. Smith the Blacksmith, use the Match Whole Word Only check box to find your text only when it appears as a whole word. If you want to find the slide on which you talked about Mr. Smith the Blacksmith's mit, for example, type **mit** for the Find What text and check the Match Whole Word Only box. That way, the Find command looks for *mit* as a separate word. It doesn't stop to show you all the *mit*s in Smith and Blacksmith.

✔ If you find the text you're looking for and decide that you want to replace it with something else, click the Replace button. This step changes the Find dialog box to the Replace dialog box, which is explained in the following section.

✔ To make the Find dialog box go away, click the Close button or press the Escape key.

Replacing Text

Suppose that the Rent-a-Geek company decides to switch to athletic consulting, so it wants to change the name of its company to Rent-a-Jock. Easy. Just use the handy Replace command to change all occurrences of the word *Geek* to *Jock*. These steps show you how:

1. **Move to the first slide in the presentation.**

   Better start from the beginning.

2. **Invoke the Edit⇨Replace command.**

   The keyboard shortcut is Ctrl+H. I have no idea why. In any case, the Replace dialog box, shown in Figure 2-4, appears.

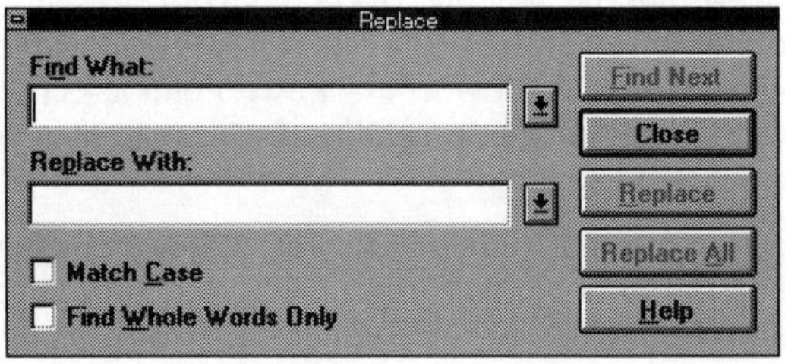

Figure 2-4:
The Replace
dialog box.

3. **In the Find What box, type the text you want to find.**

   This is the text that you want to replace with something else (*Geek*, in the example).

4. **Type the replacement text in the Replace With box.**

   This is the text that you want to use to replace the text you typed in the Find What box (*Jock*, in the example).

5. **Click the Find Next button.**

   PowerPoint finds the first occurrence of the text.

6. **Click the Replace button to replace the text.**

   Read the text first to make sure that it found what you were looking for.

7. **Repeat the Find Next and Replace sequence until you're finished.**

   Click Find Next to find the next occurrence, click Replace to replace it, and so on. Keep going until you have finished.

If you're absolutely positive that you want to replace all occurrences of your Find What text with the Replace With text, click the Replace All button. This step dispenses with the Find Next and Replace cycle. The only problem is that you're bound to find at least one spot where you didn't want the replacement to occur. Replacing the word *mit* with *glove,* for example, results in Sgloveh rather than Smith.

Always save your file before you do a find-and-replace. Undo doesn't work for find-and-replace, and the potential for totally messing up your presentation is very real.

Rearranging Your Slides in Slide Sorter View

Slide view is the view you normally work in to edit your slides, move things around, add text or graphics, and so on. But Slide view has one serious limitation: it doesn't enable you to change the order of the slides in your presentation. To do that, you have to switch to Slide Sorter view or Outline view.

Outline view is useful enough — and complicated enough — to merit its own chapter, so it's covered in Chapter 3. But Slide Sorter view is easy enough to discuss here.

These steps show you the procedure:

1. **Switch to Slide Sorter view.**

Click the Slide Sorter view button in the bottom left corner of the screen or use the View⇨Slide Sorter command. PowerPoint switches to Slide Sorter view, as shown in Figure 2-5.

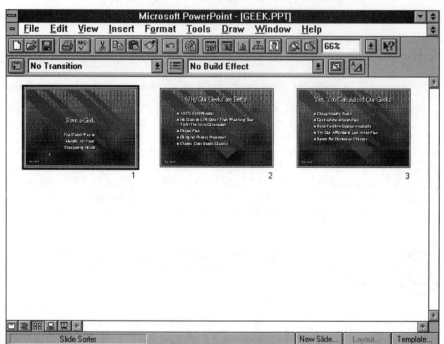

Figure 2-5:
Slide Sorter
view.

2. **To move a slide, click and drag it to a new location.**

   Point to the slide and then press and hold down the left mouse button. Drag the slide to its new location and release the button. PowerPoint adjusts the display to show the new arrangement of slides.

3. **To delete a slide, click the slide to select it and press the Del key.**

   The Del key works on an entire slide only in Slide Sorter view. You also can use the Edit⇨Delete Slide command.

New Slide... 4. **To add a new slide, click the slide you want the new slide to precede and click the New Slide button.**

   The New Slide dialog box appears so that you can choose the layout for the new slide. To edit the contents of the slide, return to Slide or Outline view using the view buttons or the View command.

If your presentation contains more slides than fit on-screen at one time, you can use the scroll bars to scroll the display. Or you can change the zoom factor to make the slides smaller. Click the down arrow next to the zoom size in the toolbar menu and choose a smaller zoom percentage, or just type a new zoom size into the toolbar's zoom size area. (See Figure 2-6.)

Figure 2-6:
The
Standard
toolbar's
zoom size
area.

Zoom size area

Slide Sorter view may seem kind of dull and boring, but it's also the place where you add jazzy transition and build effects to your slides. For example, you can make your bullets fall from the top of the screen like bombs and switch from slide to slide by using strips, wipes, or blinds. All this cool stuff is described in Chapter 10.

Chapter 3

Doing It in Outline View

In This Chapter

- What is Outline view?
- Focusing on substance, not form
- The many ways to add a slide in Outline view
- Promotions, demotions, and the lateral arabesque
- The collapse of the outline

You probably have already noticed that most presentations consist of slide after slide of bulleted lists. You may see a chart here or there and an occasional bit of clip art thrown in for comic effect, but the bread and butter of presentations is the bulleted list. It sounds boring, but it's the best way to make sure that your message gets through.

For this reason, presentations lend themselves especially well to outlining. Presentations are light on prose but heavy in the point and subpoint department — and that's precisely where outlines excel. PowerPoint's Outline view enables you to focus on your presentation's main points and subpoints. In other words, it enables you to focus on *content* without worrying about *appearance*. You can always switch back to Slide view to make sure that your slides look good. But when you want to make sure that your slides make sense, Outline view is the way to go.

Switching to Outline View

PowerPoint normally runs in Slide view, which displays slides one at a time in a what-you-see-is-what-you-get manner. Outline view shows the same information, but in the form of an outline. You can switch to Outline view in two ways:

✔ Using the View➪Outline menu command.

✔ Clicking the Outline view button on the status bar (shown in the margin), near the bottom left corner of the PowerPoint window.

Figure 3-1 shows an example of a presentation in Outline view.

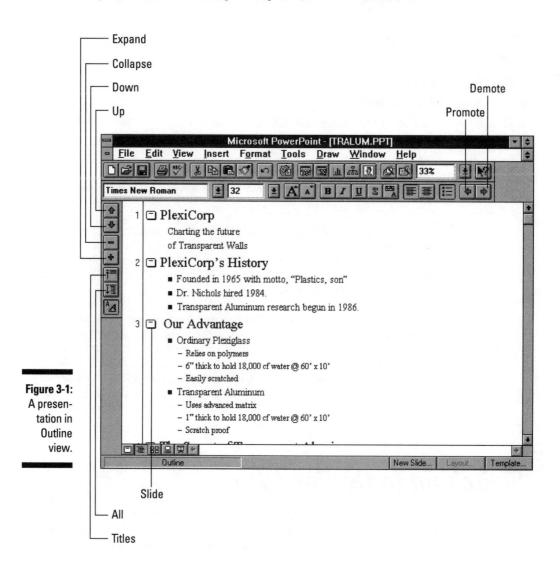

Figure 3-1:
A presentation in Outline view.

Understanding Outline View

The key to understanding PowerPoint's Outline view is realizing that Outline view is just another way of looking at your presentation. The outline is not a separate entity from the presentation. Instead, switching to Outline view takes the data from your slides and redisplays it in the form of an outline. Any changes you make to the presentation while in Outline view are automatically reflected in the presentation when you return to Slide view, and any changes you make while in Slide view automatically appear when you switch to Outline view. The reason is that Slide view and Outline view are merely two ways of displaying the content of your presentation.

There are a few important things to notice about Outline view:

- ✔ The outline is made up of the titles and body text of each slide. Any other objects you have added to a slide — such as pictures, charts, and so on — are not included in the outline. Also, if you add any text objects to the slide in addition to the basic title and body text objects that are automatically included when you create a new slide, the additional text objects are not included in the outline.

- ✔ Each slide is represented by a high-level heading in the outline. The text of this heading is drawn from the slide's title, and a button that represents the entire slide appears next to the heading. Also, the slide number appears to the left of the slide button.

- ✔ Each text line from a slide's body text appears as an indented heading, subordinate to the slide's main title heading.

- ✔ As Figure 3-1 shows, an outline can contain subpoints that are subordinate to the main points on each slide. PowerPoint enables you to create as many as five heading levels on each slide, but your slides probably will get too complicated if you go beyond two headings. You can find more about working with heading levels in the section "Promoting and Demoting Paragraphs," later in this chapter.

- ✔ When you switch to Outline view, the Drawing toolbar on the left side of the PowerPoint window changes to the Outline toolbar. Each of the buttons on this toolbar is explained in this chapter. In addition, the two buttons (the left- and right-facing arrows) on the far right side of the Formatting toolbar come into play when you work in Outline view. They're also explained in this chapter.

- ✔ Figure 3-1 shows three complete slides in Outline view. In Slide view, only one slide at a time can be seen. By presenting your content more concisely, Outline view enables you to focus on your presentation's structure. Of course, only the smallest of presentations fits entirely on-screen even in Outline view, so you still have to use the scroll bars to view the entire presentation.

Selecting and Editing an Entire Slide

When you work in Outline view, you often have to select an entire slide. PowerPoint provides three ways to do that:

- ✔ Click the slide's slide button.
- ✔ Click a slide's number.
- ✔ Triple-click anywhere in the slide's title text.

When you select an entire slide, the slide title and all its body text are highlighted. In addition, any extra objects that are on the slide but that are not shown in Slide view are selected as well.

To delete an entire slide, select it and then press the Del key.

To cut or copy an entire slide to the Clipboard, select it and then press Ctrl+X (cut) or Ctrl+C (copy). You can then move the cursor to any location in the outline and press Ctrl+V to paste the slide from the Clipboard.

To duplicate a slide, select it and then invoke the Edit⇨Duplicate command or press Ctrl+D. This step places a copy of the selected slide immediately in front of the selection.

Selecting and Editing One Paragraph

You can select and edit an entire paragraph along with all its subordinate paragraphs. Just click the bullet next to the paragraph you want to select or triple-click anywhere in the text. To delete an entire paragraph along with its subordinate paragraphs, select it and then press the Del key.

To cut or copy an entire paragraph to the Clipboard along with its subordinates, select it and then press Ctrl+X (cut) or Ctrl+C (copy). You can then press Ctrl+V to paste the paragraph anywhere in the presentation. To duplicate a paragraph, select it and then invoke the Edit⇨Duplicate command or press Ctrl+D.

Promoting and Demoting Paragraphs

To *promote* a paragraph means to move it up one level in the outline. If you promote the "Relies on polymers" line in Figure 3-1, for example, that line becomes a separate main point under the "Our Advantage" slide rather than a subpoint under "Ordinary Plexiglass." If you promote it again, it becomes a separate slide.

To *demote* a paragraph is just the opposite: the paragraph moves down one level in the outline. If you demote the "Dr. Nichols hired 1984." paragraph in Figure 3-1, it becomes a subpoint under "Founded in 1965 . . . ." rather than a separate main point.

Promoting paragraphs

To promote a paragraph, place the cursor anywhere in the paragraph and then perform any of the following techniques:

- ✔ Click the Promote button (shown in the margin) on the right side of the Formatting toolbar.
- ✔ Press the Shift+Tab key.
- ✔ Use the keyboard shortcut Alt+Shift+left arrow.

The paragraph moves up one level in the outline pecking order.

You cannot promote a slide title. Slide title is the highest rank in the outline hierarchy.

If you want to promote a paragraph and all its subordinate paragraphs, click the point's bullet or triple-click anywhere in the paragraph. Then promote it. You can also promote text by dragging it with the mouse. See the section "Dragging paragraphs to new levels," later in this chapter.

Demoting paragraphs

To demote a paragraph, place the cursor anywhere in the paragraph and then do any of the following:

- ✔ Click the Demote button (shown in the margin) on the right side of the Formatting toolbar.
- ✔ Press the Tab key.
- ✔ Use the keyboard shortcut Alt+Shift+right arrow.

The paragraph moves down one level in the outline pecking order.

If you demote a slide title, the entire slide is subsumed into the preceding slide. In other words, the slide title becomes a main point in the preceding slide.

To demote a paragraph and all its subparagraphs, click the paragraph's bullet or triple-click anywhere in the paragraph text. Then demote it. You can also demote text by dragging it with the mouse. See the following section, "Dragging paragraphs to new levels."

Be sensitive when you demote paragraphs. Being demoted can be an emotionally devastating experience.

Dragging paragraphs to new levels

When you move the mouse pointer over a bullet (or the slide button), the pointer changes from a single arrow to a four-cornered arrow. This arrow is your signal that you can click the mouse to select the entire paragraph (and any subordinate paragraphs). You also can use the mouse to promote or demote a paragraph along with all its subordinates.

To promote or demote with the mouse, follow these steps:

1. **Point to the bullet you want to demote or promote.**

   The mouse pointer changes to a four-cornered arrow. To demote a slide, point to the slide button. (Remember that you cannot promote a slide. It's already at the highest level.)

2. **Click and hold the mouse button down.**

3. **Drag the mouse to the right or left.**

   The mouse pointer changes to a double-pointed arrow, and a vertical line appears that shows the indentation level of the selection. Release the button when the selection is indented the way you want. The text is automatically reformatted for the new indentation level.

If you mess up, press Ctrl+Z to undo the promotion or demotion. Then try again.

Adding a New Paragraph

To add a new paragraph to a slide, move the cursor to the end of the paragraph you want the new paragraph to follow and press the Enter key. PowerPoint creates a new paragraph at the same outline level as the preceding paragraph.

If you position the cursor at the beginning of a paragraph and press the Enter key, the new paragraph is inserted *in front of* the cursor position. If you position the cursor in the middle of a paragraph and press the Enter key, the paragraph is split in two.

After you add a new paragraph, you may want to change its level in the outline. To do that, you must promote or demote the new paragraph. To create a subpoint for a main point, for example, position the cursor at the end of the main point and press the Enter key. Then demote the new paragraph. For details about how to promote or demote a paragraph, see the section "Promoting and Demoting Paragraphs," earlier in this chapter.

Adding a New Slide

You can add a new slide in many ways when you're working in Outline view. This list shows the most popular methods:

- ✔ Promote an existing paragraph to the highest level. This method splits a slide into two slides. In Figure 3-1, for example, you can create a new slide by promoting the "Transparent Aluminum" paragraph. That step splits the "Our Advantage" slide into two slides.

- ✔ Add a new paragraph and then promote it to the highest level.

- ✔ Place the cursor in a slide's title text and press the Enter key. This method creates a new slide before the current slide. Whether the title text stays with the current slide, goes with the new slide, or is split between the slides depends on the location of the cursor within the title when you press Enter.

- ✔ Place the cursor anywhere in a slide's body text and press Ctrl+Enter. This method creates a new slide immediately following the current slide. The position of the cursor within the existing slide doesn't matter; the new slide is always created after the current slide. (The cursor must be in the slide's body text for this method to work, though. If you put the cursor in a slide title and press Ctrl+Enter, the cursor jumps to the slide's body text without creating a new slide.)

| New Slide... |

- ✔ Place the cursor anywhere in a slide and click the New Slide button (shown in the margin).

   (My, aren't there a number of ways to create a new slide in Outline view?)

- ✔ Place the cursor anywhere in the slide and invoke the Insert➪New Slide command or its keyboard shortcut, Ctrl+M.

- ✔ Select an existing slide by clicking the slide button or triple-clicking the title and then duplicate it by using the Edit➪Duplicate command or its keyboard shortcut, Ctrl+D.

Because Outline view focuses on slide content rather than on layout, new slides are always given the basic Bulleted List layout, which includes title text and body text formatted with bullets. If you want to change the layout of a new slide, you must return to Slide view and click the Layout button to select a new slide layout.

Moving Text Up and Down

Outline view is also handy for rearranging your presentation. You easily can change the order of individual points on a slide, or you can rearrange the order of the slides.

Moving text up or down by using the keyboard

To move text up or down, first select the text you want to move. To move just one paragraph (along with any subordinate paragraphs), click its bullet. To move an entire slide, click its slide button.

To move the selected text up, use either of the following techniques:

- ✔ Click the Up button on the Outline toolbar (shown in the margin) on the left side of the screen.
- ✔ Press Alt+Shift+up arrow.

To move the selected text down, use either of the following techniques:

- ✔ Click the Down button on the Outline toolbar (shown in the margin) on the left side of the screen.
- ✔ Press Alt+Shift+down arrow.

Dragging text up or down

To move text up or down by using the mouse, follow these steps:

1. **Point to the bullet next to the paragraph you want to move.**

   The mouse pointer changes to a four-cornered arrow. To move a slide, point to the slide button.

2. **Click and hold the mouse button down.**

3. **Drag the mouse up or down.**

   The mouse pointer changes again to a double-pointed arrow, and a horizontal line appears, showing the horizontal position of the selection. Release the mouse when the selection is positioned where you want.

Be careful when you're moving text in a slide that has more than one level of body text paragraphs. Notice the position of the horizontal line as you drag the selection; the entire selection is inserted at that location, which may result in subpoints being split up. If you don't like the result of a move, you can always undo it by pressing Ctrl+Z.

Expanding and Collapsing the Outline

If your presentation has many slides, you may find it difficult to grasp its overall structure even in Outline view. Fortunately, PowerPoint enables you to *collapse* the outline so that only the slide titles are shown. Collapsing an outline does not delete the body text; it merely hides it so that you can focus on the order of the slides in your presentation.

Expanding a presentation restores the collapsed body text to the outline so that you can once again focus on details. You can collapse and expand an entire presentation, or you can collapse and expand one slide at a time.

Collapsing an entire presentation

To collapse an entire presentation, you have two options:

- Click the Show Titles button on the Outline toolbar (shown in the margin) on the left side of the screen.
- Press Alt+Shift+1.

Expanding an entire presentation

To expand an entire presentation, try one of these methods:

- Click the Show All button on the Outline toolbar (shown in the margin) on the left side of the screen.
- Press Alt+Shift+A.

Collapsing a single slide

To collapse a single slide, position the cursor anywhere in the slide you want to collapse. Then do one of the following:

- Click the Collapse Selection button on the Outline toolbar, on the left side of the screen.
- Press Alt+Shift+– (the minus sign).

Expanding a single slide

To expand a single slide, position the cursor anywhere in the title of the slide you want to expand. Then perform one of the following techniques:

 ✔ Click the Expand Selection button on the Outline toolbar (shown in the margin) on the left side of the screen.

 ✔ Press Alt+Shift++ (the plus sign).

Showing and Hiding Formats

The idea behind Outline view is to shield you from the appearance of your presentation so that you can concentrate on its content. With PowerPoint, you can take this idea one step further by removing the text formatting from your outline. The outline shown in Figure 3-1 includes text formatting. As you can see, the text for slide titles appears larger than the body text, and the bullet character varies depending on its level in the outline hierarchy.

Figure 3-2 shows the same outline with text formatting hidden. All text is displayed in the same vanilla font, and fancy bullet characters are replaced by simple bullets. The advantage of this layout is that you can see more of the outline on-screen. Notice that part of slide 4 is now visible; in Figure 3-1, you can see only the first three slides.

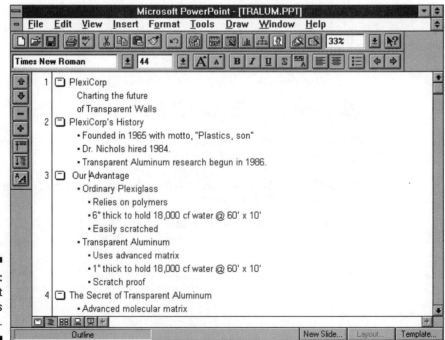

Figure 3-2:
The text
formatting is
hidden here.

To hide character formatting in Outline view, do one of the following:

- ✔ Click the Show Formatting button on the Outline toolbar (shown in the margin) on the left side of the screen.

- ✔ Press the slash key (/), the one on the numeric keypad, just above the number 8.

To restore formatting, just click the Show Formatting button or press the slash key again.

Hiding character formatting does not remove the formatting attributes from your presentation. It simply hides them while you're in Outline view so that you can concentrate on your presentation's content rather than on its appearance. Hiding character formatting removes not only character fonts and fancy bullets but also basic character styles, such as italics, bold, and underlining. Too bad. Hiding formats would be more useful if it still showed these basic character styles.

Chapter 4

Don't Forget Your Notes!

*E*ver had the fear — or maybe the actual experience — of showing a beautiful slide, complete with snappy text and perhaps an exquisite chart, and suddenly forgetting why you included the slide in the first place? You stumble for words. "Well, as you can see, this is a beautiful chart, and, uh, this slide makes the irrefutable point that, uh, well, I'm not sure — are there any questions?"

Fear not! One of PowerPoint's slickest features is its capability to create speaker notes to help you get through your presentation. You can make these notes as complete or as sketchy as you want or need. You can write a complete script for your presentation or just jot down a few key points to refresh your memory.

The best part about speaker notes is that you are the only one who sees them. They don't actually show up on your slides for all the world to see. Instead, notes pages are printed separately. There's one notes page for each slide in the presentation, and each notes page includes a reduced version of the slide so that you can keep track of which notes page belongs to which slide.

To add speaker notes to a presentation, you must switch PowerPoint to Notes Pages view. Then you just type away.

Don't you think that it's about time for a short chapter? Although notes pages are one of PowerPoint's slickest features, creating notes pages isn't all that complicated — hence the brevity of this chapter.

Understanding Notes Pages View

Notes Pages view shows the speaker notes pages that are created for your presentation. There is one notes page for each slide in a presentation. Each notes page consists of a reduced version of the slide and an area for notes. Figure 4-1 shows an example of a presentation shown in Notes Pages view.

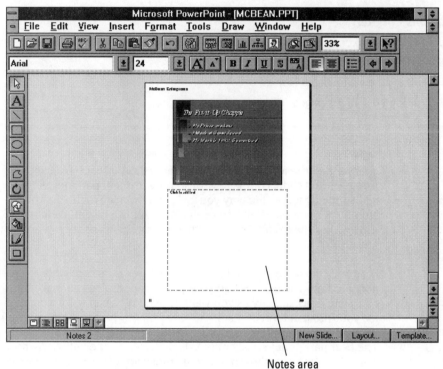

Figure 4-1:
A presentation in Notes Pages view.

Notes area

You can switch to Notes Pages view in two ways:

- ✔ Click the Notes Pages view button (shown in the margin) to the left of the horizontal scroll bar.
- ✔ Use the View⇨Notes Pages command.

Unfortunately, no keyboard shortcut is available to switch directly to Notes Pages view. To add notes to a presentation, just click the notes text object and begin typing.

When you first switch to Notes Pages view, the display probably will be too small for you to read the speaker notes. To enlarge the display, click the down arrow next to the zoom setting to reveal a list of zoom settings and pick the one that works best for you. A zoom factor of 66 or 75 percent is usually about right. (You can also type any zoom factor you like directly into the zoom size field.)

Adding Notes to a Slide

To add notes to a slide, follow this procedure:

1. **In Slide or Outline view, move to the slide to which you want to add notes.**

2. **Switch to Notes Pages view.**

3. **Adjust the zoom factor if necessary so that you can read the notes text.**

4. **Scroll the display if necessary to bring the notes text into view.**

5. **Click the notes text object, where it reads *Click to add text*.**

6. **Type away.**

The text you type appears in the notes area. As you create your notes, you can use any of PowerPoint's standard word processing features, such as cut, copy, and paste. Press the Enter key to create new paragraphs.

Figure 4-2 shows a notes page displayed with a zoom factor of 75 percent and with some notes typed.

After you have switched to Notes Pages view, you don't have to return to Slide view or Outline view to add notes for other slides. Use the scroll bar or the PageUp and PageDown keys to add notes for other slides.

My Notes Don't Fit!

If your notes don't fit in the area provided on the notes page, you have two options: increase the size of the text area on the notes page or create a second notes page for a slide.

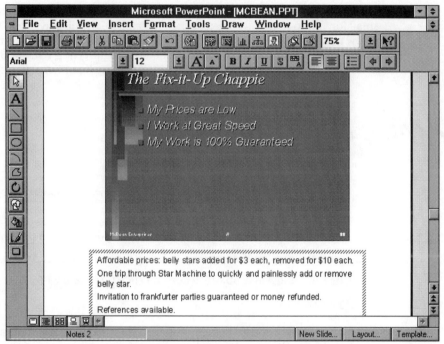

Figure 4-2:
Notes that
are en-
larged for
your reading
pleasure.

Increasing the size of the text area on a notes page

To increase the size of the text area on a notes page, follow this procedure:

1. **Make the notes page slide object smaller by grabbing a corner of the slide object (by clicking it) and dragging it to a smaller size. After you have shrunk the slide, move it to the top of the page.**

2. **Increase the size of the notes page text area by clicking it and then dragging the top love handle up.**

Figure 4-3 shows a notes page with a smaller slide and a larger area for notes.

Changing the size of the slide and text areas while you're in Notes Page view changes those areas for only the current page; other pages are unaffected. To change the size of these areas for all notes pages, switch to Notes Master view and make the adjustment. (Masters aren't covered until Chapter 8, but if you want to experiment, you can switch to Notes Master view by using the View⇨Master⇨Notes command.)

To create the largest possible area for notes on a notes page, delete the slide area altogether. Just click it and press the Del key. If you do that, you find that it's all too easy to get your notes pages mixed up so that you cannot tell which notes page belongs with which slide. Include page numbers on both your slides and your notes pages to help keep them in sync or type each slide's title at the top of the notes page. (Page numbers are set up for slides and notes pages by the Pick-a-Look wizard.)

Adding an extra notes page for a slide

PowerPoint doesn't provide any way to add more than one page of notes for each slide. But these steps show a trick that accomplishes essentially the same thing:

1. **Create a new slide immediately following the slide that requires two pages of notes.**

   Do this step in Slide, Outline, or Notes Pages view.

2. **Switch to Notes Pages view and move to the notes page for the slide you just created.**

   Delete the slide object at the top of this notes page by clicking it and pressing the Del key. Then extend the notes text area up so that it fills the page by clicking it and then dragging the top center love handle up.

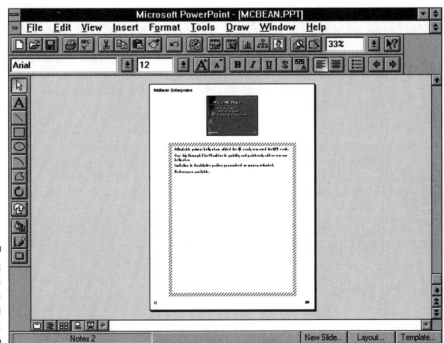

Figure 4-3:
A notes page with more room for notes.

3. Type the additional notes for the preceding slide on this new notes page.

Add a heading, such as "Continued from slide 23," at the top of the text to help you remember that this portion is a continuation of notes from the preceding slide.

4. Use the Tools⇨Hide Slide command to *hide* the slide.

You can use this command from any view. The Hide Slide command hides the slide, which means that it isn't included in an on-screen slide show.

The result of this trick is that you now have two pages of notes for a single slide, and the second notes page doesn't have an image of the slide on it and is not included in your slide show.

If you're printing overhead transparencies, you may want to uncheck the Print Hidden Slides check box in the Print dialog box. That way, the hidden slide isn't printed. Be sure to recheck the box when you print the notes pages, though. Otherwise, the notes page for the hidden slide isn't printed either — and the reason you created the hidden slide in the first place was so that you can print a notes page for it!

Think twice before creating a second page of notes for a slide. Do you really have that much to say about a single slide? Maybe the slide has too much content to begin with and should be split into two slides.

Adding a New Slide from Notes Pages View

If you're working on the notes for a slide and you realize that you want to create a new slide, you don't have to return to Slide view or Outline view. Just click the New Slide button on the status bar or use the Insert⇨New Slide menu command to add the new slide.

If you want to work on the slide's appearance or contents, however, you must switch back to Slide or Outline view. You cannot modify a slide's appearance or contents from Notes Pages view.

To revert quickly to Slide view from Notes Pages view, double-click the notes page's slide area.

Printing Notes Pages

Notes pages don't do you much good if you can't print them. These steps show you how to do so.

1. **Summon the File⇨Print command.**

   The Print dialog box appears.

2. **Use the Print What list box to choose the Notes Pages option.**

3. **Make sure that the Print Hidden Slides box is checked if you want to print notes pages for hidden slides.**

4. **Click the OK button or press the Enter key.**

Figure 4-4 shows the Print dialog box with the Notes Pages option selected so that notes pages rather than slides are printed.

If you have just printed slides on overhead transparencies, don't forget to reload your printer with plain paper. You probably don't want to print your speaker notes on transparencies!

More information about printing is in Chapter 6.

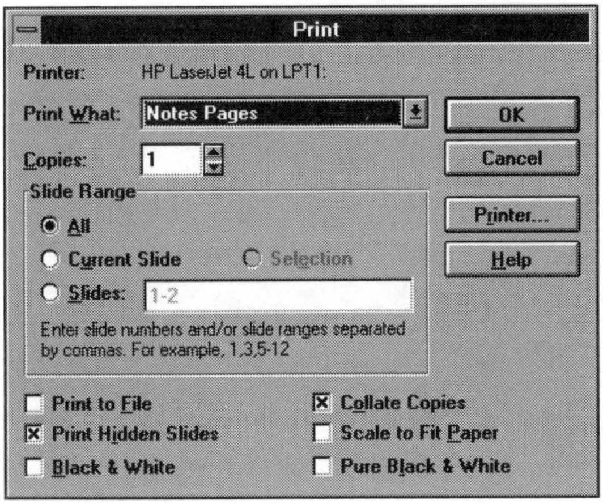

Figure 4-4:
The Print dialog box, set up to print notes pages.

Print dialog box:

Printer: HP LaserJet 4L on LPT1:

Print What: Notes Pages

Copies: 1

Slide Range
- All
- Current Slide
- Selection
- Slides: 1-2

Enter slide numbers and/or slide ranges separated by commas. For example, 1,3,5-12

OK
Cancel
Printer...
Help

- Print to File
- X Print Hidden Slides
- Black & White
- X Collate Copies
- Scale to Fit Paper
- Pure Black & White

Random Thoughts About Speaker Notes

This section provides some ideas that may help you make the most of your notes pages.

If you're giving an important presentation for a large audience, you may want to consider using notes pages to write a complete script for your presentation. For less formal presentations, more succinct notes are probably better.

Use notes pages to jot down any anecdotes, jokes, or other asides you want to remember to use in your presentation.

If you prefer to hand write your notes, you can print blank notes pages. Don't bother adding notes to your presentation, but use the File⇨Print command to print notes pages. The resulting notes pages have a reduced image of the slide at the top and a blank space in which you can handwrite your notes later.

You may also consider providing blank notes pages for your audience. The File⇨Print command can print audience handouts that contain two, three, or six slides per page, but these handout pages leave no room for the audience members to write notes.

Chapter 5

Avoiding Those
Embarrassing Speling Errors

*S*pelling errors in a word processing document are bad, but at least they're small. In a PowerPoint presentation, spelling errors are small only until you put the transparency or the 35mm slide in the projector. Then they get all blown out of proportion. Nothing is more embarrassing than a two-foot-tall spelling error.

Fortunately, PowerPoint has a pretty decent spell checker. It also has two other nifty features to help catch innocent typographical errors before you show your presentation to a board of directors: a capitalization whirligig that fixes your capitalization (capital idea, eh?) and a period flinger that ensures that each line either does or does not end with a period.

Checking Your Spelling

I was voted Worst Speller in the Sixth Grade. Not that that qualifies me to run for vice president or anything, but it shows how much I appreciate computer spell checkers. Spelling makes no sense to me. I felt a little better after watching *The Story of English* on public television. Now at least I know who to blame for all the peculiarities of English spelling — the Angles, the Norms (including the guy from "Cheers"), and the Saxophones.

Thank goodness for PowerPoint's spell checker. It works its way through your presentation, looking up every word in its massive list of correctly spelled words and bringing any misspelled words to your attention. It performs this task without giggling or snickering. It gives you the opportunity, in fact, to tell it that *you* are right and *it* is wrong and that it should learn how to spell words the way you do.

The following steps show the procedure for checking a presentation's spelling:

1. **If the presentation you want to spell check is not already open, open it.**

   It doesn't matter which view you're in. You can spell check from any of these views: Slide, Outline, Notes Pages, or Slide Sorter.

2. **Fire up the spell checker.**

    Click the Spelling button on the Standard toolbar, press F7, or use the Tools⇨ Spelling command.

3. **Tap your fingers on your desk.**

   PowerPoint is searching your presentation for embarrassing spelling errors. Be patient.

4. **Don't be startled if PowerPoint finds a spelling error.**

   If PowerPoint finds a spelling error in your presentation, it switches to the slide that contains the error, highlights the offensive word, and displays the misspelled word along with a suggested correction, as shown in Figure 5-1.

5. **Choose the correct spelling or laugh in PowerPoint's face.**

   If you agree that the word is misspelled, scan the list of corrections that PowerPoint offers and click the one you like. Then click the Change button. If you like the way you spelled the word in the first place (maybe it's an unusual word that isn't in PowerPoint's spelling dictionary or maybe you like to spell like Chaucer did), click the Ignore button. Watch as PowerPoint turns red in the face.

6. **Repeat Steps 4 and 5 until PowerPoint gives up.**

   When you see the following message:

   Finished spell checking entire presentation

   you're finished.

The remainder of this section presents some random thoughts to ponder as you spell check your presentations.

PowerPoint always spell checks your entire presentation from start to finish. Unlike Microsoft Word's spell checker, you cannot check the spelling for a single word or a selected range. Too bad. On the other hand, you don't have to worry about returning to the top of the document before running the spell checker. PowerPoint always checks spelling for the entire presentation, beginning with the first slide.

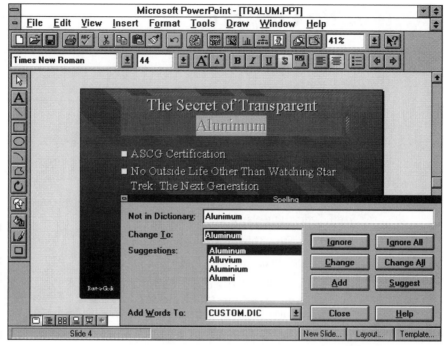

PowerPoint checks the spelling for titles, body text, notes, and text objects added to slides. It doesn't check the spelling for embedded objects, however, such as charts or graphs.

If PowerPoint cannot come up with a suggestion or if none of its suggestions is correct, you can type your own correction and click the Change button. If the word you type isn't in the dictionary, PowerPoint asks you whether you're sure that you know what you're doing. Double-check and click OK if you really mean it.

If you want PowerPoint to ignore all occurrences of a particular misspelling, click the Ignore All button. Likewise, if you want PowerPoint to correct all occurrences of a particular misspelling, click the Change All button.

If you get tired of PowerPoint always complaining about a word that's not in its standard dictionary (such as PlexiCorp), click Add to add the word to the custom dictionary. If you cannot sleep at night until you know more about the custom dictionary, read the following sidebar entitled "Don't make me tell you about the custom dictionary."

Capitalizing Correctly

PowerPoint's Change Case command enables you to capitalize the text in your slides properly. These steps show how to use it:

1. **Select the text you want to capitalize.**

2. **Invoke the Format⇨Change Case command.**

   The Change Case dialog box appears (see Figure 5-2).

3. **Study the options for a moment and then click the one you want.**

   The options follow:

   Sentence case: The first letter of the first word in each sentence is capitalized. Everything else is changed to lowercase.

   lowercase: Everything is changed to lowercase.

   UPPERCASE: Everything is changed to capital letters.

   Title Case: The first letter of each word is capitalized. PowerPoint is smart enough to leave certain words, such as *a* and *the* lowercase, but you should double-check to ensure that it worked properly.

   tOGGLE cASE: This option turns capitals into lowercase and turns lowercase into capitals, for a ransom-note look.

4. **Click OK or press Enter and check the results.**

Don't make me tell you about the custom dictionary

PowerPoint's spell checker uses two spelling dictionaries: A standard dictionary, which contains untold thousands of words all reviewed for correctness by George Bernard Shaw himself (just kidding!), and a *custom dictionary,* which contains words you have added by clicking the Add button when the spell checker found a spelling error.

The custom dictionary lives in a file named CUSTOM.DIC, which makes its residence in the \WINDOWS\MSAPPS\PROOF directory. Other Microsoft programs that use spell checkers — most notably Microsoft Word — share the same custom dictionary with PowerPoint. So, if you add a word to the custom dictionary in Word, PowerPoint's spell checker knows about the word too.

What if you accidentally add a word to the dictionary? Then you have a serious problem. You have two alternatives. You can petition Noah Webster to have your variant spelling officially added to the English language, or you can edit the CUSTOM.DIC file, search through the file until you find the bogus word, and delete it. CUSTOM.DIC is a standard text file, so you can edit it with just about any text editor, including Notepad, the jiffy editor that comes free with Windows.

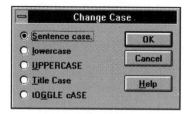

Figure 5-2:
The Change
Case dialog
box.

The speller cannot tell the difference between *your* and *you're, ours* and *hours,* or *angel* and *angle,* and so on. In other words, if the word is in the dictionary, PowerPoint passes it by regardless of whether you used the word correctly. PowerPoint's spell checker is no substitute for good, old-fashioned proofing. Print your presentation, sit down with a cup of cappuccino, and *read* it.

Always double-check your text after using the Change Case command to make sure that the result is what you intended.

Slide titles almost always should use title case. The first level of bullets on a slide can use either title or sentence case. Lower levels should usually use sentence case.

Avoid uppercase, if you can. It's harder to read and looks like you're shouting.

To Period or Not to Period. Period.

One dead giveaway of poor proofing is a slide in which some of the lines end with periods and others don't. Fortunately, PowerPoint has a Periods command that enables you to add or remove periods from the end of each line in a selection of text. These steps show how to use it:

1. **Select the text you want to periodicalize.**

   Periodicolate? Emperiod? I never pass up an opportunity to coin a new word!

2. **Invoke the Format➪Period command.**

   The Periods dialog box pops up (see Figure 5-3).

3. **To add periods, check A̲dd Periods. To remove them, check R̲emove Periods.**

4. **Click OK or press the Enter key.**

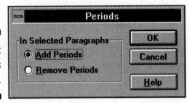

Figure 5-3:
The Periods
dialog box.

Double-check your text to make sure that the periods have been added or removed satisfactorily.

If your bullets consist of full sentences, they should end with periods. If they are sentence fragments, leave the periods off. (If your bullets are a mixture of complete sentences and sentence fragments, rewrite them so that they are all either one or the other.)

When in doubt, no one is going to sue you if you leave the periods off when you should include them or if you include them when you should leave them off, as long as you're consistent. Use periods on every bullet in the slide or on none of them.

Chapter 6

Printing Your Presentation Any Which Way You Please

⬢⬢⬢

In This Chapter

▶ Printing slides

▶ Printing handouts

▶ Printing speaker notes

▶ Printing an outline

▶ Whoa! Why doesn't it print?

⬢⬢⬢

*T*he Print command. The Printmeister. Big presentation comin' up. Printin' some slides. The Printorama. The Mentor of de Printor. Captain Toner of the Good Ship Laseroo.

Don't worry — there's no one waiting to ambush you with annoying one-liners when you print a PowerPoint presentation. Just a handful of boring dialog boxes with boring check boxes. Point-point, click-click, print-print. (Hey, humor me, OK? The French think that I'm a comic genius!)

Printing Stuff

To print slides or any other part of a presentation, you must first conjure up the Print dialog box. You can do this in more ways than the government can raise revenue without calling it a tax, but the four most common are shown in this list:

✔ Choose the File⇨Print command.

✔ Press Ctrl+P.

✔ Press Ctrl+Shift+F12.

 ✔ Click the Print button on the Standard toolbar (shown in the margin).

Any of these actions summons the Print dialog box, shown in Figure 6-1. This box grants you three wishes, but with two limitations: It cannot kill anyone (ix-nay on the illing-kay), and it cannot make anyone fall in love with you.

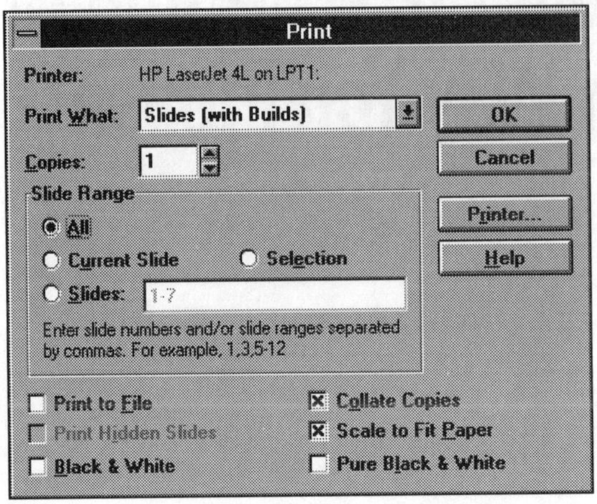

Figure 6-1:
The Print
dialog box.

After you have unleashed the Print dialog box, click the OK button or press the Enter key to print all the slides in your presentation. Or fiddle around with the settings to print just a select group of slides or more than one copy, or to print handouts, speaker notes, or an outline. This chapter shows you the treasures that lie hidden in this dialog box.

Printing can be es-el-oh-double-ewe. PowerPoint politely displays a status box to keep you informed of its progress, so at least you know that the darn program hasn't gone AWOL on you.

Don't panic if your printer doesn't start spewing forth pages immediately after the Print dialog box goes away. PowerPoint printouts tend to demand a great deal from the printer, so sometimes the printer has to work for a while before it can produce a finished page. Be patient. The Printer wizard has every intention of granting your request.

Oh, by the way, if you see a vague error message that says something like this:

Put paper in the printer, dummy!

try putting paper in the printer.

What do you want to print?

The Print What field in the Print dialog box enables you to select which type of output you want to print. The following choices are available:

- *Slides (with Builds):* Prints slides. If you have used the Build command with a slide, a separate page is printed for each bulleted item on the slide. The first page has just the first bulleted item; the second page shows the first and second bullets; and so on. Builds are covered in Chapter 10.

- *Slides (without Builds):* Prints slides but ignores builds. One page is printed for each slide, whether or not you have used the Build command for the slide.

- *Notes pages:* Prints speaker notes.

- *Handouts (2 Slides per Page):* Prints audience handout pages. Each handout page shows two slides.

- *Handouts (3 Slides per Page):* Prints audience handout pages. Each handout page shows three slides.

- *Handouts (6 Slides per Page):* Prints audience handout pages. Each handout page shows six slides.

- *Outline view:* Prints an outline of your presentation.

Select the type of output you want to print and then click the OK button or press the Enter key. Off you go!

When you're printing slides to be used as overhead transparencies, print a proof copy of the slides on plain paper before committing the output to transparencies. Transparencies are too expensive to print on until you're sure that your output is just right.

To change the orientation of your printed output from Landscape to Portrait mode (or vice versa), use the File⇨Slide Setup command. You can find more information about this command in Chapter 8.

To print handouts with two, three, or six slides per page, PowerPoint naturally must shrink the slides to make them fit. Because slides usually have outrageously large type, the handout slides are normally still readable, even at their reduced size.

Printing more than one copy

The Copies field in the Print dialog box enables you to tell PowerPoint to print more than one copy of your presentation. You can click one of the arrows next to this field to increase or decrease the number of copies, or you can type directly in the field to set the number of copies.

Near the bottom of the dialog box is a check box labeled Collate Copies. If this box is checked, PowerPoint prints each copy of your presentation one at a time. In other words, if your presentation consists of ten slides and you select three copies and check the Collate Copies box, PowerPoint first prints all ten slides of the first copy of the presentation, and then all ten slides of the second copy, and then all ten slides of the third copy. If you do not check the Collate Copies box, PowerPoint prints three copies of the first slide, followed by three copies of the second slide, followed by three copies of the third slide, and so on.

The Collate Copies option saves you from the chore of manually sorting your copies. If your presentation takes forever to print because it's loaded down with heavy-duty graphics, however, you probably can save time in the long run by unchecking the Collate Copies box. Why? Because many printers are fast when it comes to printing a second or third copy of a page. The printer may spend ten minutes figuring out how to print a particularly complicated page, but after it figures it out, the printer can chug out umpteen copies of that page without hesitation. If you print collated copies, the printer must labor over each page separately for each copy of the presentation it prints.

Printing part of a presentation

When you first use the Print command, the All option is checked so that your entire presentation is printed. The other options in the Slide Range portion of the Print dialog box enable you to tell PowerPoint to print just part of your presentation. In addition to All, you have three options:

✔ *Current Slide:* Prints just the current slide. Before you invoke the Print command, you should move to the slide you want to print. Then check this option in the Print dialog box and click OK. This option is handy when you have made a change to one slide and you don't want to reprint the entire presentation.

✔ *Selection:* Prints just the portion of the presentation you selected before invoking the Print command. This option is easiest to use in Outline or Slide Sorter view. First, select the slides you want to print by dragging the mouse to highlight them. Then invoke the Print command, click the Selection box, and click OK.

✔ *Slides:* Enables you to select specific slides for printing. You can print a range of slides by typing the beginning and ending slide numbers, separated by a hyphen, as in **5-8** to print slides 5, 6, 7, and 8. Or you can list individual slides, separated by commas, as in **4,8,11** to print slides 4, 8, and 11. And you can combine ranges and individual slides, as in **4,9-11,13** to print slides 4, 9, 10, 11, and 13.

To print a portion of a presentation, first call up the Print dialog box by using the File➪Print command, pressing Ctrl+P, or clicking the Print button on the Standard toolbar. Next, select the Slide Range option you want. Then click OK or press the Enter key.

What are all those other check boxes?

The Print command has six check boxes. They cling to the bottom of the dialog box, hoping to slip by unnoticed. This list shows you what they do:

✔ *Print to File:* Use this option if you have a friend lucky enough to have that new $20,000 Binford color LaserBlaster 32-MegaDot printer. Print to File asks you for a filename and then sends your print output to the file you indicate. You then can copy that file to a floppy disk, pack it over to your friend's computer, and print it on his or her printer by issuing a command similar to this one:

copy cheap.prt lpt1: /b

In this grisly example, CHEAP.PRT is the name of the print file that was created by way of the Print to File option. Don't forget the /B doohickey; the command doesn't work without it.

If your buddy has a new $20,000 Binford color LaserBlaster 32-MegaDot printer, she or he can probably afford a copy of PowerPoint. If the computer that has the printer you want to use also has a copy of PowerPoint, don't bother with the Print to File option. Just save your PowerPoint presentation file to a floppy disk, airmail it to your friend's computer, and print it from there directly from PowerPoint.

✔ *Collate Copies:* This option was already covered in the section "Printing more than one copy." Look there for advice about using this option.

✔ *Print Hidden Slides:* You can *hide* individual slides by way of the Tools➪Hide Slide command. After a slide is hidden, it does not print unless you check the Print Hidden Slides option in the Print dialog box.

In Figure 6-1, this option is shaded, which indicates that it is not available. That happens when the presentation being printed doesn't have any hidden slides. The Print Hidden Slides option is available only when the presentation has hidden slides. Chapter 10, "A Time of Transition," has more information about hidden slides, if you're curious.

✔ *Scale to Fit Paper:* Adjusts the size of the printed output to fit the paper in the printer. Leave this option unchecked to avoid bizarre printing problems.

✔ *Black & White:* Prints colors as shades of gray even if you have a color printer, omits the background color, and prints all text in black. It's useful when you're printing draft copies you want to proof for typos or for printing handouts or notes pages when the reduced slides are hard to read.

✔ *Pure Black & White:* Even more black and white than Black & White. This option eliminates all shading, so objects filled with color appear only as outlines. This option is useful when even black-and-white printouts are hard to read.

Microsoft considered licensing TurnerVision technology to colorize slides printed with the Black & White option, but decided against it when it was discovered that most audiences dream in black and white when they fall asleep during a boring presentation.

Printing Boo-Boos

On the surface, printing seems as though it should be one of the easiest parts of using PowerPoint. After all, all you have to do to print a presentation is click the Print button, right? Well, usually. Unfortunately, all kinds of things can go wrong between the time you click the Print button and the time gorgeous output bursts forth from your printer. If you run into printer trouble, this section discusses some things you can check out.

Getting your printer ready

Your printer must be ready and raring to go before it can spew out printed pages. If you suspect that your printer is not ready for action, this list presents some things to check:

✔ Make sure that the printer's power cord is plugged in and that the printer is turned on.

✔ The printer cable must be connected to both the printer and the computer's printer port. If the cable has come loose, turn off both the computer and the printer, reattach the cable, and then restart the computer and the printer. (You know better, of course, than to turn off your computer without first saving any work in progress, exiting from any active application programs, and shutting down Windows. So I won't say anything about it. Not even one little word.)

✔ If your printer has a switch labeled *On-line* or *Select,* press it until the corresponding On-line or Select light comes on.

✔ Make sure that the printer has plenty of paper. (I have always wanted to write a musical about a printer that ate people rather than paper. I think that I'll call it *Little DOS of Horrors.* "Try typing this command at the DOS command prompt: **Prompt: Feed Me:**")

✔ If you're using a dot-matrix printer, make sure that the ribbon is OK. For a laser printer, make sure that the toner cartridge has plenty of life left in it.

Dealing with Windows printer stuff

Windows is loaded down with all sorts of printing capabilities, and this section is certainly not the place for a treatise about the printing features in Windows. But you may face one common Windows roadblock to printing success: choosing the right printer.

Notice in Figure 6-1 that the Print dialog box has a button labeled Printer. When you click this button, the Print Setup dialog box appears, as shown in Figure 6-2. The Print Setup dialog box lists the printers that are available for your use. choose the one you want to use by clicking it and then click the OK button to return to the Print dialog box. That's all there is to it!

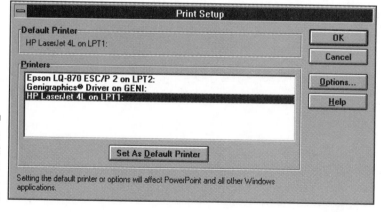

Figure 6-2:
The Print
Setup dialog
box.

You use the Print Setup dialog box only if you have more than one printer available to you. If you have two or more printers connected to your computer or if your computer is attached to a network, you use this dialog box to choose the printer you want to use.

Notice the printer named Genigraphics Driver on GENI. This printer selection doesn't represent a printer. Instead, you use it to create output that can be transferred to 35mm slides by Genigraphics Corporation. For more information about using this service, consult Chapter 11.

If your printer doesn't show up in the Printers list, your printer hasn't been installed for Windows. With an appropriate bribe, your local computer geek may be persuaded to install your printer for you. Good luck.

Part II
Dressing Up Your Presentations

The 5th Wave   By Rich Tennant

"These kidnappers are clever, Lieutenant. Look at this ransom note, the use of 4-color graphics to highlight the victim's photograph. And the fonts! They must be creating their own—must be over 35 typefaces here..."

In this part...

1 read recently that Rosanne Arnold had a slew of cosmetic surgeries as part of a take-control-of-your-life binge. The chapters in this part are all about cosmetic surgery for your presentations. You'll learn how to perform such procedures as typo-suction, chart reductions, and equation tucks.

The good news is that if health-care reform goes through, the government might even pick up the tab!

Chapter 7

Dressing Up Your Text

● ●

In This Chapter

▶ Using bold, italics, underlining, and other character effects

▶ Changing the text font and size

▶ Using bullets

▶ Lining things up

▶ Tabbing and indenting

▶ Spacing things out

● ●

A good presentation should be like a fireworks show: at every new slide, the audience gasps. O-o-o-h. A-a-a-h. The audience is so stunned by the spectacular appearance of your slides that no one bothers to really read them.

This chapter gets you on the road toward ooohs and aaahs by showing you how to format text. If you use the Pick-a-Look wizard or base your new presentations on a template, your text is already formatted acceptably. But to really pull out the pyrotechnic stops, you have to know a few basic formatting tricks.

Many of PowerPoint's text-formatting capabilities work the same as Microsoft Word's do. If you want to format text a certain way and you know how to do it in Word, try it the same way in PowerPoint. Odds are that it works.

Changing the Look of Your Characters

PowerPoint enables you to change the look of individual characters in subtle or drastic ways. You can control all these character attributes by way of the Font dialog box, which you summon by using the Format➪Font command (see Figure 7-1).

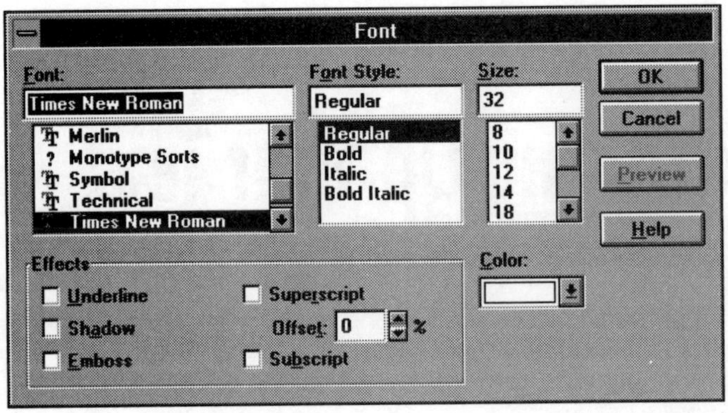

Figure 7-1:
The
cumbersome
Font dialog
box.

The Font dialog box is a bit cumbersome to use, but fortunately PowerPoint provides an assortment of shortcuts for your formatting pleasure. These shortcuts are listed in Table 7-1; the procedures for using them are described in this section.

Table 7-1	Character-Formatting Shortcuts	
Button	**Keyboard Shortcut**	**Format**
B	Ctrl+B	Bold
I	Ctrl+I	*Italic*
U	Ctrl+U	Underline
(none)	Ctrl+spacebar	Normal
 Times New Roman	Ctrl+Shift+F	Font
 32	Ctrl+Shift+P	Change point size
A	Ctrl+Shift+>	Increase point size
▲	Ctrl+Shift+<	Decrease point size
A	(none)	Text color
S	(none)	Text shadow

It's true — PowerPoint has many keyboard shortcuts for character formatting. You don't have to learn them all, though. The only ones I know and use routinely are for bold, italic, underline, and normal. Learn those and you'll be in good shape. You get the added bonus that these keyboard shortcuts are the same as the shortcuts many other Windows programs use, including Microsoft Word 6.

If you want, you can instruct these formats to gang-tackle some text. In other words, text can be bold, italic, and underlined for extra, extra emphasis. You can gang-tackle text with any combination of formats you want.

You also can remove all text formats in one swell foop by highlighting the text and pressing Ctrl+spacebar.

Most of the formatting options covered in this chapter are available only in Slide or Notes Pages view. If you try to apply a format and nothing happens, switch to Slide or Notes Pages view and try again.

Another way to summon the Font dialog box is to highlight the text you want to format and right-click the mouse. A menu appears; choose the Font option from the menu and voilá! — the Font dialog box appears.

To boldly go . . .

Want to emphasize a point? Make it bold. Remember: Martin Luther said that if you must sin, sin boldly.

To make existing text bold, follow these steps:

1. **Highlight the text you want to make bold.**

2. **Press Ctrl+B or click the Bold button on the Formatting toolbar (shown in the margin at the beginning of this section).**

To type new text in boldface, follow these steps:

1. **Press Ctrl+B or click the Bold button on the Formatting toolbar.**

2. **Type some text.**

   Make a bold effort.

3. **Press Ctrl+B or click the Bold button to return to typing normal text.**

You can use the Format➪Font command to make text bold, but who wants to mess with a cumbersome dialog box when you can click the Bold button or press Ctrl+B instead? The rule is to use whatever is easiest for you.

You can remove the bold attribute also by highlighting the bold text and pressing Ctrl+spacebar. This technique removes not only the bold attribute but also other character attributes, such as italics and underlining. In other words, it returns the text to normal.

Italics

 Another way to emphasize a word is to italicize it. To italicize existing text, follow these steps:

1. **Highlight the text you want to italicize.**

2. **Press Ctrl+I or click the Italic button on the Formatting toolbar (shown in the margin).**

To type new text in italics, follow these steps:

1. **Press Ctrl+I or click the Italic button on the Formatting toolbar.**

2. **Type some text.**

   Don't be afraid, Luke.

3. **Press Ctrl+I or click the Italic button to return to typing normal text.**

The cumbersome Format➪Font command has an italic option, but why bother? Ctrl+I and the Italic button are too easy to ignore.

 Pressing Ctrl+spacebar removes italics along with any other character formatting you applied. Use it to return text to normal or, as NASA would say, to "reestablish nominal text."

Underlines

 Back in the days of typewriters, underlining was the only way to add emphasis to text. You can underline text in PowerPoint, but you may as well use a typewriter. Underlining usually looks out of place in today's jazzy presentations, unless you're shooting for a nostalgic effect.

To underline existing text, follow these steps:

1. **Highlight the text you want to underline.**

2. **Press Ctrl+U or click the Underline button on the Formatting toolbar.**

To type new text and have it automatically underlined, follow these steps:

1. **Press Ctrl+U or click the Underline button on the Formatting toolbar.**

2. **Type some text.**

3. **Press Ctrl+U or click the Underline button to return to typing normal text.**

The Format⇨Font command enables you to underline text, but Ctrl+U or the Underline button is easier to use.

You can remove the underlines and all other character formats by highlighting the text and pressing Ctrl+spacebar.

Big and little characters

If text is hard to read or you simply want to draw attention to it, you can make it bigger than the surrounding text.

To increase or decrease the font size for existing text, follow these steps:

1. **Highlight the text whose size you want to change.**

2. **To increase the font size, press Ctrl+Shift+> or click the Increase Font Size button on the Formatting toolbar (shown in the margin).**

   To decrease the font size, press Ctrl+Shift+< or click the Decrease Font Size button on the Formatting toolbar (shown in the margin).

   To set the font to a specific size, press Ctrl+Shift+P or click the Font Size button on the Formatting toolbar and type the point size you want.

   To type new text in a different font size, change the font size by using the method in Step 2. Then type away.

Again, you can use the Format⇨Font command to change the point size, but why bother when the controls are right there on the Formatting toolbar? Only a masochist would mess with the Format⇨Font command.

Ctrl+spacebar clears font attributes, such as bold and italic, but it cannot reset the font size.

Text fonts

If you don't like the looks of a text font, you can easily switch to a different font. To change the font for existing text, follow these steps:

1. **Highlight the text whose font you can't stand.**

2. **Click the arrow next to the Font control on the Formatting toolbar (see button in margin). A list of available fonts appears. Click the one you want to use.**

   Or press Ctrl+Shift+F and then press the down-arrow key to display the font choices.

To type new text in a different font, change the font as described and begin typing. Change back to the original font when you are finished.

Yes, yes, yes — with the Format⇨Font command you change the font. But with the Font control sitting right there on the Formatting toolbar for the whole world to see, why waste time navigating your way through menus and dialog boxes?

Pressing Ctrl+spacebar does not reset the font.

If you want to change the font for all the slides in your presentation, you should switch to Slide Master view and then change the font. Details on how to do so are covered in the next chapter.

PowerPoint automatically moves the fonts you use the most to the head of the font list. This feature makes it even easier to pick your favorite font.

Don't overdo it with fonts! Just because you have 37 different typefaces doesn't mean that you should try to use them all on the same slide. Don't mix more than two or three typefaces on a slide, and use fonts consistently throughout the presentation.

The color purple

Color is an excellent way to draw attention to text in a slide if, of course, your slides print in color or you can display them on a color monitor. Follow this procedure for changing text color:

1. **Highlight the text whose color you want to change.**

2. **Click the Text Color button on the Formatting toolbar (shown in the margin).**

   A little box with color choices appears. Click the color you want to use.

To type new text in a different color, change the color and then begin typing. When you have had enough, change back to the original color and continue.

If you don't like any of the colors the Text Color button offers, click where it reads *Other color*. A bigger dialog box with more color choices appears. If you still cannot find the right shade of teal, click the More Colors button and have at it. Check out Chapter 9 if you need still more color help.

If you want to change the text color for your entire presentation, do it on the Slide Master (see Chapter 8 for details).

The shadow knows

Adding a shadow behind your text can make the text stand out against its background, which makes the entire slide easier to read. For that reason, many of the templates supplied with PowerPoint use shadows. These steps show you how to apply a text shadow:

1. **Highlight the text you want to shadow.**

2. **Click the Shadow button (shown in the margin).**

    Sorry — PowerPoint has no keyboard shortcut for this one. Oh, well. It's about time you finally learn how to use the mouse. You can set the shadow format by using the Format⇨Font command if you just can't master the mouse (or you don't have one).

Embossed text

When you emboss text, PowerPoint adds a dark shadow below the text and a light shadow above it to produce an embossed effect. Try it. It's very cool.

1. **Highlight the text you want to emboss.**

2. **Use the Format⇨Font command to pop up the Font dialog box.**

   Sorry — PowerPoint has no keyboard shortcut or toolbar button for embossing. You have to do it the hard way.

3. **Check the Emboss option.**

4. **Click the OK button.**

When you emboss text, PowerPoint changes the text color to the background color to enhance the embossed effect.

 Embossed text is hard to read in smaller point sizes. It's an effect best reserved for large titles.

Biting the Bullet

Most presentations have at least some slides that include a bulleted list — a series of paragraphs accented by special characters lovingly known as *bullets*. In the old days, you had to add bullets one at a time. Nowadays, PowerPoint comes with a semiautomatic bullet shooter that is illegal in 27 states.

To add bullets to a paragraph or series of paragraphs:

1. **Highlight the paragraphs to which you want to add bullets.**

   To add a bullet to just one paragraph, you don't have to highlight the entire paragraph. Just place the cursor anywhere in the paragraph.

 2. **Click the Bullet button (shown in the margin).**

   PowerPoint adds a bullet to each paragraph you select.

The Bullet button works like a toggle: Press it once to add bullets and press it again to remove bullets. To remove bullets from previously bulleted text, therefore, you select the text and click the Bullet button again.

If you don't like the appearance of the bullets PowerPoint uses, you can choose a different bullet character by using the Format⇨Bullet command. This command displays the Bullet dialog box, shown in Figure 7-2. From this dialog box, you can choose a different bullet character, change the bullet's color, or change its size relative to the text size.

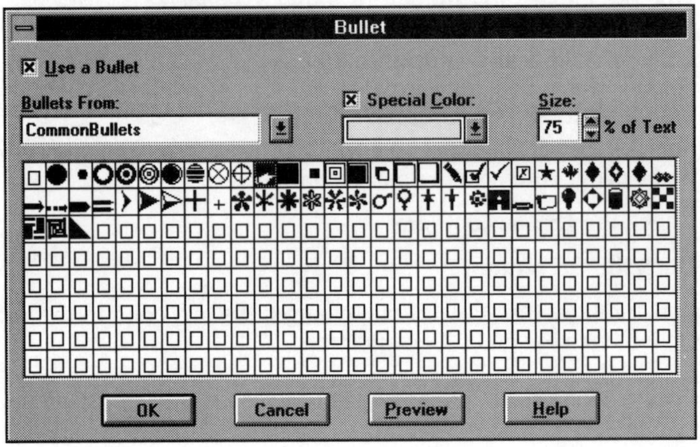

Figure 7-2:
The Bullet
dialog box.

This list shows you some pointers for using the Bullet dialog box:

✔ Notice the Use a Bullet check box in the upper left corner of the Bullet dialog box. Check this box to add a bullet to your text.

✔ Several collections of bullet characters are available for choosing bullet characters. If you don't like any of the bullet characters displayed on-screen, change the option in the Bullets From drop-down list box. Wingdings contains such useful bullets as pointing fingers, a skull and crossbones, and a time bomb. You may see other collections here as well.

> ✔ If the bullet characters don't seem large enough, increase the Size value in the Bullet dialog box. The size is specified as a percentage of the text size.
>
> ✔ To change the bullet color, check the Special Color check box and choose the color you want to use. When you click Special Color, a menu of eight color choices appears. If the color you're looking for isn't there, you can click Other Color to call forth a dialog box offering 90 color choices. If you still cannot find a color you like, click the Other Color dialog's More Colors button and pick from among 16 million colors. For more information about using colors, see Chapter 9.

You can use certain bullet characters for good comic effect in your presentations. Be creative, but also be careful. A thumbs-down bullet next to the name of your boss may get a laugh, but it may also get you fired.

Lining Things Up

PowerPoint enables you to control the way your text lines up on the slide. You can center text, line it up flush left or flush right, or justify it. You can change these alignments by using the Format⇨Alignment command, or you can use the convenient toolbar buttons and keyboard shortcuts.

Centering text

Centered text lines up right down the middle of the slide (actually, down the middle of the text object that contains the text. It appears centered on the slide only if the text object is centered on the slide).

To center existing text, follow this procedure:

1. **Select the line or lines you want to center.**

 2. **Click the Center button on the Formatting toolbar (shown in the margin) or press Ctrl+E.**

   It's true that E doesn't stand for center. Ctrl+C was already taken (for Copy, remember?), so the Microsoft jocks decided to use Ctrl+E. They consider it to be some sort of demented practical joke.

3. **Admire your newly centered text.**

   To type new centered text, skip Step 1; just click the Center button or press Ctrl+E and begin typing.

Flush to the left

Centered text is sometimes hard to read. Align the text *flush left* and the text lines up neatly along the left edge of the text object. All the bullets line up too. These steps show you how to make text flush left:

1. **Select the line or lines you want to scoot to the left.**

 2. **Click the Align Left button on the Formatting toolbar or press Ctrl+L.**

   Hallelujah! The L in Ctrl+L stands for — you guessed it — *left*.

3. **Toast yourself for your cleverness.**

   If you want to type new flush-left text, just click the Align Left button or press Ctrl+L and begin typing.

Other terms for flush left are *left justified* and *ragged right*. Just thought you may want to know.

Flush to the right

Yes, you can align text against the right edge too. I don't know why you want to, but you can.

1. **Select the line or lines you want to shove to the right.**

2. **Press Ctrl+R.**

   Sorry, PowerPoint has no button for aligning text on the right. Mercifully, the keyboard shortcut is easy to remember. R equals right — get it?

3. **Have a drink on me.**

   If you want to type new flush-right text, just press Ctrl+R and continue.

Other terms for flush right are *right justified* and *ragged left*. More cocktail party verbiage to add to your vocabulary. You'll be the hit at any nerd party.

Stand up, sit down, justify!

You also can tell PowerPoint to *justify* text: to line up both the left and right edges. The keyboard shortcut is Ctrl+J (J is for *justified*).

Messing with Tabs and Indents

PowerPoint enables you to set tab stops to control the placement of text within a text object. For most presentations, you don't have to fuss with tabs. Each paragraph is indented according to its level in the outline, and the amount of indentation for each outline level is preset by the template you use to create the presentation.

Although there's little need to, you can mess with the indent settings and tab stops if you're adventurous and have no real work to do today. Here's how you do it:

1. **Click the Slide button to switch to Slide view.**

   You cannot mess with tabs or indents in Outline view. You can do it in Notes Pages view, but Slide view is more convenient.

2. **Activate the ruler by using the View⇨Ruler command.**

   The *ruler* appears above the Presentation window. The ruler shows the current tab and indentation settings. It must be displayed if you want to change tab stops or text indents.

   Figure 7-3 shows a PowerPoint presentation with the ruler activated.

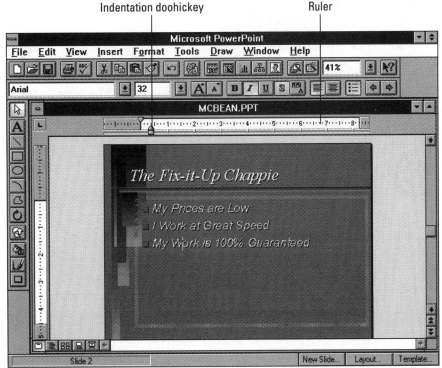

Figure 7-3:
The ruler.

3. Select the text object whose tabs or indents you want to change.

Each text object has its own tabs and indents setting. After you click a text object, the ruler shows that object's tabs and indents.

4. Click the ruler to add a tab stop.

Move the mouse pointer to the ruler location where you want to add a tab stop and then click. A tab stop appears.

5. Grab the indentation doohickey and drag it to change the indentation.

Try dragging the different parts of the indentation doohickey to see what happens. Have fun. Good luck.

If all this stuff about outline levels and demotions upsets you, refer to Chapter 3, where you can find a comforting explanation of PowerPoint outlines.

Tabs and indents can be pretty testy, but fortunately you don't have to mess with them for most presentations. If you're one of the unlucky ones, keep these pointers in mind:

✔ Each text object has its own tab settings. The tab settings for an object apply to all the paragraphs within the object, so you can't change tab settings for individual paragraphs within a text object.

✔ In PowerPoint, you press the Tab key to demote text to the next lower outline level. The traditional tabbing function is performed by pressing the Ctrl+Tab key combination. To advance text to the next tab stop, press Ctrl+Tab, not Tab.

✔ The ruler shows as many as five different indentation levels, one for each outline level. Only those levels used in the text object are shown, so if the object has only one outline level, only one indent is shown. To see additional indents, demote text within the object by pressing the Tab key.

Each text object is set up initially with default tab stops set at every inch. When you add a tab stop, any default tab stops to the left of the new tab stop disappear.

To remove a tab stop, use the mouse to drag it off the ruler (click the tab stop, drag it off the ruler, and then release the mouse button).

Don't even bother with this stuff about Tab types

PowerPoint isn't limited to just boring left-aligned tabs. In all, it has four distinct types of tabs: left, right, center, and decimal. The square button at the far left side of the ruler tells you which type of tab is added when you click the ruler. Click this button to cycle through the four types of tabs:

⌊	LTAB	Standard left-aligned tab. Press Ctrl+Tab to advance the text to the tab stop.
⌋	RTAB	Right-aligned tab. Text is aligned flush right with the tab stop.
⊥	CTAB	Centered tab. Text lines up centered over the tab stop.
⊥	DTAB	Decimal tab. Numbers line up with the decimal point centered over the tab stop.

Spacing Things Out

Feeling a little spaced out? Try tightening the space between text lines. Feeling cramped? Space the lines out a little. These steps show you how to do it all:

1. **Switch to Slide view.**

   You can change line spacing in Slide view or Notes Pages view only. Slide view is more convenient.

2. **Highlight the paragraph or paragraphs whose line spacing you want to change.**

3. **Use the Format⇨Line Spacing command.**

   Sorry, PowerPoint has no keyboard shortcut for this step. The Line Spacing dialog box, shown in Figure 7-4, suddenly appears.

Figure 7-4:
The Line
Spacing
dialog box.

Line Spacing	
Line Spacing	OK
1 ⬍ Lines ⬍	Cancel
Before Paragraph	Preview
0.2 ⬍ Lines ⬍	Help
After Paragraph	
0 ⬍ Lines ⬍	

4. Change the dialog box settings to adjust the line spacing.

Line Spacing refers to the space between the lines within a paragraph. Before Paragraph adds extra space before the paragraph, and After Paragraph adds extra space after the paragraph.

You can specify spacing in terms of lines or points. The size of a line varies depending on the size of the text font. If you specify spacing in terms of points, PowerPoint uses the exact spacing you specify, regardless of the size of the text font.

5. Click the OK button or press Enter.

Chapter 8

All About Masters and Templates

. . . .

. . . .

*W*ant to add a bit of text to every slide in your presentation? Or maybe add your name and phone number at the bottom of your audience handouts? Or place a picture of Rush Limbaugh at the extreme right side of each page of your speaker notes?

Masters are the surefire way to add something to every page. No need to toil separately at each slide. Add something to the master and it automatically shows up on every slide. Remove it from the master and — poof! — it disappears from every slide. Very convenient.

Working with Masters

In PowerPoint, a master governs the appearance of all the slides or pages in a presentation. Each presentation has four masters corresponding to the four types of output that you can print:

✔ *Slide master:* Dictates the format of your slides. You work with this master the most as you tweak your slides to cosmetic perfection.

✔ *Outline master:* Governs the appearance of printed outlines.

✔ *Handout master:* Controls the look of printed handouts.

✔ *Notes master:* Determines the characteristics of printed speaker notes.

Each master specifies the appearance of text (font, size, and color, for example), the slide's background color, and text or other objects you want to appear on each slide or page.

Each presentation has just one of each type of master. The master governs the appearance of all slides or pages in the presentation.

Masters are not optional. Every presentation has them. You can, however, override the formatting of objects contained in the master for a particular slide. This capability enables you to vary the appearance of slides when it's necessary.

The quick way to call up a master is to hold down the Shift key while you click one of the view buttons at the left side of the status bar at the bottom of the screen.

A *template* is simply a presentation used to supply the masters for a presentation. You usually choose a template when you create a new presentation, but you can change the template at any time. This feature changes the appearance of your slides but doesn't change their contents.

The Pick-a-Look wizard chooses a template and adds objects to the various masters based on the way you respond to its questions. If you tell it that you want your name to appear on each slide, for example, the Pick-a-Look wizard adds to the Slide master a text object containing your name.

Changing the Slide Master

If you don't like the layout of your slides, call up the Slide master and do something about it, as shown in these steps:

 1. **Choose the View⇨Master⇨Slide Master command or hold down the Shift key while clicking the Slide View button.**

   If you use the View⇨Master command, a submenu pops up with a listing of the four masters. Choose Slide Master to call up the Slide master.

2. **Behold the Slide master in all its splendor.**

   Figure 8-1 shows a typical Slide master. You can see the placeholders for the slide title and body text in addition to other background objects.

3. **Make any formatting changes you want.**

   Select the text you want to apply a new style to and make your formatting changes. If you want all the slide titles to be in italics, for example, select the title text and press Ctrl+I or click the Italic button on the Formatting toolbar.

   If you're not sure how to change text formats, consult Chapter 7.

4. Click the Slide View button to return to Slide view.

The effect of your Slide master changes should be apparent immediately.

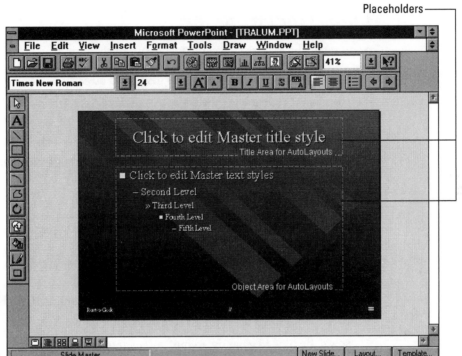

Placeholders

Figure 8-1:
A Slide
master.

PowerPoint applies character formats such as bold, italics, point size, and font to entire paragraphs when you work in Slide Master view. You don't have to select the entire paragraph before you apply a format; just click anywhere in the paragraph.

Notice that the body object contains paragraphs for five outline levels formatted with different point sizes, indentations, and bullet styles. If you want to change the way an outline level is formatted, this is the place.

You can type all you want in the title or object area placeholders, but the text you type doesn't appear in the slides. The text that appears in these placeholders is provided only so that you can see the effect of the formatting changes you apply.

You can edit any of the other objects on the master by clicking them. Unlike the title and object area placeholders, any text you type in other Slide master objects appears exactly as you type it on each slide.

Adding recurring text

To add recurring text to each slide, follow this procedure:

1. **Call up the Slide master if it's not displayed already**.

    The menu command is View➪Master➪Slide Master. Or you can Shift+click the Slide View button.

 2. **Click the Text Tool button on the Drawing toolbar.**

    This step highlights the text button. The mouse cursor turns into an upside-down cross.

3. **Click where you want to add text.**

    PowerPoint places a text object at that location.

4. **Type the text you want to appear on each slide.**

    For example: **Call Today! 1-800-555-GEEK! Don't delay! Operators standing by!**

5. **Format the text however you want (bold, for example — Ctrl+B).**

6. **Click the Slide View button to return to Slide view.**

    Now's the time to gloat over your work. Lasso some coworkers and show 'em how proud you are.

You can add other types of objects to the Slide master too. You can click the Clip Art button on the Standard toolbar (shown in the margin), for example, to insert any of the clip art pictures supplied with PowerPoint. Or you can use the Insert➪Object command to insert a WordArt Object. (Clip art is described in detail in Chapter 12; WordArt, in Chapter 16. Other types of objects are covered in the other chapters in Part III.)

After you place an object on the Slide master, you can grab it with the mouse and move it around or resize it any way you want. The object appears in the same location and size on each slide.

To delete an object from the Slide master, click it and press the Del key. To delete a text object, you must first click the object and then click again on the object frame. Then press Delete.

If you can't highlight the object no matter how many times you click it, you probably have returned to Slide view. Shift+click the Slide View button or choose the View➪Master➪Slide Master command again to call up the Slide master.

Adding the date, time, or slide number

If you want the date, time, or slide number to appear on each slide, follow the procedure described in the preceding section to insert a text object. Then type one of the following special characters in the text object:

Character	*Meaning*
//	Date
::	Time
##	Page number

When you print your presentation, PowerPoint replaces these characters with the date, time, or page number.

If you prefer, you can use the Insert➪Date, Insert➪Time, or Insert➪Page Number commands to insert a text object that contains just the date, time, or page number. After you insert the object, click and drag it with the mouse to its final resting place.

Slides are normally numbered from 1. To change the starting slide number, use the File➪Slide Setup command.

Changing the master color scheme

You can use the Slide master to change the color scheme used for all slides in a presentation. To do that, follow these steps:

1. **Choose the View➪Master➪Slide Master command or Shift+click the Slide button to summon the Slide master.**

2. **Choose the Format➪Slide Color Scheme command to change the color scheme.**

   Treat yourself to a bag of Doritos if it works the first time.

PowerPoint color schemes are hefty enough that I have devoted an entire chapter to them. Skip to Chapter 9 now if you can't wait.

If you don't have a color printer, don't waste your time messing with the color scheme unless you're going to make your presentation on-screen. Mauve, teal, azure, and cerulean all look like gray when they're printed on a noncolor laser printer.

PowerPoint's color schemes were chosen by professionals who are color-blind in no more than one eye. Stick to these schemes to avoid embarrassing color combinations! (I wish that my sock drawer came with a similar color-scheme feature.)

If you want to adjust the shading that's applied to the background slide color, choose the Format⊏⊅Slide Background command.

Changing the Outline, Handout, and Notes Masters

Like the Slide master, the Outline, Handout, and Notes masters contain formatting information that's automatically applied to your presentation. This section tells you how you can modify these masters.

Changing the Outline master

Changing the Outline master is similar to the way you change the Slide master. Follow these steps to do so:

  1. **Choose the View⊏⊅Master⊏⊅Outline Master command or hold down the Shift key and click the Outline View button.**

The Outline master appears in the Presentation window.

2. **Play with the Outline master.**

The Outline master contains a large placeholder that contains the outline. Unfortunately, you cannot change the size or position of this placeholder, nor can you change the text style used to print the outline here. But you can add or change elements you want to appear on each outline page, such as your name, a date or page number, or a logo.

3. **You're done.**

Click the Slide View button to return to Slide view or click the Outline button to return to Outline view.

4. Print an outline to check your changes.

You cannot see Outline master elements while you're working in PowerPoint. They appear only when you print an outline.

When you print an outline, PowerPoint picks up the outline text style from the Slide master, not from the Outline master. That's why the Outline master doesn't include any text in the outline placeholder.

To print an outline without any fancy text formatting, switch to Outline view and click the Show Formatting button on the Outline toolbar. This button works like a toggle: Click it once to ignore text formats and click it again to reinstate the formats.

Changing the Handout master

Guess what? Another simple procedure! Changing these masters is a matter of learning which button is which, and then changing the master to meet your needs. Follow these steps:

1. Choose the View➪Master➪Handout Master command or hold down the Shift key and click the Slide Sorter View button.

The Handout master rears its ugly head.

2. Mess around with it.

The Handout master contains immovable placeholders for slides printed two, three, and six per page. You cannot move these, resize them, or delete them. Sniff. But you can add or change elements you want to appear on each handout page, such as your name and phone number and a page number or maybe a good lawyer joke.

3. Go back.

Click the Slide View button, for example, to return to Slide view.

4. Print a handout to see whether your changes take effect.

Handout master elements are invisible until you print them, so you should print at least one handout page to check your work.

When you print handout pages, the slides are formatted according to the Slide master. You cannot change the appearance of the slides from the Handout master.

Changing the Notes master

To change the Notes master, follow these steps:

 1. **Choose the <u>V</u>iew⇨<u>M</u>aster⇨<u>N</u>otes Master command or hold down the Shift key and click the Notes View button.**

   The Notes master comes to life.

2. **Indulge yourself.**

   The Notes master contains two placeholders: One for your notes text and the other for the slide. You can move or change the size of either of these objects, and you can change the format of the text in the notes placeholder. You also can add or change elements that you want to appear on each handout page.

3. **Click the Notes button to return to Notes Pages view.**

   Admire your handiwork. Unlike you do when using the Outline master and Handout master, you don't have to print anything to check the results of changes you make to the Notes master. You can see them clearly when you switch to Notes Pages view.

At the least, you should add page numbers to your speaker notes. If you drop a stack of notes pages without page numbers, you will be up a creek without a paddle!

If public speaking gives you severe stomach cramps, add the text *Just picture them naked* to the Notes master. It works every time for me.

Using Masters

You don't have to do anything special to apply the formats from a master to your slide; all slides automatically pick up the master format unless you specify otherwise. So this section really should be titled *Not Using Masters* because it talks about how not to use the formats provided by masters.

Overriding the master text style

To override the text style specified by a Slide master or Notes master, simply format the text however you want while you're working in Slide, Outline, or Notes Pages view. The formatting changes you make apply only to the selected text. The Slide master and Notes master aren't affected.

The only way to change one of the masters is to do it directly by switching to the appropriate master view. Thus, any formatting changes you make while in Slide view affect only that slide.

If you change the slide text style and then decide that you liked it better the way it was, you can quickly reapply the text style from the Slide master by switching to Slide view and using the Format⇨Slide Layout command. A Slide Layout dialog box appears; click the Reapply button to restore text formatting to the format specified in the Slide master.

If you change the notes text style and want to revert to the text style specified in the Notes master, switch to Notes Pages view and use the Format⇨Notes Layout command. When the Notes Layout dialog box appears, check the Reapply Master check box and click OK.

The Ctrl+spacebar key combination clears all text attributes, including those specified in the Slide master or Notes master. This key combination can wreak havoc on your formatting efforts. Suppose that the Slide master specifies shadowed text. If you italicize a word and then decide to remove the italics by pressing Ctrl+spacebar, the shadow is removed as well.

Hiding background objects

Both Slide masters and Notes masters enable you to add background objects that appear on every slide or notes page in your presentation. You can, however, hide the background objects for selected slides or notes pages. These steps show you how:

1. **Display the slide or notes page you want to show with a plain background.**

2. **Summon either the Slide Background or Notes Background dialog box.**

   For Slides, use the Format⇨Slide Background command. The Slide Background dialog box appears, as shown in Figure 8-2. For notes, use Format⇨Notes Background. (The Notes Background dialog box is the same as the Slide Background dialog box; the only difference is their titles.)

3. **Uncheck the Display Objects on This Slide check box.**

   For a notes page, uncheck the Display Objects on This Notes Page check box.

4. **Click the Apply button or press Enter.**

   The background objects from the Slide master or Notes master vanish from the slide or page, respectively.

Figure 8-2:
The Slide
Background
dialog box.

Hiding background objects applies only to the current slide or notes page. Other slides or notes pages are unaffected.

If you want to remove some but not all of the background objects from a single slide, try this trick:

1. **Follow the preceding procedure to hide background objects for the slide.**

2. **Call up the Slide master (View⇨Master⇨Slide Master).**

3. **Hold down the Shift key and click each object that you want to appear on the slide.**

4. **Press Ctrl+C to copy these objects to the Clipboard.**

5. **Return to Slide view.**

6. **Press Ctrl+V to paste the objects from the Clipboard.**

7. **Choose the Draw⇨Send to Back command if the background objects obscure other slide objects or text.**

Thank Heavens for Templates

If you had to create Slide masters from scratch every time you built a new presentation, you probably would put PowerPoint back in its box and use it as a bookend. Creating a Slide master is easy. Creating one that looks good is a different story. Making a good-looking master is tough even for the artistically inclined. For right-brain nonartistic types like me, it's next to impossible.

Thank heavens for templates. When you create a presentation, PowerPoint gives you the option of stealing masters from an existing template presentation. Any PowerPoint presentation can serve as a template, including presentations you create yourself. But PowerPoint comes with more than 100 template presentations designed by professional artists who understand color combinations and balance and all that artsy stuff. Have a croissant and celebrate.

Because the templates that come with PowerPoint look good, any presentation you create by using one of them will look good too. It's as simple as that. When you pick one of PowerPoint's templates, you can rest assured that you won't get laughed out of the auditorium because your slides look like they were designed by Dan Quayle. Better still, most of your audience will assume that you designed the slides yourself. "Geez," they'll say, "I didn't realize that you were so artistic. I don't remember a word you said, but the slides were absolutely stunning!"

In addition to masters, the template also supplies the color scheme for your presentation. You can override it, of course, but you do so at your own risk. The color police are everywhere, you know. You don't want to be taken in for Felony Color Clash.

A template is simply a PowerPoint presentation file with predefined formatting settings. In fact, the file extension for template files is PPT, just like any other PowerPoint file. You can therefore use any of your own presentations as a template. If you make extensive changes to a presentation's masters, you can use that presentation as a template for other presentations you create.

Because a template is a presentation, you can open it and change it if you want.

Applying a different template

You're halfway through creating a new presentation when you realize that you can't stand the look of the slides. Oops — you picked the wrong template when you started the new presentation! Don't panic. PowerPoint enables you to assign a new presentation template at any time. These steps show you how:

Template...

1. **Choose the Format➪Presentation Template command or click the Template button on the status bar (shown in the margin).**

   The Presentation Template dialog box appears, as shown in Figure 8-3.

2. **Rummage around for a template you like better.**

Templates are stored in the following subdirectories, which correspond to the slide format you ultimately intend to use:

BWOVRHD	Black-and-white overheads
CLROVRHD	Color overheads
SLDSHOW	35mm slides
VIDSCREN	On-screen slide show

When you click a presentation, PowerPoint displays a preview of the template's appearance in the Presentation Template dialog box.

3. Click the <u>A</u>pply button or double-click the template filename to apply the template.

Make sure that you like the new template better than the first one!

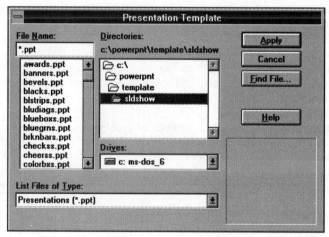

Figure 8-3:
The
Presentation
Template
dialog box.

You may still want to make minor adjustments to the Slide master to make the slides look just right.

When you apply a new template, PowerPoint copies the masters and the color scheme into your presentation. As a result, any changes you made to the presentation's masters or color scheme are lost. Too bad. If you added background objects to the Slide master (the slide number or date, for example), you have to add them again.

You don't have to worry about the new template undoing any formatting changes that you have made to individual slides. PowerPoint remembers these deviations from the master format when it applies a new template.

You also can use the Pick-a-Look wizard at any time to change the template. Use the Format⇨Pick-a-Look Wizard command. The wizard not only applies a template but also can automatically add the time, date, slide number, and a company name to the masters.

Creating a new template

If none of the templates that come with PowerPoint appeals to you, you can easily create your own. Because you can use any presentation as a template, all you have to do is create a presentation with the masters and the color scheme set up just the way you want and then call it a template. Here are a few points to remember about templates:

✔ The templates that come with PowerPoint have just one slide in them, and that slide contains a bunch of Latin gibberish. It doesn't matter how many slides are in your templates because PowerPoint ignores them and uses just the masters and the color scheme. But when you create a presentation to use strictly as a template, I suggest that you delete all slides except the title slide. Add the following Latin text to make your template look like the real McCoyus:

I-ay ade-may is-thay emplate-tay all-ay y-bay y-may-elf-say.

✔ If you want to make minor modifications to one of the supplied templates, open the template by using the File⇨Open command and then immediately save it under a new name by using the File⇨Save As command. Then change the masters and the color scheme. Don't forget to save the file again when you're finished!

✔ To make your custom templates easier to find, I suggest that you store them in a separate subdirectory. The following sidebar, "Stop me before I show you how to create a subdirectory," shows you how. Don't read it unless you have to.

Stop me before I show you how to create a subdirectory

If you create your own templates, you can store them in PowerPoint's template directories, or you can create a separate directory for them. To keep them separate, follow this procedure to create a CUSTOM subdirectory in the POWERPNT \TEMPLATE directory:

1. **In the Program Manager, start File Manager by double-clicking its icon.**

   It lives in the Main Program Manager group.

2. **Click the PowerPoint TEMPLATE directory.**

   It's safely nestled under the POWERPNT directory. If you cannot find it, use the Tree⇨Expand All command. This step reveals every subdirectory on your disk.

3. **Choose the File⇨Create Directory command.**

   A dialog box appears and asks for the name of the subdirectory you want to create. Type **CUSTOM** or whatever name you want to use.

4. **Click OK or press the Enter key.**

   The new subdirectory should appear nestled beneath the TEMPLATE directory.

5. **Exit from File Manager.**

   Choose the File⇨Exit command.

Creating a new default template

When you create a new presentation, PowerPoint asks whether you want to base the presentation on an existing template or create a blank presentation. This question is a little misleading because it suggests that the blank presentation doesn't use a template. It does — it uses a default template named DEFAULT.PPT to obtain barebones masters and a black-on-white color scheme.

If you want to create your own default template, all you have to do is save your template file by using the filename DEFAULT.PPT in the POWERPNT directory. Then, whenever you create a blank presentation, the masters and the color scheme are copied from your new default template rather than from the bland default template that comes with PowerPoint.

The procedure for creating a new default template is shown in these steps:

1. **Open the default template.**

   It's named DEFAULT.PPT and lives in the POWERPNT directory.

2. **Make any changes you want.**

   For example, add your name to the Slide master and add the page number and date to the Notes master, Outline master, and Handout master.

3. **Save your changes.**

Make a copy of the DEFAULT.PPT file before you overwrite it with your own changes. You may someday want to revert to PowerPoint's standard default template. To make a copy of the default template, open it and choose the File⇨Save As command to save it with a new name (possibly OLDEFALT.PPT).

Chapter 9

When I Am Old, I Shall Make My Slides Purple

In This Chapter

▶ Using color schemes

▶ Changing the colors in a color scheme

▶ Creating new colors

▶ Shading the slide background

▶ Coloring objects and text

▶ Copying colors from other objects

*W*elcome to the Wonderful World of Color. Here is your opportunity to unleash the repressed artist hidden deep within you. Take up your palette, grasp your brush firmly, and prepare to attack the empty canvas of your barren slides.

PowerPoint enables you to use more than 16 million colors, but you shouldn't feel obligated to use them all right away. Pace yourself. Now would be a good time to grow a goatee or to cut off your ear.

Using Color Schemes

PowerPoint's color schemes are coordinated sets of colors chosen by color professionals. Microsoft paid these people enormous sums of money to debate the merits of using mauve text on a teal background. You can use these professionally designed color schemes, or you can create your own if you think that you have a better eye than Microsoft's hired color guns.

As far as I'm concerned, PowerPoint's color schemes are the best thing to come along since Peanut M&Ms. Without color schemes, people like me would be allowed to pick and choose from among the 16 million or so colors that PowerPoint enables you to incorporate into your slides. The result is slides that can easily appear next to Cher and Roseanne in *People* magazine's annual Worst Dressed of the Year issue.

Each color scheme has eight colors, with each color designated for a particular use, as shown in this list:

- ✔ *Background color:* Used for the slide background.

- ✔ *Text-and-lines color:* Used for any text or drawn lines that appear on the slide, with the exception of the title text (described in this list). It is usually a color that contrasts with the background color. If the background color is dark, the text-and-lines color is generally light and vice versa.

- ✔ *Shadows color:* Used to produce shadow effects for objects drawn on the slide. It is usually a darker version of the background color.

- ✔ *Title text color:* Used for the slide's title text. Like the text-and-lines color, the title text color contrasts with the background color so that the text is readable. The title text usually complements the text-and-lines color to provide an evenly balanced effect. (That sounds like something an artist would say, doesn't it?)

- ✔ *Fills color:* When you create an object, such as a rectangle or an ellipse, this color is the default fill color to color the object.

- ✔ *Accent colors:* The last three colors in the color scheme. They are used for odds and ends that you add to your slide. They may be used to color the bars in a bar chart, for example, or the slices in a pie chart.

PowerPoint comes with hundreds — nay, thousands — of predefined color schemes. These schemes use 90 different background colors, with each color serving as the base for about 40 schemes (the exact number varies from color to color). Somewhere in this unfathomable collection of color schemes, you should be able to find one you like.

Each slide in your presentation can have its own color scheme. The Slide master also has a color scheme, used for all slides that don't specify their own deviant color scheme. To ensure that your slides have a uniform look, simply allow them to pick up the color scheme from the Slide master. If you want one slide to stand out from the other slides in your presentation, assign it a different color scheme.

PowerPoint picks up the initial color scheme for a presentation from the template on which the presentation is based as a part of the template's Slide master. You can change the master scheme later, but if you apply a new template, the new template's scheme overrides any change you made to the original template's color scheme.

If you don't like any of the color schemes PowerPoint provides, you can create your own. The easiest way is to choose a scheme that's close to the colors you want and then modify the scheme colors. The procedure to do so is presented later in this chapter.

You can override the master color scheme for an individual slide. You also can change the color for any object to any color in the scheme, or to any other color known to science. You get step-by-step instructions later in this chapter.

TIP

Don't get all in a tizzy about color schemes if you plan to print overhead slides on a black-and-white laser printer. The slides look dazzling on-screen, but all those stunning colors are printed in boring shades of gray.

NOTE

Metaphor alert!

If you want, you can think of the color scheme as a magic artist's palette. The artist squeezes out eight little dabs of paint to use for various elements of a painting: one for the sky, another for the mountains, and still another for the trees. Then the artist paints the picture. So far, nothing special. But here's what makes this palette magic: If the artist sets it down and picks up a different palette (with eight different little dabs of color squeezed out), the entire painting is instantly transformed to the new colors, as though the artist used the second palette all along.

This magic palette enables the artist to make subtle changes to the painting's appearance with little effort. The artist can change the painting from midday to dusk, for example, simply by switching to a palette that has a darker blue for the sky color. Or the artist can change the scene from spring to fall by switching to a palette that has yellow or orange paint rather than green paint for the trees. Or maybe switch to a winter scene by changing the mountain color to white.

PowerPoint color schemes work just like this magic palette. The color scheme gives you eight colors to work with, with each color assigned to a different slide element. If you change the color scheme, the entire presentation changes as well.

Using a different color scheme

If you don't like your presentation's color scheme, change it! The procedure is a little involved, but it's harder to explain than it is to do. Hold on to your hat:

1. **Switch to Slide Master view.**

   Shift+click the Slide View button or use the View⊅Master⊅Slide Master command.

   The fastest way to switch to Slide Master view is to hold down the Shift key while clicking the Slide View button.

2. **Choose the Format⊅Slide Color Scheme command.**

   The Slide Color Scheme dialog box appears, as shown in Figure 9-1. Notice how the eight colors of the current color scheme are displayed in this dialog box.

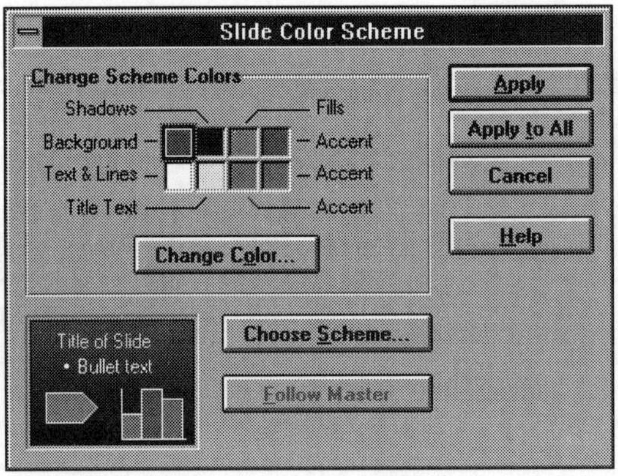

Figure 9-1:
The Slide
Color
Scheme
dialog box.

3. **Click the Choose Scheme button.**

   The Choose Scheme dialog box pops up, as shown in Figure 9-2. From this dialog box, you can choose any of the thousands of predefined schemes that PowerPoint supplies.

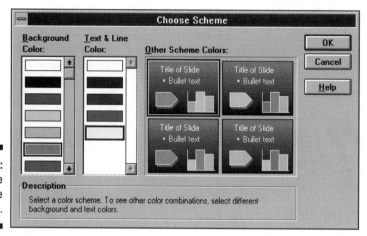

Figure 9-2:
The Choose
Scheme
dialog box.

4. Choose the colors you want to use.

Click the background color you want to use. The Background Color list box contains 90 background colors from which you can choose; use the scroll bar if the background color you want isn't visible.

When you click one of the background colors, an assortment of suitable Text & Line Colors appears. Click the one you want to use. Again, you may have to use the scroll bar if the color you want isn't immediately visible.

Clicking the Text & Line Color option summons four complete color schemes based on the Background Color and Text & Line Color you chose. These four schemes are previewed in the dialog box. Click the one you want. If you don't like any of the four color schemes that appear, go back and pick another Background Color or Text & Line Color.

5. Click the OK button or press Enter.

You return to the Slide Color Scheme dialog box, with the colors of your newly chosen color scheme displayed.

6. Click the Apply button.

This step applies the new color scheme to the Slide master, which has the effect of applying it to all the slides in your presentation (unless you override the color scheme for individual slides).

Overriding the color scheme

If you want a few slides to use a different color scheme from the rest of the presentation, you can override the color scheme for just those slides. Follow the procedure outlined in the previous section, with one important exception: *Start from Slide view rather than from Slide Master view.* That way, the change is applied to the individual slide rather than to the Slide master.

You may want to use this technique to color code your slides so that your audience has an immediate visual clue to your slide's contents. If a market-analysis presentation frequently shifts back and forth between current data and last year's data, for example, consider using a different color scheme for the slides that depict last year's data. That way, the audience is less likely to become confused.

If you click the Slide Color Scheme dialog box's Apply to All button rather than the Apply button, PowerPoint applies the scheme you chose to all the slides in the presentation. This scheme still isn't applied to the Slide master, however, unless you were in Slide Master view when you chose the Slide Color Scheme command. The Apply to All button is a convenient way to force all slides to override the Slide master's color scheme.

You can override a slide's color scheme also from Slide Sorter view. This feature is handy if you want to change the color scheme for several slides at one time. Hold down the Shift key and click each slide you want to change. Then choose the Format⇨Slide Color Scheme command, pick a new color scheme, and then click the Apply button.

To return a slide to the Slide master's color scheme, select the slide in Slide view or Slide Sorter view, call up the Format⇨Slide Color Scheme. When the Slide Color Scheme dialog box appears, click the Follow Master button and then click Apply. To return all the slides in a presentation to the Slide master's color scheme, click Follow Master and click Apply to All.

Changing colors in a color scheme

To change one or more of the colors in the current color scheme, follow this procedure:

   1. Choose the slide whose color scheme you want to change.

   To change the Slide master color scheme, Shift+click the Slide View button or use the View⇨Master⇨Slide Master command. To have your color scheme apply to only one slide, switch to Slide view and display the slide whose color scheme you want to change. To change the color scheme for several slides, switch to Slide Sorter view and hold down the Shift key while you click the slides you want to change.

2. Choose the Format⇨Slide Color Scheme command.

The Slide Color Scheme dialog box appears. Refer to Figure 9-1 if you have forgotten what it looks like.

3. Click the color box you want to change.

To change the background color, for example, click the Background Color box.

4. Click the Change Color button.

A dialog box similar to the one in Figure 9-3 appears. The title of this dialog box indicates which color you're changing (in this example, the background color).

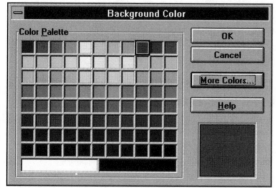

Figure 9-3:
Changing the background color.

5. Click the color you want and click OK.

If you want white or black, click the large white or black boxes at the bottom of the Background Color dialog box. Otherwise, click one of the smaller color boxes. When you click OK, you zip back to the Slide Color Scheme dialog box.

6. Choose Apply or Apply to All.

To apply the change to just the slide or slides you chose, click Apply. To apply the change to all the slides in the presentation, click Apply to All.

Be warned that after you deviate from the preselected color scheme combinations, you better have some color sense. If you can't tell chartreuse from lime, you better leave this stuff to the pros.

The dialog box in Figure 9-3 shows 88 popular colors, plus white and black. If you want to use a color that doesn't appear in the dialog box, click the More Colors button. This step whisks you away to the More Colors dialog box, shown in Figure 9-4. From this dialog box, you can construct any of the 16 million colors that are theoretically possible with PowerPoint. You need a Ph.D. in physics to figure out how to adjust the Huey, Dewey, and Louie controls, though. Mess around with this stuff if you want, but you're on your own.

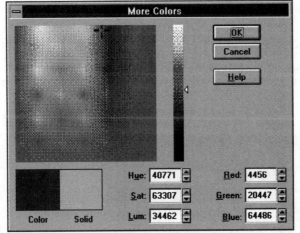

Figure 9-4:
Changing
the back-
ground
color.

Shading the slide background

You may have noticed that the slide background used in many of the PowerPoint templates is not a solid color. Instead, the color is gradually shaded from top to bottom. This shading creates an interesting visual effect. For example, look at the slide in Figure 9-5. This slide was based on the templates supplied with PowerPoint, but I modified the color scheme and the background shading to achieve the effect I wanted.

Shading for the slide background works much like the color scheme. If you apply it to the Slide master, it is picked up by every slide that follows the master. Alternatively, you can apply it to an individual slide, or you can apply it to all slides without changing the master.

These steps show you the procedure for shading the slide background:

1. **Choose the slide you want to shade.**

   To shade the background for the Slide master (and therefore for all slides that follow the master), Shift+click the Slide View button or use the View⇨Master⇨Slide Master command. To shade only one slide, switch to

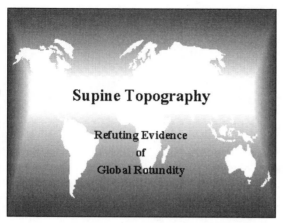

Figure 9-5:
A slide that uses back-ground shading for an interest-ing effect.

Slide view and display the slide you want to shade. To shade several slides, switch to Slide Sorter view and hold down the Shift key while you click the slides you want to shade.

2. Summon the F̲ormat⇨Slide Background command.

The Slide Background dialog box, shown in Figure 9-6, appears. Choose the shade style you want (vertical or horizontal, for example). Then choose which of the variations you want for that shade style.

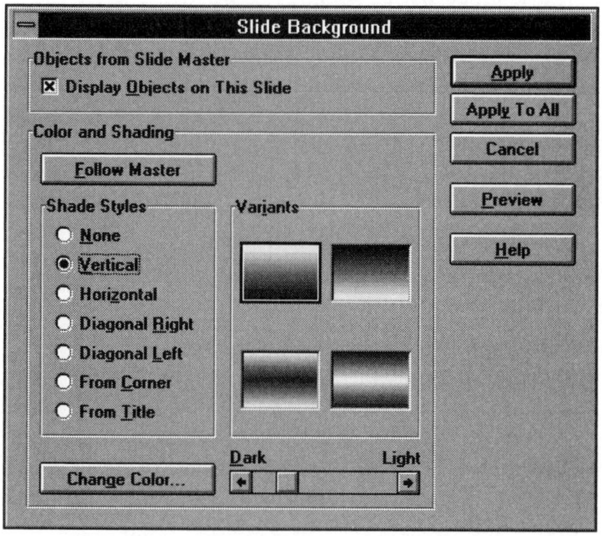

Figure 9-6:
The Slide Background dialog box.

3. Click Apply or Apply to All.

Clicking the Apply button applies the shading to just the slide or slides you chose. Clicking Apply to All applies the shading to all slides.

4. You're done.

Admire your work. Play with it some more if you don't like it.

When you apply a template, any background shading specified for the template's masters is applied along with the color scheme.

The Slide Background dialog box has a Change Color button that enables you to set the background color. This button changes the color scheme's background color as though you had used the Format⇨Slide Color Scheme command.

Coloring Text and Objects

Normally, the color scheme you choose for a slide determines the color of the various objects on the slide. If the text color is yellow, for example, all text on the slide is yellow (except the title text, which is controlled by the color scheme's Title Text color). Similarly, if the fill color is orange, any filled objects on the slide are orange.

If you change the colors in the color scheme, all the objects on the slide that follow the scheme are affected. But what if you want to change the color of just one object without changing the scheme or affecting other similar objects on the slide? No problemo. PowerPoint enables you to override the scheme color for any object on a slide. The following sections explain how.

Applying color to text

To change the color of a text object, follow these steps:

1. Highlight the text whose color you want to change.

2. Summon the Format⇨Font command.

The Font dialog box appears. Click the Color control, and a cute little Color menu appears (see Figure 9-7).

 Alternatively, click the Text Color button on the Formatting toolbar. The same cute little Color menu appears directly under the button.

3. Click the color you like from the Fill drop-down list box.

The eight colors in the Color menu are the colors from the slide's color scheme. Choose one of these colors if you want to be sure that the colors coordinate. If you're bold and trust your color sense, continue to Step 4.

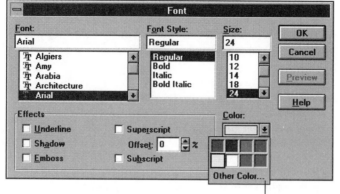

Figure 9-7:
The cute
little Color
menu.

Cute little Color menu

4. Click Other Color and choose a color you like.

The same dialog box you use to hand pick colors for the color scheme
appears. You can choose one of the 90 sensible colors displayed therein,
or you can toss caution to the wind, put on your painting clothes, and click
the More Colors button to build your own color by setting the Huey, Louie,
and Dewey buttons.

5. OK yourself back home.

You may have to click OK several times to fully unwind yourself.

Good news! If you use the Other Color option to assign a color, PowerPoint
automatically adds to the Color menu the color you chose. Figure 9-8 shows
how the Color menu may look after you have added some of your colors to it.
You can distinguish your colors from the color scheme colors because your
custom colors are underneath the Other Color option.

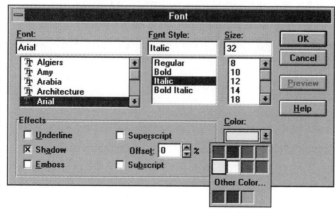

Figure 9-8:
The cute
little Color
menu with
some cute
little custom
colors
added to it.

Hey, I didn't make up the nonsense about Other Colors and More Colors. Be thankful that there aren't buttons labeled Additional Colors, Supplemental Colors, and Leftover Colors. If they had asked me (which they didn't), I would have recommended buttons labeled Good Colors, Bad Colors, and Ugly Colors.

Removing the fill color to an object

When you draw an object such as a rectangle or an ellipse, PowerPoint fills in the object with the color scheme's fill color. If you want the object to be transparent, you can remove the fill color. Follow this procedure:

1. **Choose the object you want to make transparent.**

 2. **Click the Apply Fill Defaults button on the Drawing toolbar (shown in the margin).**

   To restore the fill color from an object, click the Apply Fill Defaults button again.

The Apply Fill Defaults button works like a toggle. If you press it, PowerPoint removes the fill color, making the object transparent. If you press it again, PowerPoint restores the fill color.

 If you apply a custom color to an object as described in the next section, you can reapply the default fill color to the object by clicking the Apply Fill Defaults button twice: once to make the object transparent and then again to fill the object with the default fill color.

Applying a custom color to an object

To change the color of an object, follow these steps:

1. **Choose the object whose color you want to change.**

2. **Choose the Format➪Colors and Lines command.**

   The Colors and Lines dialog box appears. Click the Fill control and a Color menu appears, as shown in Figure 9-9.

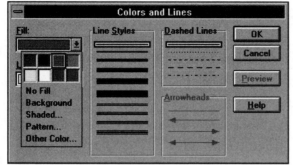

Figure 9-9:
The Colors
and Lines
dialog box
and its Color
menu.

3. Choose your color.

Choose one of the eight color schemes or choose Other Color.

4. Click OK or press the Enter key.

There are many options that you can choose in the Color submenu of the Color and Lines dialog box. I describe them here:

- ✔ If you specify No Fill, the object remains transparent — any objects behind it show through.

- ✔ If you click Background, the object is filled with the background color. Interestingly enough, any shading applied to the background also is carried through to the object. This is done in a seamless manner so that the object appears to blend in with the background.

- ✔ Click Shaded to apply shading to the object. Shading works just like background shading, which is covered earlier in this chapter, under the heading "Shading the slide background."

- ✔ Choose Pattern to assign a pattern, such as diagonal lines or polka dots, to the object. Figure 9-10 shows the dialog box that appears when you change the pattern. You can choose any of the 36 patterns, and you also can change the pattern foreground and background colors. Judicious use of yellow diagonal lines on a blue background can produce a striking Max Headroom effect.

The Colors and Lines dialog box enables you also to choose a color for the line drawn around the object, if any. Just click the Line control and choose your color, or specify No Line if you don't want a line drawn around the object.

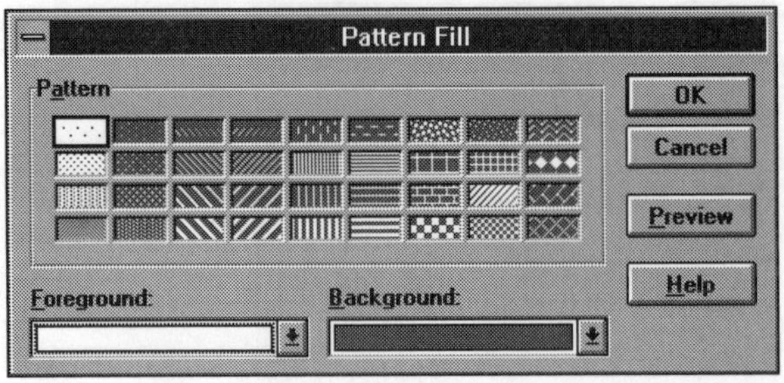

Figure 9-10:
The Pattern
Fill dialog
box.

Copying color from an existing object

If you want to force one object to adopt the color of another object, you can use a fancy tool called the *Format Painter*. It sucks up the formatting of one object and then spits it out onto another object at your command. It's a bit messy, but it gets the job done. (You should see it eat.)

To use the Format Painter, follow these steps:

1. Choose the object whose color you like.

You can select a bit of text or an entire object.

2. Click the Format Painter button on the Standard toolbar (shown in the margin).

This step sucks up the good color so that you can spit it out on other objects.

3. Click the object whose color you don't like.

This step spits the desirable color out on the object.

If you prefer the stodgy menus, choose the object whose color you want to copy and use the Format⇨Pick Up Style command. Then choose the object and use the Format⇨Apply Style command.

In addition to the fill color, the Format Painter also picks up other object attributes, such as shadows, shading, optional trim package, and aluminum alloy hubcaps.

If you want to apply one object's format to several objects, select the object whose color you like and then double-click the Format Painter. Now you can click as many objects as you want to apply the first object's format to. When you're done, press the Esc key.

Don't be spooked by the Pick Up and Apply commands on the Format menu, which seem to change themselves at random. The wording in these commands is adjusted to reflect the selected object. When you select text, the commands read *Pick Up Text Style* and *Apply To Text Style*. When you choose an object, the commands read *Pick Up Object Style* and *Apply To Object Style*. When you don't select anything, the Pick Up command is unavailable, and the Apply command changes to *Apply to Object Defaults*.

If you want to pick up an object's style and apply it as the default for all new objects you create, choose the object and use the Format⇨Pick Up Style command. Then click away from any object so that no object is selected and use the Format⇨Apply to Object Defaults command.

Chapter 10

A Time of Transition (or Slide Show FX)

* * *

In This Chapter

▶ Using slide transitions

▶ Using builds

▶ Hiding slides

▶ Running a slide show

* * *

*I*f you plan to run your presentation on your computer's screen, you can use or abuse a bag full of exciting on-screen slide show tricks. Your audience probably won't be fooled into thinking you hired Industrial Light and Magic to create your special effects, but they'll be impressed all the same. This is just one more example of how PowerPoint can make even the dullest content look spectacular.

Most of these special effects are set up from PowerPoint's Slide Sorter view. In fact, aside from providing an easy way to rearrange the order of your slides, creating special effects is Slide Sorter view's main purpose in life.

Using Slide Transitions

A *transition* is how PowerPoint gets from one slide to the next during an on-screen slide show. The normal way to segue from slide to slide is simply to cut to the new slide. Effective, but boring. PowerPoint enables you to assign any of 45 different special effects to each slide transition. For example, you can have a slide scoot over the top of the current slide from any direction, or you can have the current slide scoot off the screen in any direction to reveal the next slide. And you can use various types of dissolves, from a simple dissolve to checkerboard or venetian blind effects.

Keep in mind these points when using slide transitions:

✔ Transition effects look better on faster computers. The more powerful the computer, the more raw processing horsepower it has to implement the fancy pixel dexterity required to produce good-looking transitions.

✔ Some of the transition effects come in matched sets that apply the same effect from different directions. You can create a cohesive set of transitions by alternating among these related effects from slide to slide. For example, set up the first slide using Wipe Right, the second slide using Wipe Left, the third with Wipe Down, and so on.

✔ If you can't decide what transition effect to use, set all the slides to Random Transition. Then PowerPoint picks a transition effect for each slide at random.

Slide transitions the easy way

Here's the easy way to assign transition effects:

1. Switch to Slide Sorter view.

 Click the Slide Sorter View button or use the View➪ Slide Sorter command.

Figure 10-1 shows how PowerPoint displays a presentation in Slide Sorter view. Notice that the Formatting toolbar is replaced by the *Slide Sorter toolbar*, which enables you to apply special effects quickly for on-screen presentations.

2. Click the slide you want to create a transition for.

3. Choose the transition effect from the drop-down list box.

The Slide Sorter toolbar has two list boxes; the one on the left is for transition effects. In Figure 10-1, the transition is currently set to Cover Right.

 When you assign a transition effect to a slide, a button appears beneath the slide to indicate that the slide has a transition effect.

4. Do it to other slides.

The other slides will become jealous if you don't give them fancy transition effects too.

To get an idea of what the transition will look like, click the transition effect button beneath the slide in Slide Sorter view. PowerPoint quickly replaces the slide with the previous slide and then redisplays the slide using the transition effect you chose.

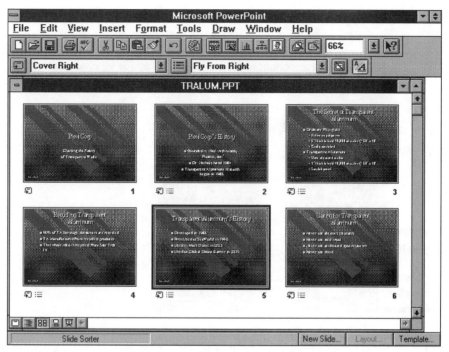

Figure 10-1:
Slide Sorter
view.

Slide transitions the hard way

You can set slide transitions also by using the menus. Here's the procedure:

1. **Head for Slide Sorter view.**

   Use the View➪ Slide Sorter command or click the Slide Sorter View button.

2. **Select the slide you want to add an effect to.**

3. **Use the Tools➪ Transition command.**

   Or, as a shortcut, click the Transition button on the Slide Sorter toolbar. Either way, the Transition dialog box, shown in Figure 10-2, appears.

4. **Choose the transition effect you want from the drop-down list box.**

5. **Choose the speed of the transition if you want.**

   Fast is almost always best, unless you're trying to fill time and you don't really have anything to say.

6. Click OK or press Enter.

PowerPoint demonstrates the transition effect you pick in the picture at the bottom right of the dialog box. Each time you pick a different effect, the picture changes from a dog to a key (or vice versa) to show you how the transition looks.

Figure 10-2:
The
Transition
dialog box.

To set up a PowerPoint slide show that runs by itself, check the Automatically After box for the slide and specify how many seconds you want the slide to display.

Using Builds

You can set up a *build effect* for any slide that has a bulleted list. When a slide has a bulleted list, the bulleted items are added to the slide one at a time. The build effect dictates the entrance made by each bullet item. You can have them appear out of nowhere, drop from the top of the screen, march in from the left or right, or do a back somersault followed by two cartwheels and a double-twist flip (talc, please!).

The build effect you choose for a slide is used for all of the bullets on that slide. However, if you pick Random Effect, a different effect is used for each bullet. Your audience will be on the edge of their collective seats, waiting to see what bullet effect is next.

Like the transition effects, some of the bullet effects come in matched sets. For example: Fly from Left, Fly from Right, Fly from Top, and Fly from Bottom. Use these effects on consecutive slides to add some continuity to your presentation.

Experts refer to build effects as *progressive disclosure*. These same people refer to jumping jacks as *two-count side-step straddle hops*.

Build effects the easy way

Here's the easy way to assign a build effect:

1. Switch to Slide Sorter view.

Use the View⇨Slide Sorter command or click the Slide Sorter View button.

2. Click the slide you want to add a build effect to.

3. Choose the build effect from the drop-down list box.

The Slide Sorter toolbar has two list boxes; the one on the right is for build effects.

When you use a build effect on a slide, PowerPoint displays a button below the slide to help you remember that you've added the build effect (shown in the margin). To remove build effects from the slide, choose No Build Effect in the drop-down list box.

Build effects the hard way

You can add build effects also by using the menus. Follow this procedure:

1. Zip over to Slide Sorter view.

Use the View⇨Slide Sorter command or click the Slide Sorter View button.

2. Click the slide you want to add an effect to.

3. Use the Tools⇨Build command.

Or click the Build button on the Slide Sorter toolbar. The Build dialog box appears. See Figure 10-3.

4. Pick a build effect from the drop-down list box.

5. Click OK or press Enter.

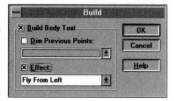

Figure 10-3:
The Build
dialog box.

If you check the <u>D</u>im Previous Points option, the bullet items that you have already shown turn a different color as PowerPoint displays each new bullet item. PowerPoint picks the color from the color scheme, but you can override it if you wish.

Hiding Slides

Suppose you're afraid that someone may challenge your claim that the world is actually flat. You want to back up your claim with a slide that provides concrete proof, but you don't want to show the slide unless someone questions your statement. Time for a hidden slide. Hidden slides are not normally displayed during the course of your slide show. When PowerPoint comes to a hidden slide, it skips over it to the next slide. But you can call up the slide at any time if necessary.

Here's how to hide a slide:

1. **Switch to Slide Sorter view.**

   Use the <u>V</u>iew⇨Sli<u>d</u>e Sorter command or click the Slide Sorter View button.

2. **Click the slide you want to hide.**

3. **Use the <u>T</u>ools⇨<u>H</u>ide Slide command.**

   Or click the Hide Slide button on the Slide Sorter toolbar.

4. **The Slide is hidden.**

   PowerPoint crosses out the slide number shown below the slide so that you can tell that the slide is hidden.

To unhide a slide, follow the above procedure again. The <u>T</u>ools⇨ <u>H</u>ide Slide command and the Hide Slide button work like toggles: use them once to hide the slide, use them again to unhide the slide.

To display a hidden slide during a slide show, type the slide number and press the Enter key. This is kind of weird because when you type the slide number, it doesn't appear on-screen anywhere. But when you press the Enter key, the slide whose number you typed is displayed. To display all of your hidden slides during a slide show, use the *H* key instead of the Enter key to advance from slide to slide.

When you print handouts or notes pages for presentations that contain hidden slides, you have the option of printing hidden slides. You should definitely print hidden slides when you print notes pages. Whether or not you print them with handouts depends on whether you want the audience to have a copy of your hidden slides.

Keep a list of the slide number for each of your hidden slides handy when you make your presentation. That way, you can find the slides quickly if you need them.

On with the Show

To start a slide show immediately, click the Slide Show button (shown in the margin). PowerPoint replaces the entire screen with the first slide of the slide show. To advance to the next slide, press Enter, press the spacebar, or click the mouse button.

Alternatively, you can use the View⊃Slide Show command. Then the Slide Show dialog box shown in Figure 10-4 appears.

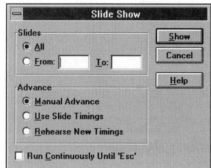

Figure 10-4:
The Slide
Show dialog
box.

With the options in the Slide Show dialog box, you can:

- ✔ Choose All to include all slides in the slide show.
- ✔ Choose From and supply starting and ending slide numbers to display a range of slides.
- ✔ Choose Manual Advance to advance from slide to slide by pressing the Enter key, pressing the spacebar, or clicking the mouse.
- ✔ Choose Use Slide Timings to advance automatically based on the timings specified for each slide.
- ✔ Choose Rehearse New Timings to have PowerPoint keep track of how long each slide is displayed as you rehearse your presentation.
- ✔ Choose Run Continuously Until Esc if you want the entire slide show to loop from the end to the beginning automatically. You must use timings for this feature to work.

Keyboard tricks during a slide show

During an on-screen slide show, you can use the keyboard to control the sequence of your presentation. Table 10-1 lists the keys you can use.

Table 10-1	Keyboard Tricks for Your Slide Show
To Do This	*Press Any of These Keys*
Display next slide	Enter, spacebar, right arrow, down arrow, PageDown, N
Display previous slide	Backspace, left arrow, up arrow, PageUp, P
Display first slide	1+Enter
Display specific slide	*Slide number*+Enter
Toggle screen black	B, period
Toggle screen white	W, comma
Show or hide pointer	A, = (equals)
Erase screen doodles	E
Stop or restart automatic show	S, + (plus)
Display next slide even if hidden	H
Display specific hidden slide	*Slide number of hidden slide*+Enter
End slide show	Esc, Ctrl+Break, – (minus)

Mouse tricks during a slide show

Table 10-2 shows some tricks you can perform with your mouse during an on-screen slide show.

Table 10-2	Mouse Tricks for Your Slide Show
To Do This	*Do This*
Display next slide	Click
Display previous slide	Right-click
Display first slide	Hold down both buttons for two seconds
Doodle	Click the doodle button at the bottom right-hand corner of the screen; then draw on the screen like John Madden (If the doodle button does not appear, press *A* or = on your keyboard or give your mouse a nudge.)

The John Madden effect

If you've always wanted to diagram plays on-screen the way John Madden does, try using the Doodle button. Here's how:

1. **Start a slide show.**

 2. **When you want to doodle on a slide, click the Doodle button.**

   The Doodle button is located at the bottom right corner of the screen. If you can't see it, try pressing *A* or pressing the equals key (=) or moving the mouse a bit.

3. **Draw away.**

   Figure 10-5 shows an example of an doodled-upon slide.

4. **To erase your doodles, press E.**

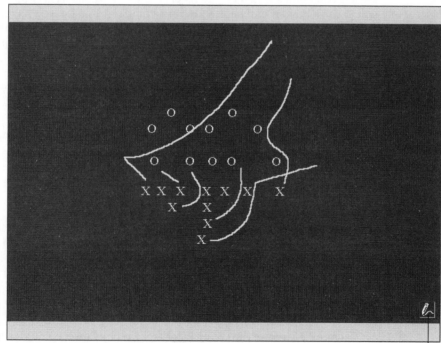

Figure 10-5:
John
Madden
would love
this
program.

Doodle button

Drawing doodles like this requires good mouse dexterity. With practice, you can learn to create all kinds of interesting doodles. Work on circling text, drawing exclamation or question marks, smiley faces, and so on.

Keep these tasty tidbits in mind when doodling:

✓ To hide the Doodle button temporarily and the mouse pointer during a slide show, press *A* or =. The button returns the moment you move the mouse, or you can press *A* or = again to summon it back.

✓ If you use the Doodle button, be sure to say "Bam" and "Pow" a lot.

✓ To turn off the Doodle button, press the equals sign (=) on your keyboard.

Taking Your Show on the Road

PowerPoint comes with a program called the *PowerPoint Viewer* that enables you to run a PowerPoint slide show on a computer that doesn't have a full-fledged copy of PowerPoint. You can't create, edit, or print presentations using Viewer, but you can run on-screen slide shows just as if you were using the full PowerPoint program.

Here's the procedure for displaying a slide show using the Viewer:

1. Start PowerPoint Viewer.

Double-click its icon, which should be hidden in the Microsoft Office Program Manager groups. Figure 10-6 shows the Viewer icon.

Figure 10-6:
The
PowerPoint
Viewer icon.

PowerPoint
Viewer

2. Select the presentation you want to show.

Figure 10-7 shows the dialog box displayed by PowerPoint Viewer. Use it to rummage through your files until you find the presentation you want.

3. Click Show.

On with the show. Break a leg, kid.

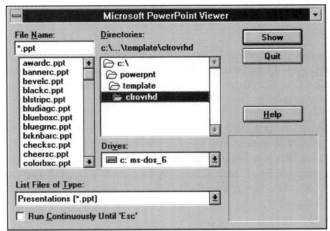

Figure 10-7:
The
Microsoft
PowerPoint
Viewer
dialog box.

Once the show is underway, you can use any of the keyboard or mouse tricks described in the section "On with the Show." You can even doodle on-screen ala John Madden.

If you have the full PowerPoint program, there's not much point in using the Viewer program instead. Viewer is designed to use on computers that don't have a copy of PowerPoint. Microsoft politely grants permission for you to copy the Viewer program to as many computers as you want. You can give it to your friends and associates. It would make a great birthday present for your mother-in-law.

If you use a desktop computer to create PowerPoint presentations and a laptop or notebook computer to run them, you don't have to install the full PowerPoint program on the laptop or notebook computer; just install the Viewer.

The Viewer program comes on a separate disk and is not automatically installed when you install PowerPoint. To install the Viewer program on a computer, insert the PowerPoint Viewer disk into a disk drive and use the Program Manager's File⇨ Run command. Then type **a:vsetup** or **b:vsetup**, depending on which disk drive you inserted the disk into. To send someone a copy of the PowerPoint Viewer, copy the entire PowerPoint Viewer disk. Use the File Manager's Disk⇨ Copy Disk command.

It's perfectly legal to give a friend a copy of the PowerPoint Viewer program along with a presentation. In fact, Microsoft specifically gives you permission to do so. This free-for-all applies only to PowerPoint Viewer, though. Don't make copies of the complete PowerPoint program for your friends unless you want to go to directly to jail (do not pass Go, do not collect $200).

If you want to set up a computer to run a slide show over and over again all day, click the Run Continuously Until Esc button.

If you do set up an unattended presentation, be sure to hide the keyboard and mouse, or unplug them from the computer once you get the slide show going. Leaving a keyboard unattended is like inviting all of the computer geeks within five miles to step up to your computer and find out what games you have.

If you're going to run a slide show on a computer other than the one you used to create the presentation, you need to make sure that the other computer has all of the fonts that your presentation uses. If it doesn't, or if you're not sure, use the File⇨ Save As command to save the file and check the Embed TrueType Fonts button. Doing so stores a copy of the fonts used by the presentation in the presentation file.

Chapter 11

Making 35mm Slides

In This Chapter

▶ Using a local photo lab

▶ Preparing a file for Genigraphics

▶ Sending a file to Genigraphics

*Y*ou can convert PowerPoint slides easily to 35mm color slides, but unless you have your own photo processing equipment, you have to deal with a photo lab to get the job done. It isn't cheap ($5–8 per slide), but the slides look great.

This chapter briefly covers what you need to know to take your presentation to a local photo lab for processing. But most of the chapter is devoted to using the Genigraphics — without doubt the most convenient way to get 35mm slides out of PowerPoint.

Using a Local Photo Lab

One way to produce 35mm slides from a PowerPoint presentation is to take the presentation files to a local photo lab with the equipment to create the slides. Call the lab first to find out the cost and to check on any special requirements they may have, such as whether you need to embed TrueType fonts when you save the file and whether they prefer you to save the file to a 5¼ inch or 3½ inch disk.

To be safe, always embed TrueType fonts and save the file to both 5¼ inch and 3½ inch disks.

You'll find photo labs that can produce computer output listed in the Yellow Pages under Computer Graphics, or perhaps under Photo Finishing. Call several and compare costs and find out how quickly they can finish the job.

Use the PowerPoint File⇨Save As command to save the presentation to disk. Take two copies of the presentation file — on separate disks — to the photo shop. Nothing is more frustrating than driving across town only to discover that something's wrong with your disk. Or, if they have a modem and if you have a modem and know how to use it, you can probably zap your presentation to them over the phone.

Carefully proof your slides using PowerPoint's Slide Show view. Run the spell checker. At $8 per slide, you don't want too many typos to slip by.

Using Genigraphics

Genigraphics is a company that specializes in computer graphics and managed to get its software bundled with PowerPoint. If you can't find a local shop that can do the job, Genigraphics is always available. You can send them your presentation on-disk, or you can send it via modem. PowerPoint even comes with a communication program specially designed for sending PowerPoint presentations to Genigraphics.

Detailed information about using Genigraphics is included with your PowerPoint documentation. Be sure to read it before sending anything to Genigraphics.

Genigraphics accepts the major credit cards or can bill you COD. If you've got clout, you may convince them to open an account. For really big presentations, they offer convenient 15- or 30-year mortgages with fixed or adjustable rates.

Preparing a presentation for Genigraphics

Genigraphics doesn't want your raw PowerPoint files. Instead, you must first create a special file by printing the presentation using the Genigraphics print driver. Sound a little tricky? It is. Here's the blow-by-blow:

1. **Open your presentation.**

   Use the File⇨Open command to find and open your file.

2. **Use the File⇨Slide Setup command to set the slides to 35mm, Landscape. Click OK.**

3. **Choose the File⇨Print command.**

   Make sure that the Print What option is set to *Slides (with Builds)* or *Slides (without Builds)*. Check the All button to print all of the slides in the presentation, or choose the Slides option and enter a range of slides to print in the dialog box next to the Slides option.

4. Click the Printer button.

The Print Setup dialog box appears, as shown in Figure 11-1.

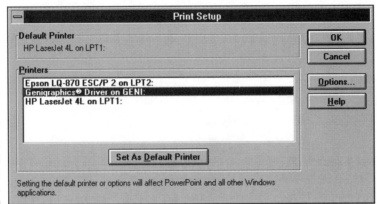

Figure 11-1:
The Print
Setup dialog
box.

5. Choose the Genigraphics Driver on GENI: option.

6. Click the Options button.

The Genigraphics Setup dialog box appears, as shown in Figure 11-2. Make
sure that the format is set to Presentation Format and that the Reduce or
Enlarge option reads 100%.

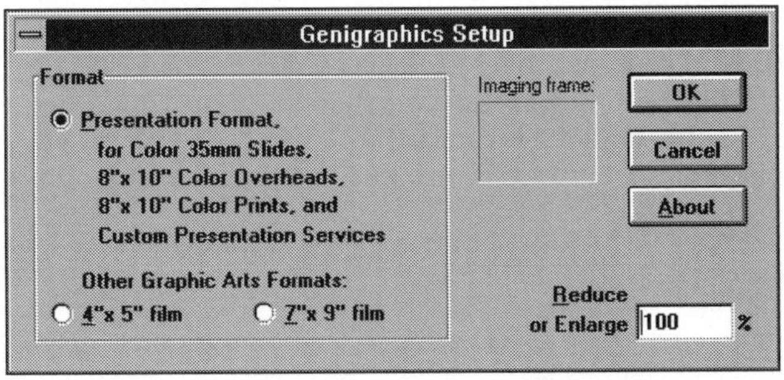

Figure 11-2:
The
Genigraphics
Setup dialog
box.

7. OK yourself back to the Print dialog box.

Click OK to return to the Print Setup dialog box; then click OK again to
return to the Print dialog box.

8. Click OK to print the presentation.

9. Fill out the job instructions.

When the Job Instructions dialog box appears, specify how many copies you want, whether you're sending the file via modem or by mail on-disk, and how you want the slides returned. See Figure 11-3.

If you don't have a modem or if you'd prefer to mail the file to Genigraphics on a disk, specify Diskette rather than Modem. A Save As dialog box pops up. Save the file on your A: or B: drive.

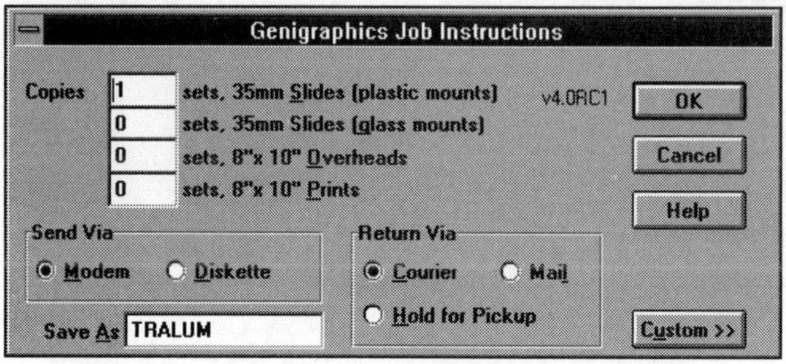

Figure 11-3:
The Job
Instructions
dialog box.

10. If any warning messages appear, heed them well.

The most common warning message is that your presentation used fonts that Genigraphics can't use. Use only TrueType fonts to avoid receiving this message.

To make sure you use only TrueType fonts in PowerPoint, use only those fonts that have the TrueType emblem displayed next to them in font drop-down lists. If you want to restrict all of your programs to TrueType fonts only, call up the Control Panel (which hides in the Main Program Manager group), double-click the Fonts button, click the TrueType button, and check the Show Only TrueType Fonts in Applications option. Wasn't that easy?

11. Pay the piper.

There's no such thing as a free lunch, and Genigraphics displays the dialog box shown in Figure 11-4 to remind you of that fact. Fill out your name and address and tell them how you intend to pay. Then click OK.

12. You're done!

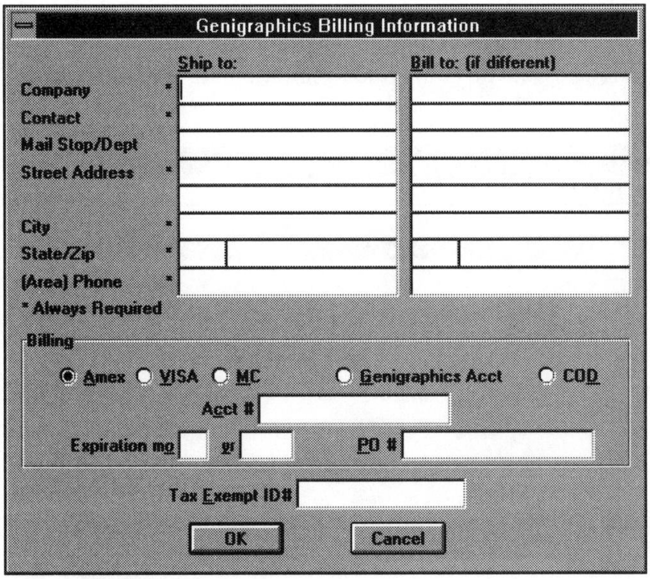

Genigraphics Billing Information

	Ship to:	Bill to: (if different)
Company *		
Contact *		
Mail Stop/Dept		
Street Address *		
City *		
State/Zip *		
(Area) Phone *		

* Always Required

Billing

○ Amex   ○ VISA   ○ MC   ○ Genigraphics Acct   ○ COD

Acct #

Expiration mo □ yr □   PO #

Tax Exempt ID#

[OK]   [Cancel]

Figure 11-4:
The Billing
Information
dialog box.

Sending the file to Genigraphics

If you have a modem and know how to use it, or even if you have a modem and
don't know how to use it, you can save time by sending your Genigraphics file
over the phone. PowerPoint even comes with a special program called
GraphicsLink that's designed to send PowerPoint files to Genigraphics.

Here's the procedure to use GraphicsLink:

1. Start GraphicsLink.

It hides in the Microsoft Office program manager group unless you have
moved it. Figure 11-5 shows its icon.

Figure 11-5:
The
GraphicsLink
icon.

GraphicsLink

GraphicsLink greets you with a list of all the PowerPoint presentations you've converted to Genigraphics files. If you can't find your presentation, use the File⇨Get File command to find the file. See Figure 11-6.

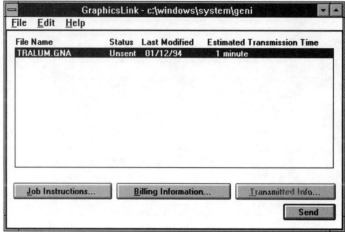

Figure 11-6:
The
wonderful
world of
Genigraphics.

2. **If you haven't already done so, use the File⇨Communications Setup command to configure the modem.**

   Set the modem port, baud rate, and all that other stuff. If you don't know how to do this, offer your local computer guru a bag of Cheetos to do it for you.

3. **Choose the file or files you want to send.**

   To select more than one file, hold down the Ctrl key while clicking the files you want to send, or hold down the Shift key while dragging to select a block of files. You also can use the Edit⇨Select All command to select all files or the Edit⇨Select Unsent command to select just files you haven't yet sent.

4. **Click the Send button to send the file(s).**

5. **Hold on to your hat.**

   Your computer gives Genigraphics a ring, sends the files, and then hangs up. It may take awhile.

You can click the Job Instructions and Billing Information buttons if you want to change the values you typed when you created the Geni file. If you hear the Genigraphics computer saying, "One ringy-dingy. Two ringy-dingy. Is this the party to whom I am speaking? <Snort snort>," hang up immediately and try again later.

After the files are successfully sent, GraphicsLink deletes them to save disk space. GraphicsLink replaces each sent file with a small report file that keeps track of the job and billing information. (Don't worry: GraphicsLink doesn't delete your actual PowerPoint files, just the file you created when you printed the presentation using the GeniGraphics printer driver.)

Part III

Pictures, Charts, and Grunts

The 5th Wave   **By Rich Tennant**

"And, as you can see by slide 8, clowning is up 20%."

In this part . . .

You'll hear nothing but yawns from the back row if your presentation consists of slide after slide of text and bulleted lists. Mercifully, PowerPoint is well equipped to add all sorts of embellishments to your slides. Clip art (pictures drawn by a real artist), drawings, graphs, organizational charts, equations, and more. You can even make your presentations belch on command.

Not that any of this is easy. That's why I devote an entire part to wrestling with these ornaments.

Chapter 12

Using the ClipArt Gallery

● ●

In This Chapter

▶ Using free pictures

▶ Finding a picture you like

▶ Moving, sizing, and stretching pictures

▶ Adding a box, shaded background, or shadow to a picture

▶ Editing a clip art picture

▶ Adding your own pictures to the ClipArt Gallery

● ●

*F*ace it: Most of us are not born with even an ounce of artistic ability. Someday, hopefully soon, those genetic researchers combing through the billions and billions of genes strung out on those twisty DNA helixes will discover *The Artist Gene*. Then, in spite of protests from the DaVincis and Monets among us (who fear that their NEA grants will be threatened), doctors will splice the little bugger into our own DNA strands so that we all can be artists. Of course, this procedure will not be without its side effects: Some will develop an insatiable craving for croissants, and others will inexplicably develop French accents. But artists we shall be.

Until then, we have to rely on clip art.

Free Pictures!

PowerPoint comes with more than 1,100 clip art pictures that you can pop directly into your presentations. These pictures were drawn by high-tech sidewalk artists who work at Microsoft and include subjects ranging from cartoons to pickaxes to maps of the Middle East.

PowerPoint's clip art pictures are managed by a program called the *ClipArt Gallery*. This nifty little program keeps track of clip art files spread out all over your hard disk and spares you the unpleasant chore of rummaging through your directories to look for that picture of Elvis you know that you have somewhere. ClipArt Gallery also takes the guesswork out of using clip art: Rather than choose a filename like ELVISFAT.PCX and hope that it's the one you remembered, you can see the clip art before you add it to your presentation.

ClipArt Gallery organizes your clip art files into categories, such as Architecture, Flags, and Gestures. This organization makes it easy to search through the 1,100 clip art images that come with PowerPoint and find just the right one. (Wouldn't it be great if the Metropolitan Museum of Art used the same categories as ClipArt Gallery?)

ClipArt Gallery works with several other Microsoft applications, most notably Microsoft Publisher. The clip art that comes with those programs is tossed in with the PowerPoint clip art so that you can easily get to it.

You also can add your own pictures to ClipArt Gallery. You may whip out a detailed replica of the Mona Lisa in Windows Paintbrush, for example, and then toss it into ClipArt Gallery.

Don't overdo it with the clip art. One surefire way to guarantee an amateur look to your presentation is to load it down with three clip art pictures on every slide. Judicious use of clip art is much more effective.

Dropping In Some Clip Art

These steps show you how to drop clip art into your presentation:

1. Move to the slide on which you want to plaster the clip art.

If you want the same clip art picture to appear on every slide, move to Master Slide view by using the <u>V</u>iew⇨<u>M</u>aster⇨Master <u>S</u>lide command (or Shift+click the Slide View button).

2. Choose the <u>I</u>nsert⇨<u>C</u>lip Art command.

Sorry, PowerPoint has no shortcut key for this command. If you like the mouse, though, you can click the Insert Clip Art button instead (shown in the margin).

It doesn't matter where you place the cursor before you choose the <u>I</u>nsert⇨<u>C</u>lip Art command. PowerPoint sticks the clip art picture right smack dab in the middle of the slide anyway. The picture will probably be way too big, so you have to move and shrink it.

3. Behold the ClipArt Gallery, in all its splendor.

After a brief moment's hesitation, the ClipArt Gallery pops up. Figure 12-1 shows what it looks like.

4. Choose the clip art picture you want.

To find the picture you want, first choose the clip art category that contains the picture (if you're not sure, make your best guess). When you first pop up the ClipArt Gallery, All Categories is the default; this category shows all the clip art pictures in your collection. To narrow your search, scroll through the Category list until you find the category you want and then click it.

Next, find the specific picture you want. ClipArt Gallery shows 12 pictures at a time, but you can display other pictures from the same category by scrolling through the pictures. When the picture you want comes into view, click it.

5. Click OK to insert the picture.

Or simply double-click the picture.

You're done.

Bammo! PowerPoint inserts the clip art picture as an object on the slide, as shown in Figure 12-2.

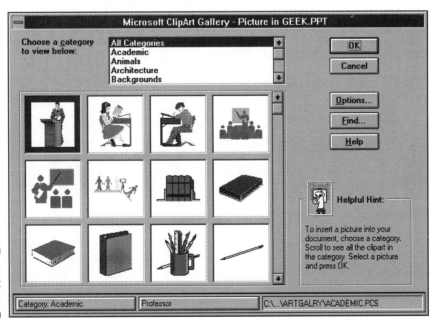

Figure 12-1:
The ClipArt
Gallery.

Handles

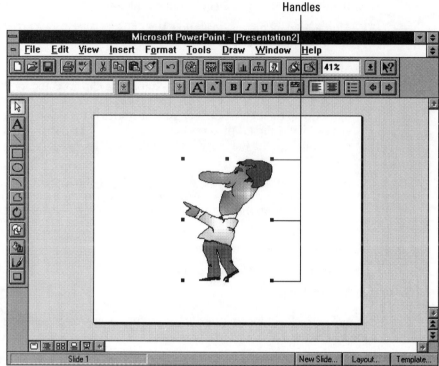

Figure 12-2:
A clip art
picture
inserted in a
presentation.

You can see that PowerPoint sticks the picture right in the middle of the slide, which is probably not where you want it. And it's probably too big. You have to wrestle with it to get it just the way you want it. See the section "Moving, Sizing, and Stretching Pictures" later in this chapter for instructions on how to force the picture into compliance.

The first time you use ClipArt Gallery after installing PowerPoint, ClipArt Gallery realizes that it hasn't added PowerPoint's clip art to the gallery. So off it goes, politely updating itself so that it can handle PowerPoint's clip art. Well, it's not really all that polite because it takes about three days (at least it seemed to take that long the first time I did it). This is a good time to get caught up on your reading or take your family to Disneyland. Mercifully, this happens only the first time you power up the ClipArt Gallery.

Notice the buttons at the bottom of the ClipArt Gallery dialog box. They tell you the current category and the name of the picture that's chosen. To change the name of the category or picture, click these buttons. Otherwise, just look at them and nod appreciatively.

At the bottom right edge of the ClipArt Gallery dialog box, you also can see the name of the file that contains the chosen picture.

If you can't find the clip art picture you're looking for, click the Find button. This step enables you to search for clip art based on the category, description, or filename. For example, you can look for all pictures that have the word *world* in their description.

Moving, Sizing, and Stretching Pictures

Because PowerPoint inserts clip art right in the middle of the slide, you undoubtedly want to move it to a more convenient location. You probably also want to change its size if it is too big.

Follow these steps to force your inserted clip art into full compliance:

1. **Click the picture and drag it wherever you want.**

   You don't have to worry about clicking exactly the edge of the picture or one of its lines; just click anywhere in the picture and drag it around.

2. **Notice the eight handles. Drag one of them to resize the picture.**

   Flip back to Figure 12-2 and notice the eight handles that surround the clip art. You can click and drag any of these handles to adjust the size of the picture. When you click one of the corner handles, the proportion of the picture stays the same as you change its size. When you drag one of the corner handles (top, bottom, left, or right) to change the size of the picture in just one dimension, you distort the picture's outlook as you go.

When you resize a picture, the picture changes its position on the slide. As a result, you can count on moving it after you resize it. If you hold down the Ctrl key while dragging a handle, however, the picture becomes anchored at its center point as you resize it. Therefore, its position is unchanged, and you probably don't have to move it.

Stretching a clip art picture by dragging one of the edge handles can dramatically change the picture's appearance. To illustrate, Figure 12-3 shows how the same clip art picture can resemble both Arnold Schwarzenegger *and* Danny DeVito. I just stretched one copy of the picture vertically to make it tall and stretched the other copy horizontally to make it, er, stout.

Figure 12-3:
Twins.

Boxing, Shading, and Shadowing a Picture

PowerPoint enables you to draw attention to a clip art picture by drawing a box around it, shading its background, or adding a shadow. Figure 12-4 shows what these embellishments look like.

Figure 12-4:
How it feels
to use
PowerPoint.

These steps show you how to use these features:

1. Click the picture you want to entomb.

2. Use the Format⇨Colors and Lines command to draw a box around the picture or to shade its background.

Figure 12-5 shows the Colors and Lines dialog box. Choose a color from the Fill list box to give the picture a background color and then choose a color from the Line list box to draw a line around the picture. You also can choose the line thickness and set up dashed lines.

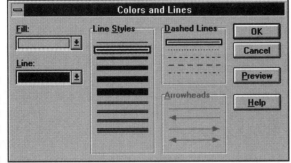

Figure 12-5:
The Colors
and Lines
dialog box.

3. Use the Format⇨Shadow command or click the Apply Shadow Defaults button to give the picture a shadow.

Figure 12-6 shows the Shadow dialog box. To add a shadow, pick a color from the Color drop-down list box. This creates a shadow that is six points below and to the right of the clip-art picture, but you can change these offsets if you wish. (A *point* is one-twelfth of an inch.)

If you click the Apply Shadow Defaults button, PowerPoint uses the shadow color from the slide's color scheme to create a shadow.

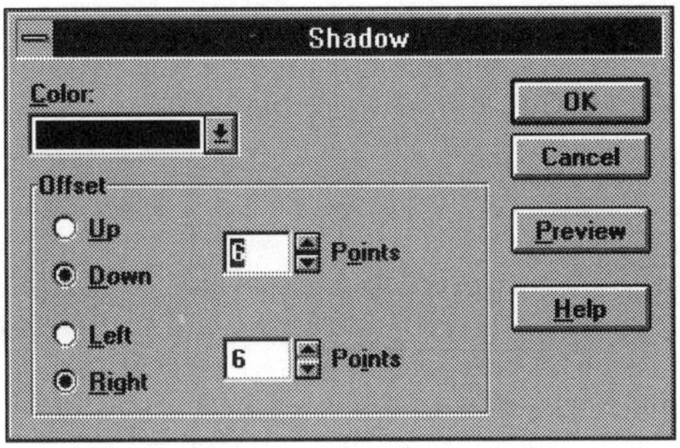

Figure 12-6:
The Shadow
dialog box.

Editing a Clip Art Picture

Sometimes one of the clip art pictures supplied with PowerPoint is close but not quite exactly what you want. In that case, you can insert the picture and then edit it to make whatever changes are needed. For example, Figure 12-7 shows the same clip art picture shown in Figure 12-2, but this time it has been edited to demonstrate the effect of telling whoppers.

You can't directly edit a clip art picture. Instead, you must first convert the picture to an equivalent bunch of PowerPoint shape objects. Then you can individually select and edit the objects using the shape editing tools described in Chapter 14.

Figure 12-7:
Always let your conscience be your guide when you edit clip art pictures.

These steps show the procedure for editing a clip art picture:

1. **Choose the picture you want to edit.**

2. **Use the Draw⇨Ungroup command to convert the picture to PowerPoint shapes that you can edit.**

   When you do, PowerPoint displays the warning message shown in Figure 12-8. If you do indeed want to convert the picture to PowerPoint shape objects that you can edit, click OK.

3. **Now you can edit the picture.**

   The clip art picture has been converted to an equivalent group of PowerPoint shape objects, so you can use PowerPoint's shape editing tools to change their appearance. You can drag any of the control handles to reshape an object, or you can change colors or add new stuff to the picture. See Chapter 14 for the details on how to edit PowerPoint shape objects.

Figure 12-8:
Throw
caution to
the wind
and ignore
this
warning.

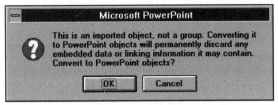

If you double-click a clip art picture that hasn't been converted to a PowerPoint object, the ClipArt Gallery is summoned so that you can choose a different clip art picture. To edit the picture, you must first convert it to PowerPoint objects. You do that using the Draw⇨Ungroup command. (I know, I know: they should have added a Draw⇨Convert command or something like that to convert a clip art picture to PowerPoint objects. Don't blame me; I'm just the messenger.)

Don't read this groupie stuff

What is all this talk of *grouping* and *ungrouping*? These are common drawing terms explained in more detail in Chapter 14. For now, consider how you can draw a simple picture of a face. You may start with a circle for the head and then add ellipses for the eyes, nose, and mouth. By the time you finish, you have five ellipse objects.

The only problem is, suppose you want to move the face you just drew to the other side of the slide. If you just clicked and dragged it, odds are you would move only the nose or one of the eyes. To move the whole thing, you have to select all five ellipses.

Wouldn't it be great if you could treat all five ellipses as a single object? That's what *grouping* is all about. When you group objects, they are treated as if they were a single object. When you click any one of the grouped objects, you click them all. Move one, they all move. Delete one, they all vanish.

What happens if after grouping the five face ellipses you discover that you made the nose too big? You have to *ungroup* them so that they become five separate objects again. Then you can select and resize just the nose.

Most complex drawings use grouping. PowerPoint clip art pictures are no exception. That's why you have to ungroup them before you can edit them. Clip art pictures have the added characteristic that when you ungroup a clip art picture, you sever its connection to the ClipArt Gallery. The picture is no longer a ClipArt Picture Object but is now merely a bunch of PowerPoint rectangles, ellipses, and free-form shapes.

Oops, this is way too much stuff about grouping for the clip art chapter. Maybe you should skip ahead to Chapter 14 if you're really this interested.

Most PowerPoint clip art pictures are constructed from groups of groups of groups of maybe more groups. To tweak the shape of an object, you must keep ungrouping it until the Ungroup command is no longer available from the Draw menu.

After you have ungrouped and edited a picture, you may want to regroup it again. You're much less likely to pull the nose off someone's face if the face is a group rather than a bunch of ungrouped ellipse objects.

When you convert a picture to PowerPoint objects, you're actually placing a copy of the ClipArt Gallery picture in your presentation. Any changes you make to the picture are reflected only in your presentation; the original version of the clip art picture is unaffected.

Adding Your Own Pictures to the ClipArt Gallery

If you're artistic and like to draw your own pictures or if you've purchased a set of clip art pictures that you use frequently, you can easily add them to the ClipArt Gallery. Then you can insert them into your presentations by using the same procedures you use to insert the clip art that comes with PowerPoint.

If you click the Options button in the ClipArt Gallery (review Figure 12-1), the Options dialog box appears, as shown in Figure 12-9.

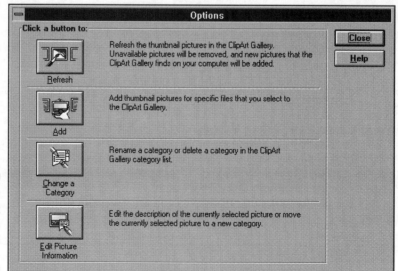

Figure 12-9:
ClipArt
Gallery's
Options
dialog box.

Don't bite your thumbnails!

What's all this talk about "refreshing the thumbnail pictures" or "adding thumbnail pictures" in the ClipArt Gallery Options dialog box? Does PowerPoint come with a bunch of pictures of people's thumbs?

Nope. The term *thumbnail picture* refers to how the ClipArt Gallery is capable of efficiently displaying those little pictures of all those clip art pictures. If ClipArt Gallery really opened each clip art file just to display those little pictures, you would never use ClipArt Gallery because it would be too danged slow.

To achieve acceptable performance, ClipArt Gallery stores all those little pictures together in one file. Whenever you add a clip art picture to the Gallery, a thumbnail picture for the clip art is

created for the picture. Then whenever you call up ClipArt Gallery, it retrieves the thumbnail pictures from the file and displays them. As a result, ClipArt Gallery doesn't have to read the clip art picture files every time you use it.

The drawback to this technique is that it's possible for ClipArt Gallery to become out of sync with the clip art files on your disk. If you modify a clip art file (perhaps by editing it with Paintbrush), for example, you have to tell ClipArt Gallery that it has to refresh its thumbnail picture. You refresh the clip art by choosing the Refresh button in the Options dialog box. If you don't, the thumbnail picture may not accurately represent the clip art picture that is inserted. Similarly, if you delete a clip art file, you should refresh ClipArt Gallery's thumbnail pictures.

From this dialog box, you can choose four options:

- ✔ *Refresh:* Scans your entire hard disk and looks for picture files that are out of sync with the thumbnail pictures in ClipArt Gallery or pictures that ClipArt Gallery doesn't yet know about. It also removes any ClipArt Gallery thumbnail sketches that belong to pictures you've deleted. (If you don't know what thumbnail pictures are — and there's no reason you should — check out the sidebar "Don't bite your thumbnails!")

  The Refresh option takes a long time to run, so don't do it if you're in a hurry.

- ✔ *Add:* Enables you to add your own clip art to the ClipArt Gallery. When you click the Add button, a dialog box pops up that enables you to thrash around on your disk drive until you find a picture that you want to add (see Figure 12-10).

- ✔ *Change a Category:* Who knows — maybe you just don't like the category names PowerPoint assigns to its clip art. You change them with this option.

- ✔ *Edit Picture Information:* Where to go if you think that the written description of a picture isn't precise.

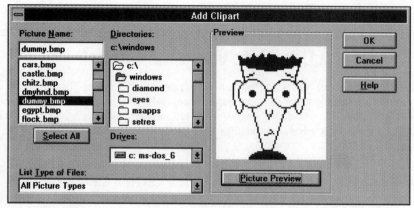

Figure 12-10:
"Hmm ... do
I really want
to add this
picture to
the ClipArt
Gallery?"

Inserting Pictures Without Using the ClipArt Gallery

PowerPoint also enables you to insert pictures directly into your document without using the ClipArt Gallery. Use this technique to insert clip art that you haven't added to the ClipArt Gallery. These steps show you how:

1. **Move to the slide on which you want to splash the clip art.**

   If you want the clip art to show up on every slide, conjure up Master Slide view with the View➪Master➪Master Slide command (or Shift+click the Slide View button).

2. **Choose the Insert➪Picture command.**

   Greet the Insert Picture dialog box, shown in Figure 12-11, with a smile.

3. **Dig through the bottom of your disk drive until you find the file you want.**

   It can be anywhere. Fortunately, the Insert Picture dialog box has all the controls you need in order to search high and low until you find the file.

4. **Click the file and then click OK.**

   You're done!

You also can paste a picture directly into PowerPoint by way of the Clipboard. Anything you can copy to the Clipboard you can paste into PowerPoint. For example, you can doodle a sketch in Paintbrush, copy it, and then zap over to PowerPoint and paste it. Voilà — instant picture!

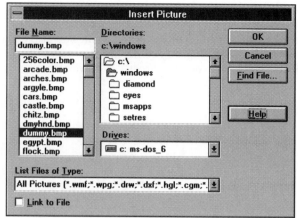

Figure 12-11:
The Insert
Picture
dialog box.

If you want to narrow your search to files of a particular type, use the List Files of Type list box. PowerPoint comes with *filters* that can convert as many as 20 different types of picture files to PowerPoint. Table 12-1 lists the formats you're most likely to use.

If the file type you want doesn't show up in the List Files of Type box, you may not have installed all the graphics filters when you installed PowerPoint. Run the PowerPoint Setup program (it's in the Microsoft Office Program Manager group) and see whether the graphics filter you want is available. Better yet, bribe your local computer guru to do this for you. This is definitely Guru Stuff.

Table 12-1	Formats for Picture Files
Format	*What It Is*
BMP	Garden variety Windows bitmap file, used by Paintbrush and many other programs
CDR	CorelDRAW!, a popular, uppercrust drawing program
DRW	Micrografx Designer or Micrografx Draw, two popular ooh-aah drawing programs
EPS	Encapsulated PostScript, a format use by some high-end drawing programs
GIF	Graphics Interchange Format, commonly found on CompuServe and often rated R
PCX	A variant type of bitmap file, also used by Paintbrush and other programs
TIF	Tagged Image Format file; another bitmap file format, used by highbrow drawing programs
WMF	Windows MetaFile, a format that many programs recognize
WPG	DrawPerfect, WordPerfect's artistic sibling

If you insert a picture by using the Insert⇨Picture command and then double-click the picture, PowerPoint throws you into the program that was used to create the file, where you can edit it any way you want. You also can ungroup the picture by using the Draw⇨Ungroup command to convert the picture to PowerPoint objects, which you can edit directly in PowerPoint.

Chapter 13

Dropping In a Chart

• •

In This Chapter

▶ Creating a chart with Microsoft Graph

▶ Moving and resizing a chart

▶ Embellishing a chart with titles, legends, and other stuff

▶ Importing chart data from a spreadsheet

• •

*O*ne of the best ways to prove a point is with numbers ("numbers don't lie"), and one of the best ways to present numbers is in a chart. Just ask Ross Perot. With PowerPoint, it's easy to add a chart to your presentation. And it's usually easy to get the chart to look the way you want. It takes a great deal of pointing and clicking, but it works.

Wouldn't it have been great if I could have talked Ross Perot into writing this chapter for me:

> "Now. Do you want to just sit around and talk about making charts or do you want to get in there and do it? Ya understand what I'm sayin'? If all you want to do is form a committee to study these charts and whatnot, I'm not your man. And don't bother me if all you want to do is import cheap charts from Mexico."

PowerPoint charts are drawn by Microsoft's latest and greatest charting program, Microsoft Graph 5. Microsoft Graph works so well with PowerPoint that you probably wouldn't know that it was a separate program if I hadn't just told you.

> "Do you mind? Now I didn't interrupt you. That was just downright rude. Now. Here's the thing. Microsoft spent something like $50 billion so that PowerPoint can make world-class charts. It took tens of thousands of talented American programmers to do it, too. Do you think that Canadian programmers could have done this? Not in a million years. This is world-class, American-made software. So stop talking about it — let's get to work."

OK, OK.

Understanding Microsoft Graph

If you've never worked with a charting program, Microsoft Graph can be a little confusing. It takes a series of numbers and renders them as a graph. You can supply the numbers yourself, or you can copy them from an Excel or Lotus 1-2-3 worksheet. Microsoft Graph can create all kinds of different charts that range from simple bar charts and pie charts to exotic doughnut charts and radar charts. Very cool, but a little confusing to the uninitiated.

This list shows some of the jargon you have to contend with when you're working with charts:

Chart or graph: Same thing. These terms are used interchangeably. A chart or graph is nothing more than a bunch of numbers turned into a picture. After all, a picture is worth a thousand numbers.

Graph object: A chart inserted on a slide. Microsoft Graph draws the chart, so whenever you try to modify the chart's appearance, PowerPoint summons Microsoft Graph.

Chart type: Microsoft Graph supports several chart types: Bar charts, column charts, pie charts, line charts, scatter charts, area charts, radar charts, Dunkin' Donut charts, and others (see Figures 13-5 and 13-6). Different types of charts are better suited to displaying different types of data.

3-D chart: Some chart types have a 3-D effect that gives them a jazzier look. Nothing special here; it's mostly a cosmetic effect.

Datasheet: Supplies the underlying data for a chart. After all, a chart is nothing more than a bunch of numbers made into a picture. The numbers come from the datasheet. It works just like a spreadsheet program, so if you know how to use Excel or Lotus 1-2-3, learning how to use the datasheet takes you about 30 seconds. The datasheet is part of the chart object, but it doesn't appear on the slide. Instead, the datasheet appears only when you edit the chart object.

Series: A collection of related numbers. For example, a graph of quarterly sales by region may have a series for each region. Each series has four sales totals, one for each quarter. Each series is usually represented by a row on the datasheet, but you can change the datasheet so that each column represents a series. Most chart types can plot more than one series. Pie charts can chart only one series at a time, however.

Axes: The lines on the edges of a chart. The X-axis is the line along the bottom of the chart; the Y-axis is the line along the left edge of the chart. The X-axis is usually used to indicate categories. Actual data values are plotted along the Y-axis. Microsoft Graph automatically provides labels for the X and Y axes, but you can change them.

Legend: A box used to identify the various series plotted on the graph. Microsoft Graph can create a legend automatically if you want one.

Microsoft Graph is a separate program, not part of the PowerPoint program. The Microsoft Graph that comes with PowerPoint 4 is the same program that comes with Excel 5. So if you know how to use Excel to create graphs, you can pretty much skip this chapter: You already know everything you need to know.

Although Microsoft Graph is a separate program, it works from within PowerPoint in a way that makes it look like it isn't a separate program. When you create or edit a chart, Microsoft Graph comes to life. But rather than pop up in its own window, Microsoft Graph sort of takes over PowerPoint's window and replaces PowerPoint's menus and toolbars with its own. This magic is accomplished with an elaborate arrangement of smoke and mirrors known as *OLE 2*. If you don't have anything else to do, check out the sidebar "Stop me before I tell you about OLE" to find out more about this cool feature.

Microsoft Graph has its own Help system. To see Help information for Microsoft Graph, first call up Microsoft Graph by inserting a graph object or double-clicking an existing graph object. Then press F1 or use the Help menu.

Creating a Chart

To add a chart to your presentation, you have two options:

- ✔ Create a new slide by using an AutoLayout that includes a chart object.
- ✔ Add a chart object to an existing slide.

It's easier to create a new slide by using an AutoLayout because the AutoLayout positions other elements on the slide for you. If you add a chart to an existing slide, you probably have to adjust the size and position of existing objects to make room for the chart object.

Inserting a new slide with a chart

This step-by-step procedure shows you how to insert a new slide that contains a chart:

1. **Move to the slide you want the new slide to follow.**

2. **Click the New Slide button on the status bar.**

   The New Slide dialog box, shown in Figure 13-1, appears.

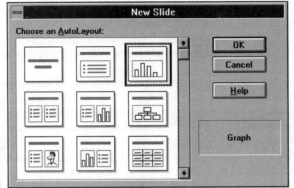

Figure 13-1:
The New
Slide dialog
box.

Stop me before I tell you about OLE

If you read anything about Windows these days, you can't avoid reading about OLE. Microsoft introduced OLE, which can be pronounced oh-el-ee or *ohlay* (rhymes with *Frito-Lay*), with Windows 3.1. A new version of OLE, however, known as OLE 2, was recently developed to overcome the many shortcomings in the original OLE. PowerPoint 4, Word for Windows 6, and Excel 5 are the first Microsoft application programs to take advantage of the new OLE 2 capabilities.

OLE stands for *Object Linking and Embedding*. The idea behind it is that it enables you to create documents that contain different kinds of data. Suppose that you want to include some spreadsheet data in a word processing document. With OLE, you simply insert a *spreadsheet object* in the word processing document. OLE remembers that the data was originally created by a spreadsheet program. If you want to edit the spreadsheet data, you just double-click it. OLE magically conjures up the spreadsheet program so that you can edit the data.

With the original OLE, a new window appeared when you double-clicked an embedded object to edit it. With OLE 2, embedded objects are not edited in separate windows. Instead, when you double-click an embedded object, the menus and toolbars from the embedded object's program appear to replace the main program's menus and toolbar. You can then directly edit the object. Click anywhere outside the object to restore the original program's menus and toolbars.

Some interesting tidbits about OLE follow:

- In OLE terminology, the document that contains an embedded object is called a *container,* and a program that creates a container document is called a *client.* An embedded object is called a *component,* and the program that creates it is called a *server.* These terms are important to the people who write OLE programs, but they're completely unimportant to normal people like you and me.

- Microsoft Graph isn't the only OLE program that can work with PowerPoint. Microsoft WordArt, Equation Editor, and Organization Chart are other examples of OLE, as is PowerPoint's capability to embed a Word for Windows table or an Excel worksheet.

3. Choose the slide type you want and click OK.

Several slide types include chart objects. Choose the one you want and click OK. A new slide is added. As you can see in Figure 13-2, the chart object is simply a placeholder; you have to use Microsoft Graph to complete the chart.

Figure 13-2:
A new slide with a virgin chart object.

4. Double-click the chart object to conjure up Microsoft Graph.

PowerPoint awakens Microsoft Graph from its slumber, and the two programs spend a few moments exchanging news from home. Then Microsoft Graph takes over, creating a sample chart with make-believe data, as shown in Figure 13-3.

5. Change the sample data to something more realistic.

The *datasheet*, visible in Figure 13-3, supplies the data on which the chart is based. The datasheet, displayed in a separate window, is not a part of the slide. Unfortunately, the datasheet window sits right on top of the chart, so you cannot see the chart until you close the datasheet window or move the window by dragging the title bar.

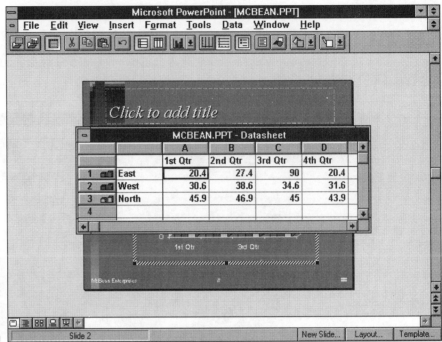

Figure 13-3:
Microsoft
Graph takes
over.

The datasheet works just like a spreadsheet program. For more information on using it, see the section "Working with the Datasheet" later in this chapter.

6. Return to the slide.

Click anywhere on the slide outside the chart or the datasheet to leave Microsoft Graph and return to the slide. You can then see the chart with the new numbers, as shown in Figure 13-4.

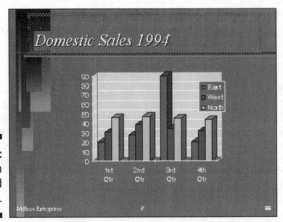

Figure 13-4:
A slide with
a finished
chart.

Inserting a chart in an existing slide

Remember that this method is the more difficult of the two methods of adding charts to your slides. Use the previous one unless you have already created your slide.

Use this procedure to add a chart to an existing slide:

1. **Move to the slide on which you want to place the chart.**

2. **Summon the Insert⊃Microsoft Graph command.**

    Or click the Insert Graph button (shown in the margin).

3. **Type your data in the datasheet.**

   Replace the sample data with your numbers.

4. **Click outside the chart to return to the slide.**

5. **Rearrange everything.**

   The chart undoubtedly falls on top of something else already on the slide. You probably will have to resize and move the chart object and perhaps other objects on the slide to make room for the chart. Or you may want to delete an unnecessary text or clip art object from the slide. See the next section, "Moving and Resizing a Chart," to learn how to move your chart around.

Moving and Resizing a Chart

You can move or resize charts the same way as you do any other PowerPoint object. To move a chart, just click the mouse anywhere in the chart and drag it to its new location. To resize a chart, click the object and then drag one of the eight love handles that appear.

Holding down the Ctrl key while resizing an object keeps the object centered over its original position. This rule holds true for charts.

If you drag one of the edge love handles (top, bottom, left, or right), the proportions of the chart are distorted. Depending on the chart type, this procedure may emphasize or deemphasize differences between values plotted on the graph.

Working with the Datasheet

The datasheet contains the numbers plotted in your Microsoft Graph chart. The datasheet works like a simple spreadsheet program, with values stored in cells that are arranged in rows and columns. Like a spreadsheet, each column is assigned a letter, and each row is assigned a number. You can identify each cell in the datasheet, therefore, by combining the column letter and row number, as in A1 or B17. (Bingo!)

 Ordinarily, each series of numbers is represented by a row in the spreadsheet. You can change this orientation so that each series is represented by a column by clicking the By Column button on the toolbar (shown in the margin) or by using the Data⇨Series in Columns command.

The first row and column in the datasheet are used for headings and are not assigned a letter or number.

If you have a large number of data values that you want to chart, you may want to increase the size of the datasheet window. Unfortunately, they forgot to put the maximize button on the datasheet window, but you can still increase the size of the datasheet window by dragging any of its corners.

You can choose an entire column by clicking its column letter, or you can choose an entire row by clicking its row number. You also can choose the entire datasheet by clicking the blank box in the upper left corner of the datasheet.

You can change the font used in the datasheet by using the Format⇨Font command. You also can change the numeric format with the Format⇨Number command. Changing the font and number format for the datasheet affects not only the way the datasheet is displayed but also the format of data value labels included in the chart.

Although the datasheet resembles a spreadsheet, you cannot use formulas or functions in a datasheet. If you want to use formulas or functions to calculate the values to be plotted, use a spreadsheet program, such as Excel, to create the spreadsheet and then import it into Microsoft Chart. (Or create the chart in Excel rather than in PowerPoint and then import the Excel Chart into the PowerPoint presentation by using the Insert⇨Object command or copy it into PowerPoint by way of the Clipboard.)

 If the datasheet disappears, you can summon it again by clicking the Datasheet button on the toolbar (shown in the margin).

If you copy data from another application such as Excel and then paste it into the datasheet using the Edit⇨Paste Link command, you are greeted with the *Chart wizard*, a dialog box that confronts you with simple questions such as

"Would you like a legend?" or "How about lunch?" Answer the questions to create a basic chart, but feel free to embellish the chart using the procedures in the following sections.

Changing the Chart Type

Microsoft Graph enables you to create 14 basic types of charts. Each type of chart conveys information with a different emphasis. Sales data plotted in a column chart may emphasize the relative performance of different regions, for example, and the same data plotted as a line chart may emphasize the increase or decrease in sales over time. The type of chart that's best for your data depends on the nature of the data and which aspects of it you want to emphasize.

Fortunately, PowerPoint doesn't force you to decide the final chart type up front. You can easily change the chart type at any time without changing the chart data. These steps show you how:

1. **Double-click the chart to activate Microsoft Graph.**

2. **Summon the Format⇨Chart Type command.**

   Microsoft Graph displays the Chart Type dialog box, shown in Figure 13-5 and Figure 13-6. From this dialog box, you can choose the chart type you want to use. The chart types are arranged in two groups: two-dimensional and three-dimensional. Figure 13-5 shows the 2-D types; Figure 13-6 shows the 3-D types. To switch from the 2-D group to the 3-D group, click the 3-D radio button.

3. **Click the chart type you want.**

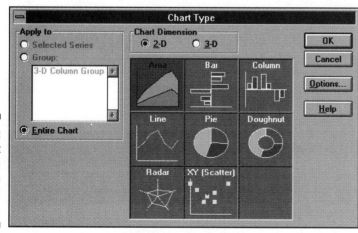

Figure 13-5:
The Chart Type dialog box shows the 2-D chart types.

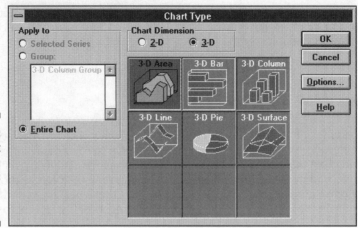

Figure 13-6:
The Chart
Type dialog
box shows
the 3-D
chart types.

4. **To use a variant of the chart type, click the Options button and choose the chart subtype.**

For example, the 3-D column chart type has subtypes that enable you to place columns for the different series next to one another, on top of one another, or behind one another.

5. **Click OK and you're done.**

Another way to summon the Chart Type dialog box is to double-click the chart object and then right-click the chart. When the quick menu appears, choose the Chart Type command.

You can change the chart type another way by using the Chart Type button on Microsoft Graph's toolbar. When you click the down arrow next to the button, a palette of chart types appears, as shown in Figure 13-7. All 14 basic chart types are available from this menu, but if you want to choose a subtype, you must use the Format⇨Chart Type command.

Figure 13-7:
The
Chart Type
button is a
shortcut for
assigning
chart types.

One more way to change the chart type is to use an AutoFormat. See the section "Applying an AutoFormat" at the end of this chapter for more information.

If you choose one of the 3-D chart types, you can adjust the angle from which you view the chart by using the Format⇨3-D View command. Experiment with this one; it's kind of fun.

Unlike chart types, the characters in most modern novels come in only two-dimensional varieties.

Embellishing a Chart

Microsoft Graph enables you to embellish a chart in many ways: You can add titles, labels, legends, and who knows what else. You add these embellishments by using the Insert menu command.

Adding chart titles

Microsoft Graph enables you to add two types of titles to your chart: a chart title, which describes the chart's contents, and axis titles, which explain the meaning of each chart axis. Most charts use two axes: the *value axis* and the *category axis*. Some 3-D chart types use a third axis called the *series axis*.

These steps show the procedure for adding any of these title types:

1. Choose the Insert⇨Titles command.

The Titles dialog box, shown in Figure 13-8, appears.

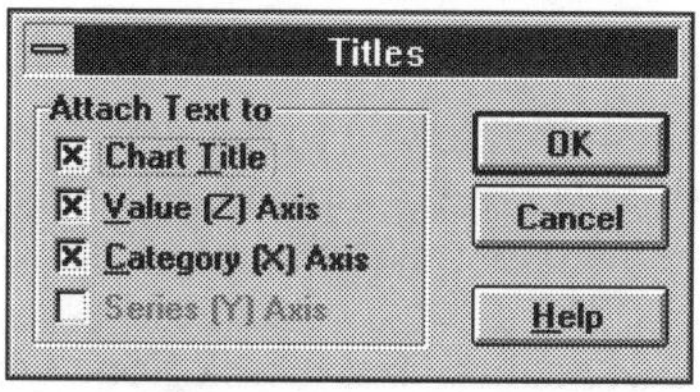

Figure 13-8:
The Titles
dialog box.

Titles

Attach Text to
☒ Chart Title
☒ Value (Z) Axis
☒ Category (X) Axis
☐ Series (Y) Axis

OK
Cancel
Help

2. Check the type of title you want to insert and then click OK.

3. Click the title and type some text.

4. Move the title, if you want, by dragging it with the mouse.

5. Change the font, if you want, by using the Format⇨Font command.

In most cases, the slide title serves as a chart title for a chart included on a PowerPoint slide. If that's the case, there's no need to use a chart title.

The value axis title is sometimes handy for pointing out that sales are in thousands or millions or that the number of hamburgers served is in the billions. The category axis title is a good place to add a note, such as Sales by Quarter.

To remove a title, click it and press the Del key. Or follow the procedure in this section and uncheck the title you want to remove.

Adding a label

A *label* is the text that's attached to each data point plotted on the chart. You can tell Microsoft Graph to use the actual data value for the label, or you can use the category heading for the label.

To add a label, follow this step-by-step procedure:

1. **Conjure up the Insert⇨Data Labels command.**

2. **From the Data Labels dialog box, choose whether you want to create a label (from the headings in the data table) or use the actual data value for each point plotted on the chart. Then click OK.**

3. **To change the format used for the labels, choose a label and summon the Format⇨Selected Data Labels command. Then set the pattern, font, number format, and alignment that you want.**

4. **If a data label isn't positioned where you want it, move it by clicking it and then dragging it to a new location.**

For most slide types, data labels add unnecessary clutter without adding much useful information. Use labels only if you think that you must back up your chart with exact numbers.

Some chart types — such as pie charts — enable you to display a percentage rather than an exact value as the label. This type of label is very helpful because percentages are often difficult to judge from an unlabeled pie chart.

To remove labels, follow the steps in this section, but check None when the Data Labels dialog box appears. Or click the label you want to remove and press the Del key.

Adding a legend

A *legend* explains the color scheme used in the chart. If you want a legend to appear in your chart, follow these steps:

1. **Invoke the Insert⇨Legend command.**

2. **Move the legend by dragging it with the mouse or resize it by clicking it and dragging one of its control handles.**

   To remove the legend, click it and press Del.

To change the format of the legend, click the legend and then use the Format⇨Selected Legend command.

Microsoft Graph enables you to create a legend, but you're on your own if you need a myth or fable.

Applying an AutoFormat

Microsoft Graph's AutoFormats are a combination of a chart type and other chart elements, such as legends, labels, fonts, and colors. Think of AutoFormats as templates for charts.

Each type of chart format is appropriate for a particular type of data. For example, if your data shows how expenses break down into various categories, use a pie chart. To show how sales have increased or decreased over time, use a column chart or a line chart. Use common sense to pick the chart type that's right for your data.

To apply an AutoFormat, follow these steps:

1. **Double-click the chart to edit it.**

2. **Use the Format⇨AutoFormat command.**

   The AutoFormat dialog box, shown in Figure 13-9, comes to life.

3. **Choose the AutoFormat that you want to use.**

   The various formats are arranged in Galleries by chart type. First, choose the basic chart type from the Galleries list. Then choose the format you want to use.

4. **Click OK and you're done.**

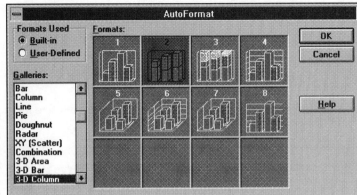

Figure 13-9:
The
AutoFormat
dialog box.

You can apply a different AutoFormat to a chart at any time. When you do, the chart type, color scheme, and other characteristics of the chart change, but the data remains the same.

Chapter 14
Drawing on Your Slides

● ●

In This Chapter

▶ Drawing lines and fancy shapes

▶ Adding text to an object

▶ Changing colors and line types

▶ Changing shapes

▶ Understanding layers and groups

▶ Lining things up

● ●

Chim-chiminey, chim-chiminey, chim-chim cheroo,
I draws what I likes and I likes what I drew. . . .

Art time! Everybody get your crayons and glue and don an old paint shirt.
You're going to cut out some simple shapes and paste them on your
PowerPoint slides so that people will either think that you are a wonderful artist
or scoff at you for not using clip art.

This chapter covers PowerPoint's drawing features. PowerPoint isn't a full-
featured drawing program like CorelDRAW!, but it gives you some rudimentary
drawing tools to spice up your charts with a bit of something here and a bit of
something there.

Some General Drawing Tips

PowerPoint's drawing tools aren't as powerful as the tools provided with a full-
featured drawing program like CorelDRAW! or Illustrator, but they are powerful
enough to create some pretty fancy pictures. Before getting into the specifics of
how to use each tool, this section describes a handful of general tips for
drawing pictures.

Zoom in

When you work with PowerPoint's drawing tools, increase the zoom factor so that you can draw more accurately. I often work at 200, 300, or even 400 percent when I'm drawing. To change the zoom factor, click the down arrow next to the Zoom Control button (near the right side of the Standard toolbar) and choose a zoom factor from the list. Or you can click the zoom factor, type a new zoom percentage, and press Enter.

Before you change the zoom factor to edit an object, choose the object you want to edit. That way, PowerPoint zooms in on that area of the slide. If you don't choose an object before you zoom in, you probably will have to scroll around to find the right location.

Activate the Drawing+ toolbar

PowerPoint has two toolbars that provide buttons for drawing objects on slides. The basic Drawing toolbar is normally visible, but the advanced Drawing+ toolbar is hidden. To reveal it, use the View⇨Toolbars command and click the Drawing+ option. Then click OK.

Figure 14-1 shows what the PowerPoint window looks like with the Drawing+ toolbar revealed. The drawing functions provided by each button on both toolbars are explained later in this chapter.

I used PowerPoint's drawing buttons to draw the face shown in Figure 14-1. The sidebar "Don't let me tell you how I drew that funny face!" later in this chapter shows you step-by-step how I drew this face.

All the Drawing+ toolbar's functions are available from the Draw menu, so you can draw pictures without calling up the Drawing+ toolbar. If you plan to do extensive work with drawn objects, however, it's convenient to have these commands available at the click of a button.

Display the ruler

If you want to be precise about lining up objects on the slide, consider activating the ruler. If the ruler isn't displayed already, use the View⇨Ruler command to show it.

When you work with drawing objects, PowerPoint formats the ruler so that zero is at the middle of the slide. When you edit a text object, the ruler changes to a text ruler that measures from the margins and indicates tab positions.

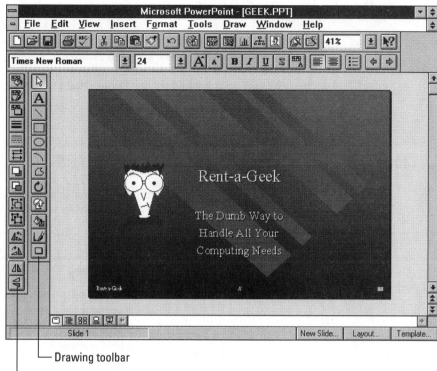

Figure 14-1:
PowerPoint
with both
Drawing
toolbars.

└─ Drawing toolbar

└─ Drawing+ toolbar

Stick to the color scheme

You can assign individual colors to each object you draw, but the point of
PowerPoint's color schemes is to talk you out of doing that. If possible, let solid
objects default to the color scheme's fill color. If you must assign a separate
color to an object, choose one of the eight colors that's a part of the color
scheme. (If you decide to arbitrarily choose one of PowerPoint's 64 million
colors for an object, a good lawyer may be able to get you off by using the
"irresistible urge" defense.)

Save frequently

Drawing is tedious work. You don't want to spend two hours working on a
particularly important drawing only to lose it all just because a comet strikes
your building or an errant Scud lands in your backyard. You can prevent
catastrophic loss from incidents such as these by pressing Ctrl+S frequently as
you work. And always wear protective eyewear.

Don't forget Ctrl+Z

Don't forget that you're never more than one keystroke away from erasing a boo-boo. If you do something silly — like forget to group a complex picture before trying to move it — you can always press Ctrl+Z to undo your last action. Ctrl+Z is my favorite and most frequently used PowerPoint key. (For left-handed mouse users, Alt+Backspace does the same thing.)

Drawing Simple Lines and Shapes

PowerPoint provides a whole row of drawing tools, located on the basic Drawing toolbar. Table 14-1 shows you what each of these drawing tools does.

Table 14-1	Basic Drawing Tools	
Drawing Tool	*What It's Called*	*What It Does*
▣	Selection button	Not really a drawing tool, but rather the generic mouse pointer used to choose objects.
▣	Text button	Adds a text object.
▣	Line button	Adds a line. You can later change the attributes of the line to create thick lines, dashed lines, or lines with arrowheads.
▣	Rectangle button	Used to draw rectangles. To make a perfect square, hold down the Shift key while you draw.
▣	Ellipse button	Draws circles and ovals. To create a perfect circle, hold down the Shift key while you draw.
▣	Arc button	Not Noah's arc, but a curved line. To create a perfect quarter-circle arc, hold down the Shift key while you draw.
▣	Freeform button	Draws polygons (remember that from ninth-grade geometry?) or irregular shapes.

Drawing Tool	What It's Called	What It Does
	Free Rotate button	When you click here, the Rotate button leaps from the water to make its escape into the open sea while Michael Jackson sings an inspiring song.
	AutoShapes button	Activates the AutoShapes toolbar, which contains a bevy of shapes you can draw, such as arrows and crosses.

To draw an object on a slide, you just click the button that represents the object you want to draw and then use the mouse to draw the object on the slide. Well, it's not always as simple as that. You'll find detailed instructions for drawing with the more important tools in the following sections.

If the Drawing toolbar has disappeared, you can make it appear again by using the View➪Toolbars command and checking the Drawing check box.

Before you draw an object, move to the slide on which you want to draw the object. If you want the object to appear on every slide in the presentation, display the Slide master by using the View➪Master➪Slide Master command or Shift+clicking the Slide View button on the status bar.

PowerPoint has two types of objects: shapes, such as circles, rectangles, and crosses; and lines and arcs. PowerPoint enables you to add text to any shape object, but you can't add text to a line or arc object.

Made a mistake? You can delete the object you just drew by pressing the Del key and then try drawing the object again. Or you can change its size or stretch it by clicking it and dragging its love handles.

Table 14-2 summarizes some handy shortcuts you can use while drawing. The last one needs a bit of explanation. If you click a drawing tool button once (such as the rectangle or ellipse button), the mouse cursor reverts to an arrow after you've drawn an object. To draw another object, you must click a drawing tool button again. If you know in advance that you want to draw more than one object of the same type, double-click the drawing tool button. Then you can keep drawing objects of the selected type till who laid the rails. To stop drawing, click the Selection Tool button (the arrow at the top of the Drawing toolbar).

I have no idea what the expression "till who laid the rails" means. One of the residents of River City (the mayor, I believe) used it in *The Music Man*, and I've always liked it ever since.

Table 14-2	Drawing Shortcuts
Shortcut	*What It Does*
Shift	Hold down the Shift key to force lines to be horizontal or vertical, to force arcs and ellipses to be true circles, to force rectangles to be squares, or to draw other regular shapes.
Ctrl	Hold down the Ctrl key to draw objects from the center rather than from end to end.
Ctrl+Shift	Hold down these two keys to draw from the center and to enforce squareness.
Double-click	Double-click any drawing button on the Drawing toolbar if you want to draw several objects of the same type.

Drawing straight and curved lines

To draw a straight line, follow this procedure:

1. **Click the Line button (shown in the margin).**

2. **Point to where you want the line to start.**

3. **Click and drag the mouse button to where you want the line to end.**

4. **Release the mouse when you reach your destination.**

The procedure for drawing an arc is the same except that you click the Arc button (shown in the margin) rather than the Line button.

You can use the Format➪Colors and Lines command to change the line color, thickness, dashes, and arrowheads for a line or arc. Or you can use buttons on the Drawing and Drawing+ toolbars to change these attributes.

You can force a line to be perfectly horizontal or vertical by holding down the Shift key while you draw.

The ends of an arc are always 90 degrees apart. In other words, an arc is always one-quarter of a circle or ellipse.

After you have drawn a line or arc, you can adjust it by clicking it and then dragging either love handle that appears.

Sorry, PowerPoint doesn't include powerful tools for drawing precise curves. If you need better curves than the Arc button can provide, get yourself a more powerful drawing program.

Drawing rectangles, squares, and circles

To draw a rectangle, follow these steps:

1. **Click the Rectangle button (shown in the margin).**

2. **Point to where you want one corner of the rectangle to be positioned.**

3. **Click the mouse button and drag to where you want the opposite corner of the rectangle to be positioned.**

4. **Release the mouse.**

The procedure for drawing a circle or ellipse is the same except that you click the Ellipse button (shown in the margin) rather than the Rectangle button.

You can use the Format⇨Colors and Lines command to change the fill color or the line style for a rectangle or circle. You also can use the buttons on the Drawing toolbars to change the color and line style.

To apply a shadow, use the Format⇨Shadow command or click the Apply Shadow Defaults button.

Hold down the Shift key while you draw to create an even square or a perfectly round circle. Also, you can adjust the size or shape of a rectangle or circle by clicking it and dragging any of its love handles.

Drawing a polygon or freeform shape

Mr. Arnold, my seventh-grade math teacher, taught me that a *polygon* is a shape that has many sides and has nothing to do with having more than one spouse (one is certainly enough for most of us). Triangles, squares, and rectangles are polygons, but so are hexagons and pentagons, as are any unusual shapes whose sides all consist of straight lines. Politicians are continually inventing new polygons when they revise the boundaries of congressional districts.

PowerPoint's Freeform button is designed to create polygons, with a twist: not all the sides have to be straight lines. The Freeform button enables you to build a shape whose sides are a mixture of straight lines and freeform curves. Figure 14-2 shows three examples of shapes I created with the Freeform button.

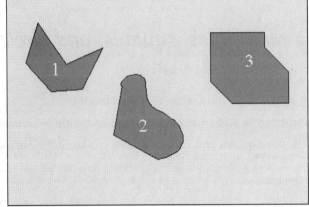

Figure 14-2:
Three
freeform
shapes.

Follow these steps to create a polygon or freeform shape:

 1. **Click the Freeform button (shown in the margin).**

2. **Click where you want the first corner of the object to be positioned.**

3. **Click where you want the second corner of the object to be positioned.**

4. **Keep clicking wherever you want a corner to be positioned.**

5. **To finish the shape, click near the first corner, the one you created in Step 2.**

   You don't have to be exact; if you click anywhere near the first corner you put down, PowerPoint assumes that the shape is finished.

You're finished! The object assumes the line and fill color from the slide's color scheme.

To draw a freeform side on the shape, hold the mouse button down when you click a corner and then draw the freeform shape with the mouse. When you get to the end of the freeform side, release the mouse button. Then you can click again to add more corners. Shape 2 in Figure 14-2 has one freeform side.

If you look at a freeform side closely, you see that it isn't freeform at all. Instead, it consists of a series of small, straight line segments that approximate the curvy line you tried to draw with the mouse. The line segments are small enough that when you view them at normal size, they appear to be a smooth curve, just as you drew it. Figure 14-3 shows a portion of shape 2 from Figure 14-2 with the zoom factor set to 300 percent so that you can see what I mean.

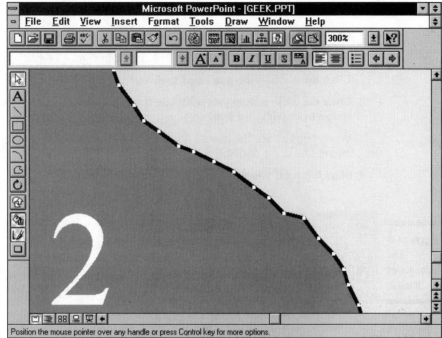

You can reshape a polygon or freeform shape by double-clicking it and then dragging any of the love handles that appear on the corners.

If you hold down the Shift key while you draw a polygon, the sides are constrained to 45-degree angles. Shape 3 in Figure 14-2 was drawn in this manner. How about a constitutional amendment requiring Congress to use the Shift key when it redraws congressional boundaries?

You also can use the Freeform button to draw a multisegmented line, called an *open shape*. To draw an open shape, follow the procedure in this section, except that you skip Step 5. Instead, double-click or press the Esc key when the line is done.

Using the AutoShape button

Rectangles and circles aren't the only two shapes PowerPoint can draw automatically. When you click the AutoShape button on the Drawing toolbar, a complete toolbar list of 24 *AutoShapes* appears. These AutoShape buttons make it easy to draw common shapes.

These steps show you how to draw an AutoShape:

 1. Click the AutoShape button on the Drawing toolbar.

The AutoShapes toolbar appears, as shown in Figure 14-4.

2. Click the AutoShape you want to draw.

3. Click the slide where you want the shape to appear and then drag the shape to the desired size.

When you release the mouse button, the AutoShape object takes on the current fill color and line style.

4. Start typing if you want the shape to contain text.

Figure 14-4:
The
AutoShapes
toolbar.

Hold down the Shift key while drawing the AutoShape to create an undistorted shape.

To dismiss the AutoShapes toolbar, double-click its control box in the upper left corner. If your AutoShapes toolbar is sitting right on top of where you want to draw the shape, move it by dragging its title bar. If you move it to the edge of the Presentation window, it sticks there like the other toolbars do.

Some AutoShape buttons — such as the Seal and Balloon buttons — cry out for text. Figure 14-5 shows how you can use the Seal shape to add a jazzy burst to a slide.

Figure 14-5:
The Seal
AutoShape
button can
make your
presentation
look like a
late-night
infomercial.

You can change an object's AutoShape at any time by choosing the object and using the Draw⇨Change AutoShape command.

Some AutoShape buttons have an extra love handle that enables you to adjust some aspect of the object's shape. For example, the arrows have a love handle that enables you to increase or decrease the size of the arrowhead. Figure 14-6 shows how you can use these extra love handles to vary the shapes produced by several AutoShape buttons. For each of the six buttons, the first object shows how the AutoShape is initially drawn; the other two objects drawn with each AutoShape button show how you can change the shape by dragging the extra handle.

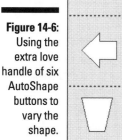

Figure 14-6:
Using the extra love handle of six AutoShape buttons to vary the shape.

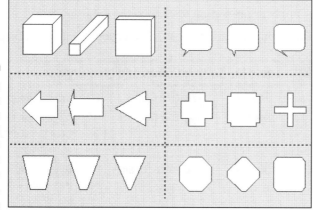

Setting the Fill Color, Line Style, and Shadow

PowerPoint objects have various attributes that you can change. The buttons for these attributes are defined in Table 14-3. These attributes are defined as follows:

Fill color: The interior color of an object. One of the eight colors from the color scheme is designated as the fill color, but you can override the color scheme's fill color and use any color you want. If the object has no fill color, the background color shows through. See Table 14-3 to learn how to change the fill color.

Line color: The color of the lines that outline the object (or in the case of a line or arc, the color of the actual line or arc). The default line color comes from the color scheme, but you can set the line color to any color you want. If the object has no line color, the lines are not visible.

Shadow color: The color of the object's shadow, normally taken from the color scheme. If the object has no shadow color, the shadow is not visible.

Line style: The thickness of the lines that outline the object.

Dashed lines: The dashing pattern used for the lines that outline the object. The default uses a solid line, but different patterns are available to create dashed lines.

Arrowheads: Lines can have an arrowhead at either or both ends. Arrowheads are used mostly on line and arc objects.

To change any of these object attributes, follow these steps:

1. **Select the object or objects you want to change.**

2. **Click the appropriate button to change the color or style.**

   Table 14-3 summarizes the toolbar buttons you can use for this purpose.

Table 14-3   Tools for Setting Colors and Line Styles

Drawing Tool	*Toolbar*	*What It's Called*	*What It Does*
	Drawing	Apply Fill Defaults	Applies the fill color from the slide's color scheme.
	Drawing	Apply Line Defaults	Applies the line color from the slide's color scheme.
	Drawing	Apply Shadow Defaults	Applies the shadow color from the slide's color scheme.
	Drawing+	Fill Color	Sets the fill color.
	Drawing+	Line Color	Sets the line color.
	Drawing+	Shadow Color	Sets the shadow color.
	Drawing+	Line Style	Sets the line width.
	Drawing+	Dashed Lines	Creates dashed lines.
	Drawing+	Arrowheads	Adds arrowheads to lines.

The three buttons on the Standard toolbar apply the fill, line, and shadow colors from the slide's color scheme. To change these default colors, change the color scheme. (To change the color scheme for the entire presentation, change the master slide's color scheme.)

If you have a dialog box fetish, you can use the Format⇨Colors and Lines command and the Format⇨Shadow command to change colors, line styles, and shadows. These commands pop up the dialog boxes shown in Figure 14-7 and Figure 14-8. Fiddle with them if you want, but I prefer the buttons.

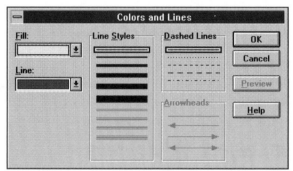

Figure 14-7:
The Colors
and Lines
dialog box.

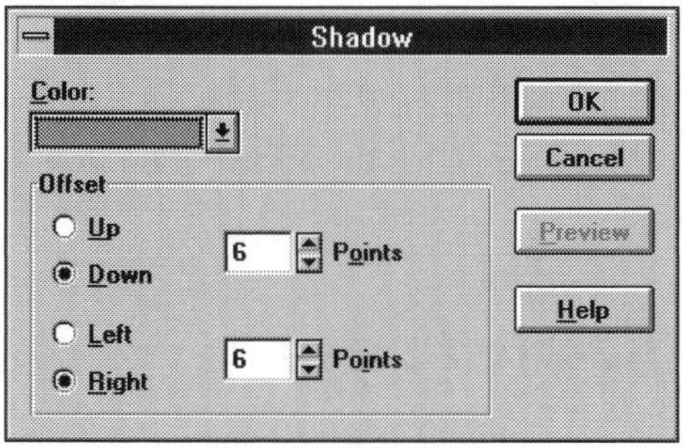

Figure 14-8:
The Shadow
dialog box.

When you experiment with shadows, be sure to try out the Embossed shadow type. It adds a dark shadow below the object and a light shadow above it to create the illusion that the object is carved out of the background. Very cool.

The color buttons on the Drawing+ toolbar all activate drop-down menus that offer color choices chosen from the color scheme and allow room for eight colors you choose. If the color you want doesn't appear on the menu, click Other Color to choose a custom color.

For more information about colors, check out Chapter 9.

Flipping and Rotating Objects

To *flip* an object means to create a mirror image of it. To *rotate* an object means to turn it about its center. PowerPoint enables you to flip objects horizontally or vertically, rotate objects in 90-degree increments, or freely rotate an object to any angle.

Flipping an object

PowerPoint enables you to flip an object vertically or horizontally to create a mirror image of the object. To flip an object, follow these steps:

1. **Choose the object you want to flip.**

 2. **Click the Flip Horizontal or Flip Vertical button on the Drawing+ toolbar (shown in the margin).**

Rotating an object 90 degrees

You can rotate an object in 90-degree increments by following these steps:

1. **Choose the object you want to rotate.**

2. **Click the Rotate Left or Rotate Right button on the Drawing+ toolbar.**

3. **To rotate the object 180 degrees, click the appropriate Rotate button again.**

Using the Free Rotate button

Rotating an object in 90-degree increments is useful sometimes, but if you want to give just a bit of slant to an object, 90-degree rotation won't do. That's when the Free Rotate button comes in handy. It enables you to rotate an object to any arbitrary angle just by dragging it with the mouse. Figure 14-9 shows an example of a slide with a rotated object. I rotated the face to give it just the right inquisitive slant.

This step-by-step procedure shows you how to use the Free Rotate button:

1. **Choose the object you want to rotate.**

 2. **Click the Free Rotate button on the Drawing toolbar (shown in the margin).**

Figure 14-9:
The slide
with the
slanted
face.

3. Drag one of the corner love handles around the object.

As you drag, an outline of the object rotates around. When you get the object's outline to the angle you want, release the mouse button, and the object is redrawn at the new angle.

To restrict the rotation angle to 45-degree increments, hold the Shift key while dragging around the corner handle.

When you hold down the Ctrl key while dragging a corner handle, the object rotates about the opposite corner handle rather than the center. Very strange, but occasionally useful.

Remember how all the bad guys' hideouts were slanted in the old "Batman" TV show? Wasn't that cool?

Drawing a Complicated Picture

When you add more than one object to a slide, several problems come up. What happens when the objects overlap? How do you line up objects so that they don't look like they were thrown at the slide from a moving car? And how do you keep together objects that belong together?

This section shows you how to use PowerPoint features to handle overlapped objects, align objects, and group objects. If you're interested in a description of how these PowerPoint features are used together to draw a picture, check out the sidebar titled "Don't let me tell you how I drew that funny face!"

NOTE

Don't let me tell you how I drew that funny face!

In case you're interested, you can follow along with the bouncing ball to see how I created the face that keeps popping up in the figures in this chapter. By studying this creature, you can get an idea of how layers and groups and alignment are used to create complicated pictures, as shown in these steps:

1. I drew this basic shape by using the Freeform button. Then I filled it with white.

(The color scheme's fill color for this slide wasn't white, so I used the Drawing+ toolbar Fill Color button to do this step.)

2. To draw the glasses, I started with the left lens, by using the Circle button to draw first a big circle (which I filled with white) and then a small circle filled with black.

Then I used the Draw⇨Align command to align the circles, both middle and center. Next, I grouped the circles and pressed Ctrl+D to duplicate the group. Then I dragged the duplicate lens to the right side of the face. Finally, I drew the two lines that connect the lenses.

3. To add the hair and body, I drew both objects by using the Freehand button and filled them both with black.

4. I drew all the facial features by using the Line button.

5. Drawing the ears was the hardest part. I used the Freeform button to draw the left ear, right on top of the lens.

After filling it with white, I used the Send Backward button over and over again, until the ear finally dropped behind the lens and face where it belonged. Then I decided that I didn't like the ear, so I deleted it and tried again. And again. And again. When I finally got it right, I duplicated it (Ctrl+D), flipped the duplicate, moved it over to the right side of the face, and used Send Backward again to move the ear behind the lens and face.

Oh, I almost forgot. The last step is to choose all objects that make up the face and group them by using the Group button or the Draw⇨Group command. That way, I don't have to worry about accidentally dismembering the face.

Changing layers

Whenever you have more than one object on a slide, the potential exists for objects to overlap one another. Like most drawing programs, PowerPoint handles this problem by layering objects like a stack of plates. The first object you draw is at the bottom of the stack; the second object is on top of the first; the third is atop the second; and so on. If two objects overlap, the one that's at the highest layer is the one that wins; objects below it are partially covered.

So far, so good — but what if you don't remember to draw the objects in the correct order? What if you draw a shape you want to tuck behind a shape you've already drawn or what if you want to bring an existing shape to the top of the pecking order? No problem. PowerPoint enables you to change the stack order, by moving objects toward the front or back so that they overlap just the way you want.

PowerPoint provides four commands for changing the stacking order:

> *Draw⇨Bring to Front:* Brings the chosen object to the top of the stack.

> *Draw⇨Send to Back:* Sends the chosen object to the back of the stack.

> *Draw⇨Bring Forward:* Brings the chosen object one step closer to the front of the stack (button is shown in the margin).

> *Draw⇨Send Backward:* Sends the object one rung down the ladder (button is shown in the margin).

Layering problems are most obvious when objects have a fill color. If an object has no fill color, any objects behind it are allowed to show through. In this case, the layering doesn't matter much.

To bring an object to the top of another, you may have to use the Bring Forward command several times. The reason is that even though the two objects appear to be adjacent, other objects may occupy the layers between them.

Line 'em up

Nothing looks more amateurish than objects dropped randomly on a slide with no apparent concern for how they line up with one another. PowerPoint provides several features that enable you to line up objects as you draw them:

> *Snap to Grid:* When Snap to Grid is on, the entire slide is overlaid by an invisible grid to which objects are aligned. Whenever you create a new object or move an existing object, it automatically sticks to the nearest grid line. To turn Snap to Grid mode on or off, use the Draw⇨Snap to Grid command.

In case you're interested, the grid spacing is 12 lines per inch.

You can't see the grid, but trust me: it's there. When you increase the zoom setting enough, you see the effects of objects snapping to it.

Guides: If you activate PowerPoint's guides, two lines — one horizontal, the other vertical — appear on-screen. These lines do not show up in printed output, but any object that comes within a pixel's breath of one of these guidelines snaps to it. Guides are a great way to line up objects in a neat row.

To display the guides, use the View⇨Guides command (use the same command again to hide them). The guides initially pop up like crosshairs centered on the slide, but you can move them to any location you want by simply dragging them with the mouse.

The keyboard shortcut to display or hide the guides is Ctrl+G.

When you move the guides, PowerPoint shows the ruler measurement for the guide as you move it. Very interesting. The whiz kids at Microsoft love to add features like that, but do you get a truly good Align command? Read on.

Align command: The Draw⇨Align command enables you to choose several objects and then line them up. You can align the objects horizontally to the top, bottom, or middle of the objects, or vertically to the left edges, right edges, or center.

Figure 14-10 and Figure 14-11 show how these Align commands work. Figure 14-10 shows three objects as they were originally drawn. Figure 14-11 shows the result of choosing all three objects and using the various Draw⇨Align commands.

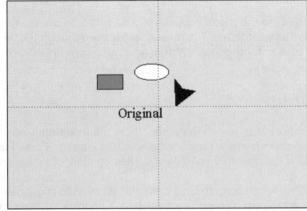

Figure 14-10:
Three
unaligned
objects.

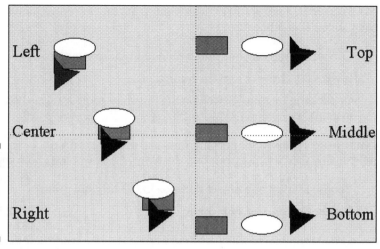

Figure 14-11:
Putting
the Align
commands
to work.

To center two or more objects, choose the objects and then use the
Draw➪Align➪Middles command followed by the Draw➪Align➪Centers command.

Unfortunately, PowerPoint has no keyboard shortcuts or toolbar buttons for
the Align commands.

Nope, the Align command isn't anything to write home about. It's OK, and gets
the job done, but it could be better. Oh, well. Time to get off the soapbox.

Group therapy

A *group* is a collection of objects that PowerPoint treats as though they were
one object. Using groups properly is one key to putting simple shapes together
to make complex pictures without becoming so frustrated that you have to join
a therapy group. ("Hello, my name is Doug, and PowerPoint drives me crazy.")

To create a group, follow these steps:

1. **Choose all objects you want included in the group.**

2. **Conjure up the Draw➪Group command.**

   Or click the Group button on the Drawing+ toolbar (shown in the margin).

To take a group apart so that PowerPoint treats the objects as individuals again, follow this procedure:

1. **Choose all objects you want included in the group.**

2. **Invoke the Draw⇨Ungroup command.**

 Or click the Ungroup button on the Drawing+ toolbar (again, in the margin).

If you create a group and then ungroup it so that you can work on its elements individually, you can easily regroup the objects. These steps show you how:

1. **Choose at least one object that was in the original group.**

2. **Use the Draw⇨Regroup command.**

PowerPoint remembers which objects were in the group and automatically includes them.

PowerPoint enables you to create groups of groups. This capability is useful for complex pictures because it enables you to work on one part of the picture, group it, and then work on the next part of the picture without worrying about accidentally disturbing the part you've already grouped. After you have several such groups, choose them and group them. You can create groups of groups of groups, and so on ad nauseum.

PowerPoint offers the following impossible-to-remember keyboard shortcuts for grouping:

Ctrl+Shift+G   Group

Ctrl+Shift+H   Ungroup

Ctrl+Shift+J   Regroup

I guess the idea is that Ctrl+Shift+G is easy to remember because G stands for Group, and H and J are adjacent to it on the keyboard. Right.

Chapter 15

Creating an Organizational Chart

. . . .

In This Chapter

▶ Creating an organizational chart

▶ Adding boxes

▶ Reorganizing your chart

▶ Adding fancy stuff

. . . .

*O*rganizational charts — you know, those box-and-line charts that show who reports to whom, where the buck ends, and who got the lateral arabesque — are an essential part of many presentations. You can draw organizational charts by using PowerPoint's standard rectangle- and line-drawing tools, but that process is tedious at best. If Jones gets booted over to advertising, it can take hours to redraw the chart.

Mercifully, Microsoft decided to toss in a program designed just for creating organizational charts. They call it — hold on to your hat — Microsoft Organization Chart. It's not as tightly integrated with PowerPoint as Microsoft Graph is, but it gets the job done. (Because Microsoft Organization Chart is a bit of a mouthful, I'll call it OrgChart from now on.)

Keep in mind that organizational charts are useful for more than showing employee relationships. You also can use them to show any kind of hierarchical structure. For example, back when I wrote computer programs for a living, I used organizational charts to plan the structure of my computer programs. They're also great for recording family genealogies, although they don't have any way to indicate that Aunt Milly hasn't spoken to Aunt Beatrice in 30 years.

Creating an Organizational Chart

You can add an organizational chart to a presentation in two ways:

- ✔ Create a new slide by using an AutoLayout that includes an organizational chart.
- ✔ Add an organizational chart to an existing slide.

The easier of the two methods is to create a new slide by using an AutoLayout. That way, the organizational chart is already positioned in the correct location on the slide. If you add an organizational chart to an existing slide, PowerPoint will probably plop it down right on top of something else important, so you have to move things around to make room for the chart.

If you create an organizational chart with more than four or five boxes, it probably won't fit within the OrgChart window. To see the whole chart, maximize OrgChart by clicking the maximize button in the upper right corner of the window.

OrgChart terms you can skip

OrgChart thrusts a bunch of specialized terminology in your face. This list explains some of the more important terms:

Manager: A box that has subordinate boxes reporting to it.

Subordinate: A box beneath a manager box that reports to it in a line relationship.

Coworker: Two or more boxes that report to the same manager.

Assistant: A box that has a staff relationship to another box rather than a line relationship. Assistant boxes are drawn differently to indicate their different relationship to the chart.

Comanagers: Two or more boxes that share subordinates. Don't you feel sorry for those subordinates?

Group: All the boxes that report to a particular manager.

Group style: The way a group of boxes are drawn to show their relationships. OrgChart has several group style options you can choose. You can freely mix group styles within the same chart.

Branch: A box and all the boxes that report directly and indirectly to it.

Connecting line: A line that shows a relationship between two boxes.

Inserting a new slide with an organizational chart

Follow these steps to add a new slide with an organizational chart:

1. Move to the slide you want the new slide to follow.

2. Click the New Slide button on the status bar.

The New Slide dialog box, shown in Figure 15-1, shows its familiar face.

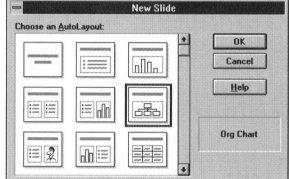

Figure 15-1:
The New
Slide dialog
box.

3. Pick the OrgChart slide type and click OK.

PowerPoint adds a new slide with a placeholder for an organizational chart (see Figure 15-2).

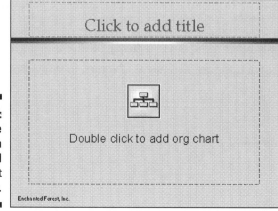

Figure 15-2:
A new slide
with an
organizational
chart
placeholder.

4. Double-click where it says *Double-click to add org chart.*

PowerPoint launches Microsoft Organization Chart, which pops up in its own window and enables you to create the chart. OrgChart starts off with a simple four-box chart, as shown in Figure 15-3.

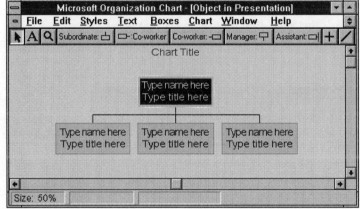

Figure 15-3:
OrgChart
starts with a
four-box
chart.

5. Draw the organizational chart.

Click the boxes that are already on the sample chart and type the names for your chart boxes. OrgChart enables you to type a name, title, and one or two comment lines for each box.

If you want to add boxes, click the Subordinate button and then click the box you want the new box to be subordinate to. (For more information about adding boxes to a chart, see the steps listed later in this chapter, under the heading "Adding Boxes to a Chart.")

Figure 15-4 shows the OrgChart window after I finished creating a simple chart with seven boxes. For the first four boxes (Doc, Sneezy, Grumpy, and Bashful), I just replaced the text *Type name here* with the names I wanted to use. I added the other three boxes by using the Subordinate button.

6. Use the File⇨Exit and Return command to return to PowerPoint.

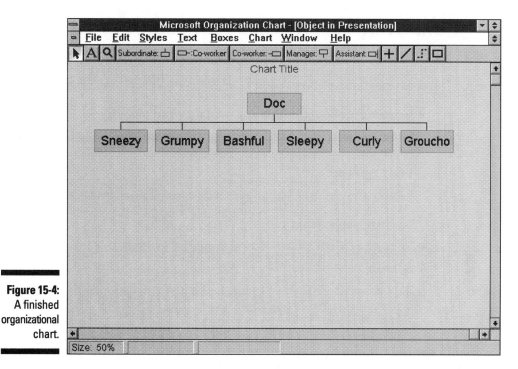

Figure 15-4:
A finished
organizational
chart.

You return to PowerPoint, where you can see your organizational chart in all its glory. Figure 15-5 shows how a finished organizational chart looks on the slide.

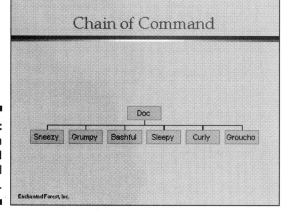

Figure 15-5:
A slide with
a finished
organizational
chart.

Inserting an organizational chart in an existing slide

These steps show you how to add an organizational chart to an existing slide:

1. **Move to the slide on which you want the chart placed.**

 2. **Click the Insert OrgChart button on the Standard toolbar (shown in the margin).**

3. **Draw the chart.**

   Replace the text *Type here* with your own text and add new boxes by choosing the Subordinate button and clicking the box you want the new box to be subordinate to.

4. **Invoke the File⇨Exit and Return command to return to PowerPoint.**

5. **Rearrange everything.**

   If the chart landed on top of something important, rearrange the objects on the slide so that everything is visible. Drag them, resize them, or delete them if you must.

Adding Boxes to a Chart

To add a new box to an organizational chart, you use one of the five box buttons listed in Table 15-1.

Table 15-1	OrgChart's Box Buttons
Box Button	*What It Does*
Subordinate:	Inserts a new box subordinate to the box you click.
⊡·:Co-worker	Inserts a coworker to the left of the box you click. The new box is subordinate to the same box as the existing box you click.
Co-worker: ⊡	Inserts a coworker to the right of the box you click. The new box is subordinate to the same box as the existing box you click.
Manager:	Inserts a manager box above the box you click.
Assistant:	Inserts an assistant box for the box you click.

Follow this general procedure for adding a new box:

1. **Click the appropriate Box button for the type of box you want to add.**

2. **Click the existing box you want the new box related to.**

3. **Type the name and, if you want, title and comments for the new box.**

   Press the Tab or Enter key to move from line to line within the box. Press the Esc key or click anywhere outside the box when you're finished.

To add several boxes, hold down the Shift key when you click the Box button. Then you can create several boxes without having to reset the Box button each time.

OrgChart automatically adjusts the size of the box based on the amount of text you type in the box. To keep the boxes small, type as little text as you can.

To insert a new manager box between an existing box and its subordinates, first select the boxes that you want to be subordinate to the new manager box. Then hold down the Ctrl key and click the Manager button.

Rearranging the Chart

Some companies continually rearrange their organizational charts. If you're the hapless chap responsible for keeping the chart up to date, you better study this section closely.

Selecting boxes

The easiest way to select a box is to click it with the mouse. To select several boxes, hold down the Shift key while clicking. Or if you're a keyboard junkie, you can use the shortcuts summarized in Table 15-2.

Table 15-2	Keyboard Shortcuts for Selecting Boxes
Keyboard Action	*What It Does*
Ctrl+G	Selects all the current box's coworkers (the boxes in the same group).
Ctrl+B	Selects an entire branch, beginning with the current box.
Ctrl+A	Selects all boxes in the chart.
Ctrl+left arrow	Selects the box to the left of the current box.
Ctrl+right arrow	Selects the box to the right of the current box.
Ctrl+up arrow	Selects the current box's manager.
Ctrl+down arrow	Selects the first box that reports to the current box.

Deleting chart boxes

To delete a box from an organizational chart, click the box to select it and press the Del key. OrgChart automatically adjusts the chart to compensate for the lost box.

When you delete a box from an organizational chart, you should observe a moment of somber silence — or throw a party. It all depends on whose name was on the box, I suppose.

Moving a box

To move a box to a different position on the chart, drag the box with the mouse until it lands right on top of the box you want it to be subordinate to. OrgChart automatically rearranges the chart to accommodate the new arrangement.

Suppose that you want to recast the organizational chart shown in Figure 15-5 to introduce a new layer of management. Figure 15-6 shows the result. To create this chart, I dragged Sneezy and Bashful over the top of Grumpy. Then I dragged Sleepy and Groucho on top of Curly.

Figure 15-6:
Rearranging the boxes on an organizational chart.

Moving a box precisely over the top of another box is a bit tricky. OrgChart clues you that you've made it by changing the color of the box. Release the mouse button as soon as you see the color change.

If you move a box by dragging it, any subordinate boxes are moved also. To move a box without moving its subordinates, select the box, press Ctrl+X to cut it to the Clipboard, select the box you want to move the cut box to, and press Ctrl+V to insert the box.

Using group styles

OrgChart enables you to arrange groups of boxes in several different ways. Suppose that you decide that the six boxes subordinate to Doc in Figure 15-5 cause the chart to be too wide. It's easy to rearrange those six boxes so that they are shown as in Figure 15-7. All you have to do is apply a different _group style_.

Figure 15-7:
Changing the group style changes the chart's appearance.

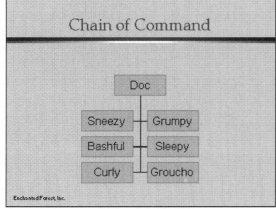

Follow this procedure to apply a group style:

1. **Select all the boxes you want rearranged.**

   Hold down the Shift key while you click the boxes.

2. **Choose the §tyles menu command.**

   The Group Styles menu appears, as shown in Figure 15-8.

3. **Click the group style you want.**

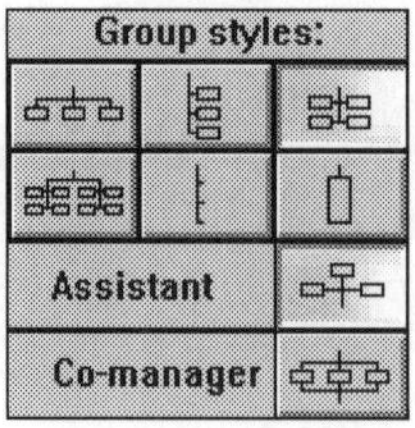

Figure 15-8:
The Group
Styles menu.

OrgChart applies the style to the boxes you selected and adjusts the chart as necessary.

Made an oops? Don't forget about the Undo command (Ctrl+Z or Alt+Backspace).

You can mix and match group styles any which way you please to create some bizarre-looking charts. Figure 15-9 shows an organizational chart in which Bashful reports to Doc as a subordinate and has an assistant named Hawkeye and two subordinate workers named Grumpy and Sneezy. Pluto and Sleepy are comanagers over Curly, Groucho, and Zonk.

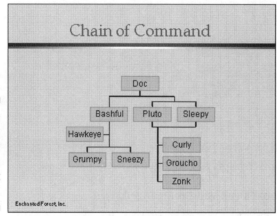

Figure 15-9:
An
organizational
chart with
different
group styles.

Formatting Chart Boxes

OrgChart enables you to apply fancy formatting options to the text in chart boxes, the boxes themselves, or the lines that connect the boxes.

Follow these steps to spruce up your boxes:

1. Select the box or boxes whose format you want to change.

2. Use the following commands to format the box text:

Text⇨Font: Changes the font and font characteristics for the box text.

Text⇨Color: Changes the text color.

Text⇨Left: Left-justifies the text.

Text⇨Right: Right-justifies the text.

Text⇨Center: Centers the text.

3. Use the following commands to format the boxes:

Boxes⇨Box Border: Assigns a border style for the box.

Boxes⇨Box Shadow: Creates a shadow effect for the box.

Boxes⇨Box Color: Sets the box color.

To add emphasis to the lines that connect the boxes, follow these steps:

1. Select the line segments you want to emphasize.

2. Use the following commands to change the line segments:

Boxes⇨Line Thickness: Sets the thickness of the lines.

Boxes⇨Line Style: Enables you to create dashed or solid lines.

Boxes⇨Line Color: Sets the line color.

Unfortunately, because OrgChart doesn't implement the expected keyboard shortcuts for text formatting, you can't make text italicized by pressing Ctrl+I or bold by pressing Ctrl+B.

One good use for these formatting options is to draw attention to a particular part of a chart. Figure 15-10 shows a chart that uses an emphasized line and a contrasting color to show the chain of command from Doc to Sneezy.

Figure 15-10:
Using box and line formats to draw attention to a certain part of the chart.

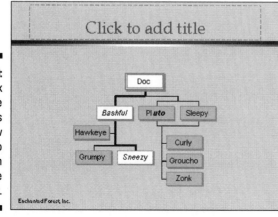

Chapter 16

Equations, WordArt, and Other Ornaments

Clip art pictures, graphs, and drawings aren't the only ornaments that you can add to your presentations. For the math nuts out there, PowerPoint comes with an Equation Editor that helps you create Einsteinian equations that make even the most resolute audience members hide under their chairs. For the typographers out there who would give their pica sticks to skew some text, there's WordArt. For all those WinWord and Excel zealots, PowerPoint includes OLE 2 links to both those programs so that you can stick a table or worksheet right in the middle of a slide. All these features are very useful — well, if you happen to need them. Otherwise, they just take up disk space.

Using Equation Editor

Steven Hawking has said that his editor told him that every mathematical equation he included in his book *A Brief History of Time* would cut the book's sales in half. So he included just one: the classic $e=mc^2$. See how easy that equation was to type? The only trick was remembering how to format the little 2 as a superscript.

My editor promised me that every equation I included in this book would double its sales, but I didn't believe her, not even for a nanosecond. Just in case, Figure 16-1 shows some examples of the equations you can create by using PowerPoint's handy-dandy Equation Editor program. You wouldn't even consider using ordinary text to try to create these equations, but they took me only a few minutes to create with Equation Editor. Aren't they cool? Tell all your friends about the cool equations you saw in this book so that they'll all rush out and buy copies for themselves.

Figure 16-1:
Eight equations that will probably not affect the sales of this book one way or another.

$$\mu_{Y \cdot X} = \overline{Y}_X \pm t_\alpha s_{Y \cdot X}\sqrt{\frac{1}{n} + \frac{(X - \overline{X})^2}{\sum X^2 - n\overline{X}^2}}$$

$$I = \frac{\sum\left(\frac{P_n}{P_0} \times 100\right)v}{\sum v}$$

$$t = \frac{\overline{X}_A - \overline{X}_B}{\sqrt{\frac{(n_A - 1)s_A^2 + ((n_B - 1)s_B^2}{n_A + n_B - 2}}\sqrt{\frac{1}{n_A} + \frac{1}{n_B}}}$$

$$f(x) = y = \sqrt[3]{\frac{x - 1}{x^2 + 1}}$$

$$\sigma_p = \sqrt{\frac{\pi(1 - n)}{n}}\sqrt{\frac{N - n}{N - 1}}$$

$$\sqrt{(x - h - c)^2 + (y - k)^2} = \left|h + \frac{c}{e^2} - x\right|e$$

$$t = \frac{b}{\frac{s_{Y \cdot X}}{\sqrt{\sum X^2 - n\overline{X}^2}}}$$

$$d_1^* = -z_{\alpha/2}\sqrt{P_c(1 - P_c)\left(\frac{1}{n_A} + \frac{1}{n_B}\right)}$$

Equation Editor is a special version of a gee-whiz math program called MathType, from Design Science.

Equation Editor also comes with Microsoft Word for Windows. If you have WinWord and already know how to use its Equation Editor, you're in luck: they're identical.

You don't have to know anything about math to use Equation Editor. I don't have a clue what any of the equations in Figure 16-1 do, but they sure look great, don't they?

Don't forget to tell your friends how great the equations in Figure 16-1 are. They alone are worth the price of the book.

Equation Editor has its own complete Help system. After you're in Equation Editor, press F1 or use the Help command to call up complete information about using it.

Adding an equation to a slide

To add an equation to a slide, follow these steps:

1. Use the Insert⇨Object command.

Alternatively, create a new slide by using one of the AutoLayouts that includes an Object placeholder. Then double-click the Object placeholder. Either way, the Insert Object dialog box appears, as shown in Figure 16-2.

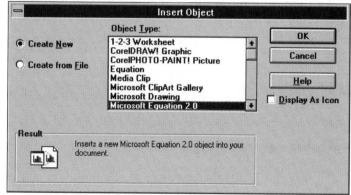

Figure 16-2:
The Insert
Object
dialog box.

2. Choose Microsoft Equation 2.0 from the Object Type list box and then click OK.

This step summons Equation Editor, which argues with PowerPoint for a few moments about who's really in charge. Then it replaces PowerPoint's menus with its own and pops up the floating Equation toolbar that's chock-full of mathematical doohickeys (see Figure 16-3).

A *floating toolbar* is nothing more than a window jammed full of toolbar buttons. Floating toolbars have a nasty habit of getting in the way, but you can move them by dragging them by their title bars.

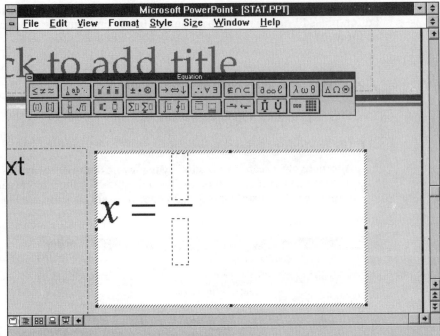

Figure 16-3:
Creating an
equation
with
Equation
Editor.

3. Start typing your equation.

The variables and basic operators, such as plus and minus signs, are easy enough. But how do you get those fancy symbols, such as square root and summation? The answer lies in the Equation toolbar.

4. To add a symbol that's not on the keyboard, use one of the buttons in the top row of the Equation toolbar.

Each button yields a menu of symbols, most of which only J. Robert Oppenheimer could have understood. There's nothing special about the tools in the top row of the Equation toolbar; they simply insert special characters into your equation. The magic of Equation Editor lies in the bottom row on the toolbar, which enables you to build the parts of the equation that have elements stacked on top of one another, such as fractions, superscripts, and roots.

5. To add a stacked symbol, use one of the buttons in the bottom row of the Equation toolbar.

Each button in the bottom row of the toolbar is attached to a menu of *templates,* which you use to create stacked symbols. Most templates include a symbol and one or more *slots,* in which you type text or insert other symbols. Back in Figure 16-3, for example, I used a template to create a fraction. You can see that the fraction template consists of a horizontal stroke with a slot for the numerator above and the denominator below.

To complete this fraction, I can type a number in each slot. Or I can add another symbol or template to make the equation more interesting. Most equations consist of templates nestled within the slots of other templates. The beauty of it is that Equation Editor adjusts the equation on the fly as you add text or other templates to fill a slot. If you type something like **ax2+bx+c** in the top slot, for example, Equation Editor stretches the fraction bar accordingly.

To move from one template slot to the next, press the Tab key.

6. **When you're done, click anywhere outside the equation.**

   Equation Editor bows out, enabling PowerPoint to restore its menus and toolbars. You can now drag the equation object to change its size or location.

Confused? I don't blame you. After you latch on to the idea behind templates and slots, you can slap together even the most complex equations in no time. But the learning curve here is steep. Stick with it.

Did you notice how big the equation is in Figure 16-3? That's because I was working at 100 percent zoom before I inserted the equation object. After you're in the Equation Editor, you cannot increase the zoom factor, so you may want to switch to a higher zoom factor before you insert the equation.

The *denominator* is the bottom part of a fraction, not an Arnold Schwarzenegger movie.

Sometimes Equation Editor leaves behind droppings that obscure the clean appearance of the equation. When that happens, use the View⇨Redraw command to clean up the equation.

Spend some time exploring the symbols and templates available on the toolbar. There's enough stuff here to create a presentation on how to build your own atomic bomb. (None of the equations in Figure 16-1 has anything to do with atomic bombs. Honest.)

Editing an equation

To edit an equation, follow these steps:

1. **Double-click the equation.**

   This step summons Equation Editor.

2. **Make your changes.**

   For example, suppose you just doubled the mass of Jupiter by typing a *4* when you meant *2*. Just click the 4 to select the template that contains it, and then type a 2 in its place.

3. Click outside the equation when you're done.

All the standard Windows editing tricks work in Equation Editor, including the Ctrl+X, Ctrl+C, and Ctrl+V shortcuts for cutting, copying, and pasting text, respectively.

Typing text

Equation Editor watches any text you type in an equation and does its level best to figure out how the text should be formatted. If you type the letter x, for example, Equation Editor assumes that you intend for the x to be a variable, so the x is displayed in italics. If you type **cos**, Equation Editor assumes that you mean the cosine function, so the text is not italicized.

You can assign several different text styles to text in an equation:

Math: The normal equation style. When you use the Math style, Equation Editor examines text as you type it and formats it accordingly by using the remaining style types.

Text: Text that is not a mathematical symbol, function, variable, or number.

Function: A mathematical function such as *sin, cos,* and *log.*

Variable: Letters that represent equation variables, such as *a, b,* or *x.* Normally formatted as italic.

Greek: Letters from the Greek alphabet that use the Symbol font.

Symbol: Mathematical symbols, such as +, =, summation, and integral. Based on the Symbol font.

Matrix-Vector: Characters used in matrices or vectors.

You can change the text style by using the Style commands, but you should normally leave the style set to Math. That way, Equation Editor can decide how each element of your equation should be formatted.

On occasion, Equation Editor's automatic formatting doesn't work. Type the word **cosmic**, for example, and Equation Editor assumes that you want to calculate the cosine of the product of the variables *m, i,* and *c.* When that happens, highlight the text that was incorrectly formatted and use the Style⇨Text command.

Equation Editor's default text sizes are designed for use with Word for Windows, not PowerPoint. They are much too small. If you plan to use Equation Editor exclusively with PowerPoint, use the Size⇨Define command and double all the point sizes shown in the dialog box that's displayed. (You can always revert to the default sizes by using the Size⇨Define command and clicking the Defaults button.)

Don't use the spacebar to separate elements in an equation — let Equation Editor worry about how much space to leave between the variables and the plus signs. The only time you should use the spacebar is when you're typing two or more words of text formatted with the Text style.

The Enter key has an interesting behavior in Equation Editor: It adds a new equation slot, immediately beneath the current slot. This technique is sometimes a good way to create stacked items, but it's best to use an appropriate template instead.

Using WordArt

WordArt is a little program that takes a snippet of ordinary text and transforms it into something that looks like you paid an ad agency an arm and a leg to design. And the best part is that it's free! Figure 16-4 is an example of what you can do with WordArt in about three minutes. Pretty nifty, eh?

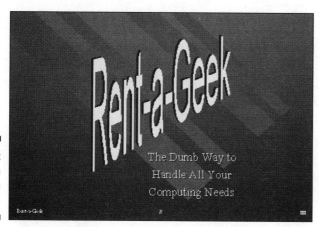

Figure 16-4:
You too can
do this with
WordArt.

Once again, you're in luck if you already know how to use WordArt in Word for Windows. WordArt is the same in PowerPoint and Word for Windows.

Follow these steps to transform mundane text to something worth looking at:

1. **Use the Insert⇨Object command.**

Or insert a new slide by using one of the AutoLayouts that includes an Object placeholder and then double-click the placeholder. Either way, the Insert Object dialog box appears like a flash.

2. **Choose Microsoft WordArt 2.0 from the Object Type list box and then click OK.**

A number of other object types may have infiltrated the list; if so, just scroll until you find WordArt 2.0. When you finally find it, click OK to conjure up WordArt. Like the other OLE 2 add-ons, WordArt and PowerPoint spend a few moments discussing how the Seahawks should fare next season. Then WordArt takes over PowerPoint's menus and toolbars and replaces them with its own.

3. **Type some text in the *Enter Your Text Here* dialog box.**

4. **Pick a shape from the shape list, on the left side of the toolbar.**

The text is skewed to conform to the shape you choose. Figure 16-5 shows how the screen looked after WordArt took over and I typed some text and picked a shape.

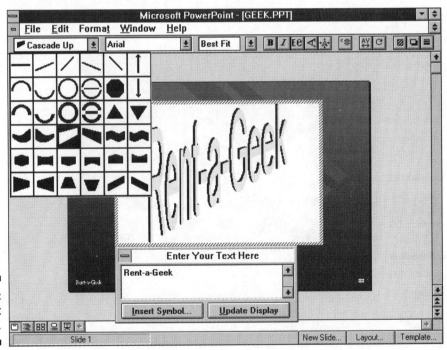

Figure 16-5:
WordArt
takes over.

5. Fool around with other WordArt controls.

The various controls available on the WordArt toolbar are summarized in Table 16-1. Experiment as much as you want until you get the text to look just right.

6. Click anywhere outside the WordArt frame to return to the slide.

Table 16-1		WordArt Buttons
Button	*Name*	*What It Does*
B	Bold	Makes the text bold.
I	Italic	Makes the text italic.
Ee	Even Height	Makes all characters the same height, whether they are upper- or lowercase.
◁	Flip	Flips letters on their sides.
A	Stretch	Stretches the text to fill the selected shape.
≣	Align	Displays a menu of alignment choices (Center, Left, Right, plus three types of justification).
AV	Spacing Between Characters	Displays a dialog box that enables you to adjust spacing.
C	Rotate	Displays a dialog box that enables you to rotate the text.
▨	Shading	Selects a pattern or color for the text.
▢	Shadow	Selects one of several shadow types for the text.
▬	Border	Adjusts the thickness of the text outline.

Don't forget that, in PowerPoint's eyes, a WordArt object is not text. You can't edit it just by clicking it and typing. Instead, you have to double-click it to conjure up WordArt and then edit the text from within WordArt.

WordArt is used most often to create a company logo for the master slide or for the title slide.

Adding a Word Table or Excel Worksheet

If you want to create a slide that has columnar information, don't struggle with trying to line up the text by using PowerPoint's crude tab stops. Instead, take advantage of PowerPoint's capability to create an OLE 2 link with Word for Windows to embed a Word table. When you insert a Word table, all of Word's features for creating and editing a table are available to you from within PowerPoint.

Figure 16-6 shows an example of a Word table inserted into a PowerPoint slide. Notice the gridlines that mark the individual table cells. These were created by using WinWord's table-formatting commands, not PowerPoint's line-drawing button.

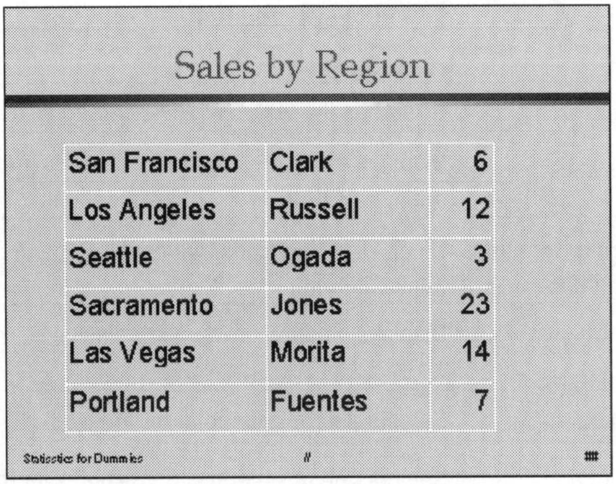

Figure 16-6:
A Word
table
inserted
into a
PowerPoint
slide.

Sales by Region		
San Francisco	Clark	6
Los Angeles	Russell	12
Seattle	Ogada	3
Sacramento	Jones	23
Las Vegas	Morita	14
Portland	Fuentes	7

Statistics for Dummies

You can also insert an Excel worksheet into a PowerPoint presentation. This capability gives you access to Excel's advanced features for calculating values with sophisticated formulas and functions.

For these features to work, you must have Word for Windows 6 or Excel 5 installed on your computer. Older versions of Word for Windows or Excel don't work.

Inserting a Word table

Follow these steps to insert a Word table:

1. **Create a new slide by using the Table AutoLayout and double-click the Table placeholder.**

   This step creates a slide with a placeholder for a Word table. Alternatively, you can use the Insert⇨Microsoft Word Table command or click the Insert Microsoft Word Table button on the Standard toolbar (shown in the margin). Either way, the Insert Word Table dialog box pops up, as shown in Figure 16-7.

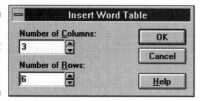

2. Dial the table size you want.

The default table size of two columns by two rows is undoubtedly too small. Increase the columns-and-rows setting as necessary.

3. Click OK.

Microsoft Word and PowerPoint argue about health-care reform for a few moments and then Word plops down its menus and toolbars right on top of PowerPoint's and wraps a ruler around the table. Have a look at Figure 16-8 to see what I mean.

Standard Word toolbars

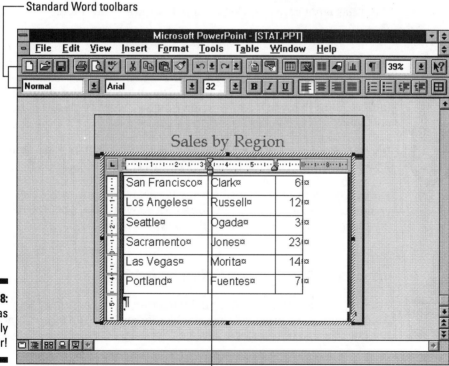

Figure 16-8:
Word has
completely
taken over!

Column marker

4. Type some text into the table cells.

Click the cell in which you want to type text or press the Tab key to move from cell to cell. To adjust the width of a column, drag the column marker on the ruler.

5. Add a border if you're in a daring mood.

To add a border, click the Border button on the Formatting toolbar (shown in the margin). This step pops up the Borders toolbar, shown in Figure 16-9. Click the cells you want to add border lines to and then click the various Border toolbar buttons to add the borders.

Figure 16-9:
WinWord's
Borders
toolbar.

6. Click anywhere outside the table to return to the slide.

Marvel at the greatness of your work.

Don't forget that even though it looks like text on-screen, PowerPoint thinks of the text as a Word table. To edit it, you have to double-click and wait while WinWord and PowerPoint get together. The OLE 2 link for embedding a Word table requires that you have Word for Windows Version 6 installed on your computer.

Don't try to cram more than four columns into a table. Remember that folks have to be able to read the table from the back of the room.

For the complete Lowe-down on using Word tables, run — don't walk — to the computer store or bookstore and pick up a copy of *More Word For Windows 6 For Dummies* (IDG Books Worldwide), by yours truly.

Inserting an Excel worksheet

Inserting an Excel Worksheet is similar to inserting a Word table. No AutoLayout format provides a placeholder for an Excel worksheet, however, nor does the Insert menu have an Excel Worksheet command.

The two options for inserting a worksheet are shown in this list:

You must have Excel 5 for this feature to work.

  ✔ Use the Insert⇨Object command and browse for Excel Worksheet.

  ✔ Click the Insert Microsoft Excel Worksheet button on the Standard toolbar
  (shown in the margin).

After you've inserted the worksheet, you can toil with it by using Excel's
worksheet-editing tools. When you're done, click anywhere outside the
worksheet to return to the slide.

Chapter 17
Multimedia Gags

* *

* *

*W*hat's all the rage about multimedia these days? You would think that some computer geek in Sunnyvale just invented talking movies. Multimedia technology has progressed almost to the point where a $3,000 computer can belch realistically and play six seconds of *The African Queen* almost as well as a $159 VCR can.

Oh, well. It's a trendy business, and I wouldn't be caught dead not including a chapter about multimedia gags in a PowerPoint book. Mercifully, this chapter is short because there's not really much you can do with sound and video in PowerPoint except paste them on a slide and play them when you run the slide show on your computer.

Adding Sound to a Slide

It used to be that the only sound you could get from your computer was a sterile *beep*. Nowadays, you can make your computer talk almost as well as the computers in the *Star Trek* movies. Or you can give them a sophomoric sense of audible distaste. At last, the computer can be as obnoxious as the user!

There's a catch. Your computer must be equipped with a *sound card* to play these types of sounds. Apple Macintosh users love to brag that every Macintosh ever made has had sound capabilities built right in while poor PC users still have to purchase a separate sound card to make their computers burp as well as a Mac. Fortunately, sound cards are getting less and less expensive. Cheap ones can be had for about $50 nowadays, and fairly good ones go for about $150.

All about sound files

Computer sounds are stored in *sound files,* which come in two varieties:

> *Wave files:* Contain digitized recordings of real sounds, such as Darth Vader saying, "I find your lack of faith disturbing" or DeForest Kelly (that's Dr. McCoy, for you non-Trekkers) saying, "He's dead, Jim." Windows comes with four WAV files: CHIMES.WAV, CHORD.WAV, DING.WAV, and TADA.WAV. Notice that these files all have names that end with WAV.

> *MIDI files:* Contain music stored in a form the sound card's synthesizer can play. Windows comes with one: CANYON.MID. All MIDI files have names that end in MID.

To insert a sound into a PowerPoint presentation, all you have to do is paste one of these sound files into a slide. Then when you run the presentation in Slide Show view, you can have the sounds play automatically during slide transitions, or you can play them manually by clicking the Sound button.

You're more likely to use wave files than MIDI files in a PowerPoint presentation. MIDI files are great for playing music, but the wave files enable you to add truly obnoxious sounds to a presentation.

The four WAV sounds that come with Windows are pretty boring, but fortunately we have no national shortage of sound files. You can download them from just about any on-line system (such as CompuServe), purchase them in collections from computer software stores, or beg, borrow, or steal them from your computer-geek friends. Most computer geeks gladly offer you a disk full of *Star Trek* sounds in exchange for a large bag of Cheetos.

If you have a microphone, you can plug in to your sound card, and you can even record your own sounds. Move your computer into the living room some weekend and rent the following movies:

- ✔ *Star Wars*
- ✔ Any *Pink Panther* movie
- ✔ *The Great Muppet Caper*
- ✔ *Star Trek IV* and *Star Trek VI*
- ✔ *The African Queen*
- ✔ *2001: A Space Odyssey*
- ✔ *Annie Hall, Bananas,* or *Sleeper*

Have a ball!

Sound files consume large amounts of disk space. A typical two-second sound clip can take up 25K of precious disk real estate. It doesn't seem like much, but it adds up. (The main reason I installed the new disk compression program that comes with MS-DOS 6 — DoubleSpace — is to make room for my collection of Pink Panther sound files.)

How to insert a sound in PowerPoint

To make your PowerPoint presentation as obnoxious as possible, follow these steps:

1. **Move to the slide to which you want to add the sound.**

2. **From Program Manager, start the Sound Recorder application.**

   Hold down Alt and press Tab repeatedly until Program Manager returns to your screen. Sound Recorder hides in the Program Manager Accessories group. Figure 17-1 shows its icon; double-click it to wake it up.

Figure 17-1:
The Sound
Recorder
icon, which
hides in the
Accessories
group.

3. **Stare at the Sound Recorder window a minute to get your bearings.**

   Figure 17-2 shows what it looks like. The wavy line in the middle is a waveform image of the current sound file.

Figure 17-2:
The Sound
Recorder
dialog box.

4. Use the File⇨Open command to open the sound file you want to insert.

You may have to rummage through your hard disk until you find the file. Keep looking; it's there somewhere.

5. Click the Play button (shown in the margin) to make sure that you found the right sound.

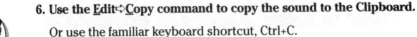

6. Use the Edit⇨Copy command to copy the sound to the Clipboard.

Or use the familiar keyboard shortcut, Ctrl+C.

7. Pop over to PowerPoint.

Press Alt+Tab until PowerPoint comes back to life.

8. Use the Edit⇨Paste command to paste the sound.

Or use the venerable Ctrl+V keyboard shortcut. The sound is pasted as a button right smack-dab in the middle of the slide. I usually move it and enlarge it a little so that I can see it better. Figure 17-3 shows a slide with a sound button.

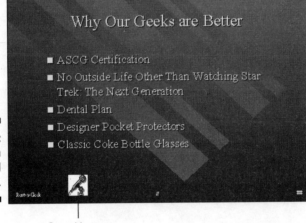

Figure 17-3:
A slide with
a sound
button.

Sound button

9. Double-click the sound button to hear the sound.

Ta-da!

Playing a sound during a slide show

By default, embedded sounds play automatically in a slide show during the transition into the slide that contains the sound or when you click the sound button. You can change this behavior by selecting the sound in Slide view and using the Tools⇨Play Settings command. This step summons the Play Settings dialog box, shown in Figure 17-4.

Figure 17-4:
The Play
Settings
dialog box.

Check the When Click on Object check box if you want to be able to play the sound at will by clicking its button.

If the Hide While not Playing check box is checked, the sound button is hidden during the slide show except when the sound is playing. This situation makes it difficult to click the button, so you should uncheck this box if you want to play the sound at will during the slide show.

Check the When Transition check box to cause the sound to play automatically during the transition into the slide. You also can click the Starts radio button to play the sound at the beginning of the transition or the Ends radio button to play the sound when the transition ends. And you can add a time delay so that the sound isn't played immediately.

If you check When Transition, the sound also plays during each build if you specified a build effect for the slide. Hearing the same sound over and over again can get pretty boring, so I avoid using build effects and transition sounds together on the same slide.

Removing a sound

If you finally come to your senses and realize that sounds are a bit frivolous, you can easily remove them. To remove a sound, click it and press the Del key.

Adding Video to a Slide

Welcome to the MTV era of computing. If your computer has the chutzpah, you can add small video clips to your presentations and play them at will. I'm not sure why you would want to, but hey, who needs a reason?

Adding a video clip to a slide is similar to adding a sound clip. There's a crucial difference, however, between video clips and sound bites: Video is meant to be *seen* as well as *heard*. An inserted video should be given ample space on your slide.

Oh, and you think that sound files are big? Wait till you see how big video files are. Ha! The whole multimedia revolution is really a conspiracy started by hard disk manufacturers.

To work with video clips, you have to get the new version of the Windows Media Player. You can purchase Microsoft Video for Windows from a computer software store, or you can obtain a scaled-back version called *Run-time Video for Windows* from CompuServe.

This procedure shows how to add a video clip to a slide:

1. **Create a new slide by using an AutoLayout that has a placeholder.**

   Alternatively, you can use the Insert⇨Object command, but then you have to rearrange the other objects on the slide to accommodate the video.

2. **Double-click the Object placeholder to conjure up the Insert Object dialog box.**

   See Figure 17-5.

3. **Choose Media Clip as the object type and then click OK.**

   This step runs the new Media Player, shown in Figure 17-6.

4. **Use the File⇨Open command to open a video file.**

   Video files have names that end in AVI. If you can't find the movie you want, hunt around until you locate it.

5. **Use the File⇨Exit and Return command to return to PowerPoint.**

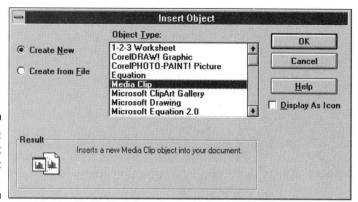

Figure 17-5:
The Insert
Object
dialog box.

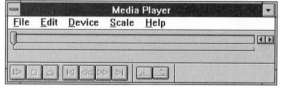

Figure 17-6:
The Media
Player.

The video clip is inserted into the object placeholder. To play it, double-click it.

Like sound objects, video clips can be set to play automatically during the slide transition. Use the Tools⇨Play Settings command to set the play options.

To improve the quality at which the movie plays back, try making the video object smaller by dragging one of its corner love handles.

Like I said, video clips are big, big, big. Sure, you can find them on CompuServe, but it costs a small fortune in connect charges to download them. Best to buy them in collections from computer stores. You need a CD-ROM drive because that's how most movie clips are distributed.

To learn more about video and multimedia in general, check out *More Windows For Dummies* (IDG Books Worldwide), by Andy Rathbone. I don't get a nickel for making this plug, but I figure you can probably use more help here.

Part IV
Working with Files

"AND TO COMPLETE OUR MULTI MEDIA PRESENTATION,..."

In this part...

*N*o matter how hard you try, you cannot avoid dealing with files. After all, the basic function of PowerPoint and just about any other program, for that matter, is to create files. If all you ever do is create files, pretty soon your hard disk resembles my feeble attempts at gardening: The good stuff is choked nearly to death by giant eight-foot weeds you should have pulled out months ago. Like a garden, your hard disk — along with its directories and files — must be tended.

The chapters in this part are a file-management gardening guide. They explore the intricacies of working with PowerPoint files, coexisting with other types of files, keeping track of your files, and using the Windows equivalent of Mr. McGreggor, lovingly known as File Manager.

Chapter 18

Files, Files, Files

● ●

In This Chapter

▶ Editing several presentations all at once

▶ Stealing slides from another PowerPoint file

▶ Saving summary information

● ●

S ure, you probably already know how to click the New button to create a new file, the Open button to retrieve an existing file, and the Save button to save a file. But there's much more to working with files than clicking these three buttons. This chapter covers the all-important and ever-so-boring topic of working with PowerPoint files. Have fun.

Editing More Than One Presentation at a Time

Some people like to do just one thing at a time: start a task, work on it till it's done, and then put away their tools. These same people sort their canned goods by food group and have garages that look like the hardware department at Sears.

Then there are people like me, who work on no fewer than 12 things at a time, would just as soon leave canned goods in the bag arranged just the way the kid at the grocery store tossed them in, and haven't been able to park both cars in the garage since before the kids were born.

Apparently, a few of the latter type work at Microsoft because they decided to enable you to open as many as nine PowerPoint files at a time. Now you're getting somewhere!

To open more than one presentation file, just keep using the File⇨Open command. PowerPoint places each file you open in its own Presentation window that's contained within the PowerPoint window. This Presentation window is normally maximized to fill all the available space within the PowerPoint window, so you can see only one Presentation window at a time. But you can switch between windows by choosing the window you want with the Window command or by pressing Ctrl+F6 to pop from window to window.

PowerPoint enables you to display the windows for each open file in three ways:

Cascaded: The Presentation windows are stacked atop one another, as shown in Figure 18-1. This arrangement enables you to see the title bar of each window. To switch to a window other than the one on top, click its title bar or any other portion of the window you can see. This step sucks the window up to the top of the stack. To cause all Presentation windows to fall into a cascaded stack, use the Window⇨Cascade command.

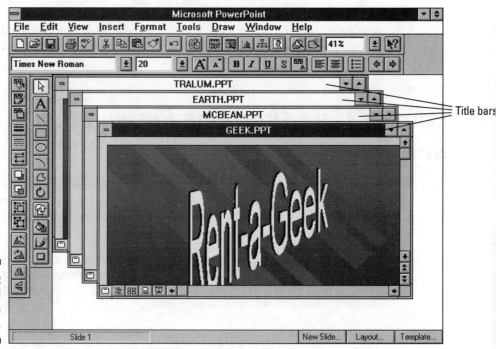

Figure 18-1:
Cascaded
Presentation
windows.

Tiled: The Presentation windows are arranged side-by-side, as shown in Figure 18-2. This arrangement enables you to see a small portion of each presentation, though the more files you have open, the smaller this portion gets. To arrange all Presentation windows in tiled form, use the Window⇨Arrange All command.

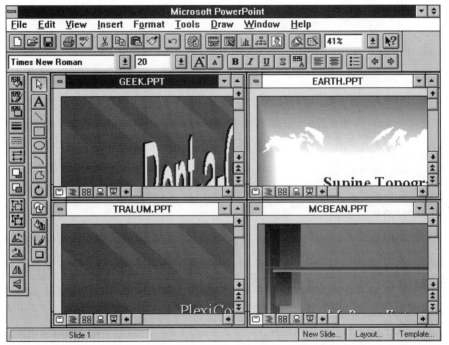

Figure 18-2:
Tiled
Presentation
windows.

Minimized: The windows become icons that appear within the PowerPoint window, as shown in Figure 18-3. To shrink a Presentation window to an icon, click the window's minimize button. To restore the window, double-click the icon.

Figure 18-3:
Minimized
Presentation
windows.

Even though you can open umpteen Presentation windows, only one is active at a time. While you work on one presentation, the others lie dormant, praying to the ASCII gods that you won't neglect them forever.

To copy something from one file to another, switch to the first file's window, copy the object to the Clipboard (by using the normal Copy command), and then switch to the second file's window and paste away.

Most other Windows programs that enable you to open multiple documents, including Word for Windows 6 and Excel 5, work the same as PowerPoint. So learning the menu commands and keyboard shortcuts for working with more than one Presentation window in PowerPoint pays off because you use the same menu commands and keyboard shortcuts in other programs.

PowerPoint offers a handful of keyboard shortcuts for bouncing around between Presentation windows. They're summarized for your reading pleasure in Table 18-1.

You can quickly change the size of a Presentation window so that it's just big enough to show the entire slide at the current zoom factor by using the Window⇨Fit to Page command.

Table 18-1	Keyboard Shortcuts for Multiple Windows
Shortcut	*What It Does*
Ctrl+F6	Moves you to the next Presentation window.
Shift+Ctrl+F6	Moves you to the previous Presentation window.
Ctrl+F10	Maximizes a Presentation window.
Ctrl+F5	Returns a window to its normal size.
Ctrl+F4	Closes a document window.

Here are a couple of tips for working with multiple windows:

- ✔ You can open more than one file with a single pass through the File➪Open command. Just hold down the Ctrl key while you click each file you want to open or use the Shift key to select a block of files. When you click the OK button, all the files you selected open, each in its own window.

- ✔ Some men especially love to use the Ctrl+F6 shortcut to flip from one window to the next. They sit there at the computer, beer in hand, flipping incessantly from window to window and hoping to find a football game or a boxing match.

- ✔ If you want to shut down a window, use the File➪Close command, press Ctrl+W, or double-click in the window's control box. If the file displayed in the window contains changes that haven't been saved to disk, PowerPoint asks you whether you want to save the file first.

Don't bother reading this stuff about the Multiple Document Interface

If you're into Windows trivia, you may be interested to know that PowerPoint's capability to open more than one file at a time conforms to a Microsoft standard called *Multiple Document Interface,* lovingly abbreviated as *MDI.* Other programs that conform to MDI include Microsoft's Word for Windows and Excel.

A non-MDI program can open only one file at a time; every time you open a new file, the current file is closed. The Windows accessory programs, such as Write and Paintbrush, are non-MDI programs. Most new full-figured programs use MDI, but you still occasionally run across a non-MDI program. Just a few weeks ago I bought Microsoft Publisher 2, and guess what? No MDI. You can work on only one Publisher document at a time. Hmmm. Will they ever learn?

One side benefit of MDI is that all the mouse and keyboard shortcuts for working with document windows work the same for all programs that confess the MDI creed. So if you remember that Ctrl+F6 flips from window to window in PowerPoint, you already know how to flip from window to window in Word or Excel.

Stealing Slides from Other Presentations

What do you do when you're plodding along in PowerPoint and realize that you want to copy slides from an old presentation into the one you're working on now? You steal the existing slides, that's what you do. No need to reinvent the wheel, as they say.

You can steal slides from other presentations in two ways. The easier method is to insert all the slides from an existing presentation into the file you're working on. PowerPoint has a menu command designed to do specifically that, so you don't have to think about it. If you need just a few slides from another file, you can open them both and copy slides individually from one file to the other. This technique takes a little more concentration, though.

Stealing a whole presentation

To steal all of an existing presentation and stash it in the presentation you're working on, follow these steps:

1. **Move to the slide you want the stolen slides to follow.**

2. **Conjure up the Insert⇨Slides from File command.**

   This step displays the dialog box shown in Figure 18-4.

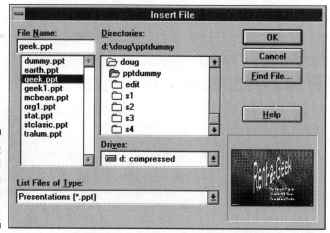

Figure 18-4:
The Steal Slides from File dialog box (ha ha).

3. **Snoop around on your hard disk until you find the presentation you want to steal. Highlight it and then click OK.**

   You're done.

As the slides are copied into the presentation, they are adjusted to match the master slide layout for the new presentation. Embedded charts are even updated to reflect the new color scheme.

Stealing slides is a felony in most states, and if you transmit the presentation across state lines by way of a modem, the feds may get involved — which is good, but it pretty much guarantees that you'll get off scot-free.

The Insert⇨Slides from File command copies all the slides in the file. You can't tell PowerPoint to copy just certain slides, but you can delete any slides you don't need after the file has been copied. This technique is easiest to do in Slide Sorter or Outline view. If you need just a few slides, it may be easier to use the dragon-drop technique, described next.

Stealing just a few slides

The Insert⇨Stolen Slides from Other Files command is good if you want to plant all the slides, or at least most of them, from an old presentation into a new one. If you want to borrow only a few slides, though, follow these steps:

1. **Open the new file and switch to Slide Sorter view.**

2. **Open the old presentation and switch to Slide Sorter view.**

3. **Use the Window⇨Arrange All command to tile the windows.**

4. **Hold down the Ctrl key, click and drag the slide you want to steal right across the window boundary to the new presentation, and deposit it wherever you please.**

   This technique is affectionately known as *dragon-dropping* by perverted Windows junkies. Watch where you step.

If you don't hold down the Ctrl key when you drag the slide, the slide is *moved*, not copied. In other words, the slide is really stolen from the old presentation and relocated to the new presentation. This situation probably isn't what you want. Holding down the Ctrl key while doing a dragon-drop moves a *copy* of the slide to the new presentation.

To move several slides at a time, first select them by holding down the Shift key while you click each slide you want to steal. Then dragon-drop them into the new presentation.

Saving Summary Information

PowerPoint stores summary information with each PowerPoint presentation file you create. *Summary information* includes the filename and directory, the template assigned to the file, and some information you can type: the presentation's title, subject, author, keywords, and comments.

If you use PowerPoint much of the time and have trouble remembering which file is which, the summary info can help you keep your files sorted. It's also handy if you know that you created a presentation about edible spiders last year but can't remember the filename. Just use the File➪Find File command to search for all files with the keyword *spider* in the summary info. (The Find File command is covered in Chapter 20.)

To view or set the summary information for a file, follow these steps:

1. **Open the file, if it isn't already open.**

2. **Conjure up the File➪Summary Info command.**

   The Summary Info dialog box appears, as shown in Figure 18-5.

3. **Type whatever summary info you want to store along with the file.**

   The Title field in the Summary Info dialog box is automatically filled in with whatever you type in the first slide's title placeholder, and the Author field is filled in with your name. (PowerPoint asked for your name when you installed it, remember?)

4. **Click OK.**

5. **Save the file (Ctrl+S or File➪Save).**

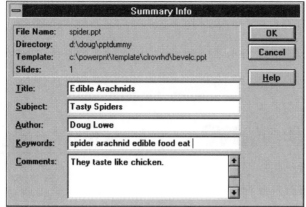

Figure 18-5:
The
Summary
Info dialog
box.

When you fill out the Summary Info screen, spend a few moments thinking about which keywords you may use to look for the file later on. Choosing descriptive keywords makes the file much easier to find.

If you want to include summary information with every PowerPoint file you create, use the Tools⇨Options command and check the Prompt for Summary Info option (see Figure 18-6).

Figure 18-6:
Setting the
Prompt for
Summary
Info option.

The 5th Wave
By Rich Tennant

"IT WAS BETWEEN THAT AND NEW CLASSROOM COMPUTERS."

Chapter 19

Those Durn Foreign Files

In This Chapter

▶ Importing a text file

▶ Exporting a presentation to a word processor

▶ Saving a slide as a graphics file

*I*n the spirit of NAFTA, this chapter shows you how to exchange data with files created by other programs. Sure, it would be nice if we could build a brick-walled protectionist fortress around ourselves and never even acknowledge the existence of other programs, but that wouldn't be — as a former president would say — prudent. Other programs are here to stay, so we had better learn to get along.

The technical term for loading a file created by some other program and converting it to PowerPoint format is, appropriately enough, *importing.* You can import all sorts of file types into PowerPoint: Word for Windows documents, other word processing documents, generic DOS text files, and files created by other presentation programs.

The converse of importing, naturally, is *exporting.* PowerPoint can import more file formats than it can export. I guess the folks at Microsoft want you to convert the competition's files to PowerPoint but not the other way around.

Importing a Foreign File

You have just spent three weeks writing a detailed proposal for a new project, and your boss has just decided that he wants *you* to make the presentation. He expects you to create top-quality 35mm slides based on the proposal, a 60-page Word for Windows document. What do you do?

If you have low self-esteem, you plummet from the sixth-floor window. Otherwise, you just import the document into PowerPoint and get to work. With luck, PowerPoint's text-conversion routines recognize headings in the document and convert them to an outline suitable for presentation. It doesn't always work the way you hope, but it's a start, anyway.

PowerPoint can import not only Word for Windows files but also other file types. Here's the complete list of text file types PowerPoint admits:

Word for Windows: PowerPoint works with Word for Window's outline feature to convert a document to a presentation. Each level-1 heading starts a new slide, with lower-level headings converted to slide text. Paragraphs not assigned a heading style are ignored.

Other word processors: To import a document created by another word processor, first use that word processor's conversion feature to store the document as a Rich Text Format (RTF) file. If the word processing program uses heading styles, they are properly converted to PowerPoint outline levels. If not, PowerPoint guesses at the outline structure by examining how paragraphs are indented.

DOS text files: PowerPoint can read plain old-fashioned DOS text files, sometimes called *ASCII files.* (ASCII is pronounced *ask-ee.*) Most word processors can save files in ASCII format, and the Windows Notepad program and the DOS Edit command work with ASCII files. PowerPoint looks for tabs at the beginning of each line to figure out how to construct an outline from the file.

Competitors' presentation files: PowerPoint converts presentation files created by Harvard Graphics or Lotus Freelance.

Creating a presentation from a foreign file

This procedure shows you how to create a new presentation from a foreign file:

1. **Use the File⇨Open command.**

   The Open dialog box appears.

2. **Pick the file type.**

   Scroll through the List Files of Type list box until you find the one you want (see Figure 19-1).

3. **Choose the file you want to import.**

   You may have to rummage about to find it.

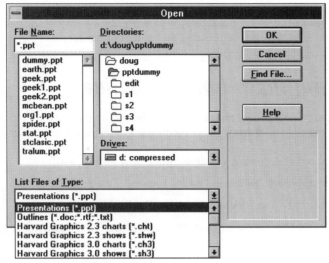

Figure 19-1:
Importing a
foreign file.

4. Click OK.

The file is imported; PowerPoint does its best to construct a reasonable outline from the file.

5. Apply a template.

Click the Template button in the bottom left corner of the status bar and choose an appropriate template.

6. Edit the outline.

The outline imported from the file probably needs a bit of work. Have fun.

Can't convert the file? It may be that you (or someone else) decided to leave out the text-conversion filters when PowerPoint was installed. Grab your original installation disks, pop up the Microsoft Office Program Manager group, and fire up the PowerPoint Setup program. Check to see that the text converters and the presentation converters are installed. Or, better yet, offer a bag of Doritos to your local computer guru. He or she will gladly install the missing converter, do a back flip, and may even recite *The Walrus and the Carpenter* from Alice in Wonderland.

Don't expect perfection when you import a document. PowerPoint does its best to guess at the outline structure of the document, but sometimes it gets confused. Be patient and be prepared to do some heavy editing.

The PowerPoint customs officers don't allow immigrant word processing files to bring their graphics with them. You have to copy any charts or pictures you want to include in the presentation. The easiest way to do that is to fire up both the word processor and PowerPoint at the same time and then copy graphics from the word processing document to PowerPoint by way of the Clipboard. (You press Ctrl+C to copy and Ctrl+V to paste, remember?)

Inserting slides from an outline

You can insert slides from an outline directly into an existing presentation by using the Insert⇨Slides from Outline command. Here's the procedure:

1. **Move to the slide that you want your new slides to follow.**

   For best results, switch to Outline view or Slide Sorter view.

2. **Activate the Insert⇨Slides from Outline command.**

   The Insert Outline dialog box, shown in Figure 19-2, appears.

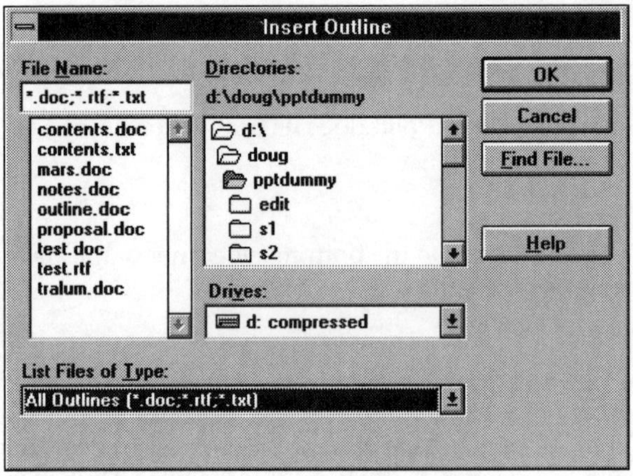

Figure 19-2:
The Insert
Outline
dialog box.

3. **Find the file that contains the outline you want to copy.**

4. **Click OK.**

5. **Review the outline and edit as necessary.**

   It probably won't work exactly as you expect, but it should be close.

The outline can be a Word for Windows document, a document exported from another word processor in Rich Text Format (RTF), or a plain ASCII file.

The new slides are formatted by using the master slide that's already in place.

Exporting an Outline

PowerPoint enables you to save a presentation's outline by using Rich Text Format (RTF), a format for word processing documents that is recognized by just about every word processing program ever written. Here's the procedure:

1. **Activate the File➪Save As command.**

   The Save As dialog box appears.

2. **Choose Outline (RTF) in the Save Files as Type list box.**

   See Figure 19-3.

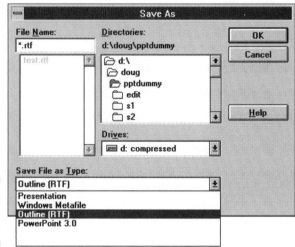

Figure 19-3:
Creating an
outline file.

3. **Type a filename.**

4. **Click OK.**

To open the outline file by using Microsoft Word for Windows, just use the File➪Open command. Choose RTF as the file type to search for. WinWord automatically recognizes that the file is stored in RTF format and offers to convert it.

To open the outline file with other word processors, you may have to use an Import command or a separate conversion program.

Saving Slides as Graphic Files

Just spent hours polishing a beautiful slide and wish that you could find a way to save the slide as a graphics file so that you can import it into another program, such as Word for Windows or a desktop publishing program? You've come to the right place. Fancy that.

PowerPoint has the capability to save any slide in a presentation as a separate graphics file by using the Windows MetaFile (WMF) format. Just follow these steps:

1. **Open the presentation and move to the slide you want to save as a graphic.**

   You can do this in Slide view or in Slide Sorter view — whatever suits your fancy.

2. **Use the File⇨Save As command.**

3. **Pick Windows MetaFile as the file type.**

4. **Type a filename without the extension.**

   The extension WMF is automatically appended to the end of the filename, so you don't have to type it.

5. **Click OK.**

   The slide is saved as a Windows MetaFile, suitable for framing in Word, Publisher, CorelDRAW!, Pagemaker, or any other program that can import WMF files.

Chapter 20
Managing Your Files

● ●

In This Chapter

▶ Using filenames you can remember

▶ Using directories wisely

▶ Finding lost files

▶ Copying files

▶ Creating new directories

▶ Deleting files

▶ Creating new directories

▶ Backing up your files

● ●

*M*y first computer had two disk drives; each drive held 360K of data. A year later, I had a gargantuan 10M hard disk and wondered how I would keep track of two or three hundred files I would store on the disk. (I never thought I would fill it up either.) Today I have more than 400M of disk space, with nearly 10,000 files. It's a miracle I can find anything.

This chapter talks about the mundane task of managing your files: keeping track of where they are, giving them names that help you remember what they contain, and — perhaps most important — backing them up so that you have a spare copy for safekeeping.

Organizing Your Files

The first step in managing your files is organizing them so that you can find them when you need them. You must do only two things to organize your files, but you must do them both well: use filenames you can remember and use directories wisely.

Using filenames that you can remember

Every file must have a name that conforms to the sadistic filenaming conventions adopted by the DOS moguls many years ago. Unfortunately, DOS limits your filenames to a total of 11 characters: 8 for the name itself and 3 for the extension. Sometimes it's tough to concoct good, descriptive filenames that stay within the 11-character limit.

Picking filenames that don't violate the filenaming rules is the easy part. The hard part is obeying the rules and still coming up with names that make sense. The key, obviously, is to abbreviate. It would be great if you could assign a name like PowerPoint Edible Arachnid Presentation For Arachnid Expo '94, but that's well beyond the 11-character limit. A more likely filename is AREXPO94.PPT.

Be consistent about how you name files. If AREXPO94.PPT is the presentation file for Arachnid Expo '94, use AREXPO95.PPT for next year's Expo.

As tempting as it may be, don't use filename extensions other than PPT for PowerPoint presentations. That's just asking for trouble.

Filename characters are a precious commodity. You get only eight, so don't waste them. For example, naming the Expo '94 presentation file EX94PRES.PPT wastes half the filename characters on redundant information: All PPT files are presentations, so there's no need to include PRES in the filename to identify the file as a presentation.

If your presentation includes speaker notes, add the filename to the bottom of the page on the Notes master. That way, the filename is printed on each speaker notes page, which makes it easier to file later.

Using directories wisely

The biggest file-management mistake most beginners make is to dump all their files in one directory. This technique is the electronic equivalent of storing all your tax records in a shoe box. Sure, all the files are there, but it's next to impossible to find anything. Show the shoe box to your accountant on April 14, and you'll be lucky if she or he stops laughing long enough to show you how to file for an extension.

Use directories to impose organization on your files. Don't just dump all your files into one directory. Instead, create a separate directory for each project and dump all the files for each project into its directory. Suppose that you're charged with the task of presenting a market analysis every month. You can create a directory named MKTANAL to store the PowerPoint files for these reports. Then each month's PowerPoint file is named by using the month and year: JAN94.PPT, FEB94.PPT, MAR94.PPT, and so on. (If you're not up to snuff on how directories work, see the sidebar, "Don't read this directory stuff if you can avoid it.")

DOS enables you to create directories within directories to give your hard disk even more organization. Carrying our market-analysis presentation one step further, suppose that quite a few files are required to assemble each report: perhaps a master PowerPoint presentation file, several Excel worksheet files, a WinWord document or two, and who knows what else. To keep these files separate, you can create subdirectories named JAN94, FEB94, MAR94, and so on within the MKTANAL directory. All the files required for a given month's market analysis are stored in the appropriate subdirectory. Very slick, eh?

You can read the steps for creating a new directory later in this chapter, under the heading "Creating a new directory." Isn't that clever?

This list includes some tips for working with directories:

- ✔ Store as few files as possible in the root directory. The *root directory* is kind of like a fire lane, which should be kept free for emergency vehicles at all times.

- ✔ Don't store PowerPoint presentation files in the \POWERPNT directory. The \POWERPNT directory is where all PowerPoint's program files belong. You don't want your own files mingling with them.

- ✔ There's no reason you can't store files that belong to different application programs together in the same directory. Each file's extension identifies the program that created the file. No need to segregate.

- ✔ Don't forget to clean out your directories periodically by deleting files that you no longer need.

- ✔ There is no limit to the number of files you can store in a directory, nor is there a limit to the number of directories you can create. The only exception to this rule is that the root directory can have no more than 254 files and subdirectories. That's why you should keep the root directory free from unnecessary files.

Don't read this directory stuff if you can avoid it

A *directory* is the means by which DOS keeps track of the files on your hard disk. Without directories, your hard disk would resemble the yarn basket after the cat ran amok.

Every file on a disk must have a *directory entry*, which is nothing more than a notation in a directory that lists the file's name and its location on-disk. Think of the directory as a guest registry for a bed-and-breakfast, and you have the idea. The guest registry lists the name of each occupant and the occupant's room number. In a similar way, a disk directory lists each file by name and its disk "room number."

Every disk has a least one directory, called the *root directory.* You can create additional directories to impose structure on your files. These additional directories are sometimes called *subdirectories,* but the terms *directory* and *subdirectory* are generally used interchangeably. The only time it is considered bad form to do so is when you're referring to the root directory. Because the root directory is not subordinate to any other directory, it is not properly called a subdirectory. Refer to the root directory as a subdirectory, and you'll be banished from computer geekdom forever ('tis a consummation devoutly to be wished).

Secrets of the Find File Command

PowerPoint comes with a slick little command called Find File that does more than just find files: It doubles as a mini-File Manager from which you can perform routine file-management chores such as deleting old files, copying files to other directories, and creating new directories.

PowerPoint's Find File command is very similar to the Find File command in Word for Windows 6. If you already know how to use WinWord's Find File command, you're in luck. You can put this book down right now and get back to work. Or you can prop the book up so that it looks like you're reading about the Find File command while you take a nap.

Rummaging for files

Find File's basic purpose in life is to help you rummage about in your hard disk looking for lost files. If you already know the name of the file you're after and you have a pretty good idea of what directory it's in, don't bother with Find File. Just pop up the Open command and navigate through the various directories until you see the file you're after. But if you aren't certain about the filename or the directory, Find File is an answer to your prayer.

Follow these steps to find missing files:

1. Use the File⇨Find File command.

The Find File dialog box miraculously appears, as Figure 20-1 shows.

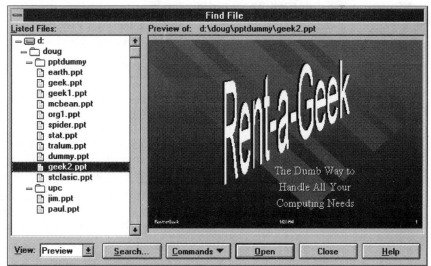

Figure 20-1:
Find File to
the rescue!

The first time you use the Find File command, the Search dialog box shown
in Figure 20-2 appears. It enables you to tell Find File which type of file
you're looking for and which disk drive you want to search. Leave the File
Name field set to *.PPT, but change the Location field if you want to look
for files on a different drive. Then click OK.

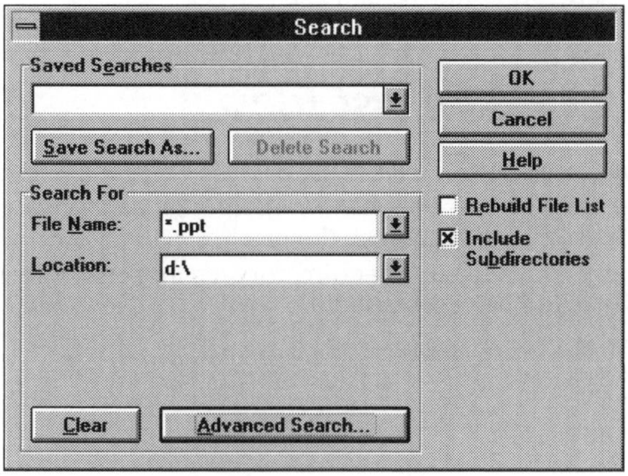

Figure 20-2:
The Search
dialog box.

2. **Rummage through the files displayed in the file list until you find the one you're after. Then highlight it.**

Notice that a picture of each presentation's title slide is displayed in the Find File dialog box. This display helps you determine when you have found the right file.

3. **Click the Open button to open the file.**

Here are some tips for rummaging for files:

✔ You also can get to Find File from the Open command by clicking the Find File button in the Open dialog box.

✔ If you don't see the title slide preview, examine the View drop-down list in the bottom left corner of the Find File dialog box. You can set it to Preview to see the title slides, File Info to see file information such as the creation date and file size, or Summary to see each file's summary information (title, subject, author, keywords, and comments). Chapter 18 explains how to add this summary information to your files, in case you're interested.

✔ You can call up the Search dialog box at any time by clicking the Search button. Then you can specify a different drive to search or change the file type so that all files are displayed rather than just PowerPoint files.

✔ If you like typing DOS paths and filenames, you can type a directory path in the Location field in the Search dialog box and a filename with wild cards in the File Name field. This step restricts the search to a particular directory and includes only files that match the filename pattern you supply.

✔ Make sure that the Include Subdirectories box in the Search dialog box is checked if you want the search to include subdirectories of the directory listed in the Location field.

✔ That Saved Searches list box in the Search dialog box is for fanatics who feel compelled to use the Find File command as often as humanly possible. Feel free to completely ignore it.

Searching for really lost files

OK, you've rummaged through Find File's list of files long enough. You know that the file is there, but you just can't find it. Time for an *advanced search*. Put on your protective eyewear, batten down the hatches, and follow these steps:

1. **Call up the File➪Find File command.**

The Find File dialog box appears.

2. **Punch the Search button.**

The Search dialog box rears its ugly head.

3. **Close your eyes and click Advanced Search.**

4. **Open your eyes and survey the Advanced Search dialog box.**

See Figure 20-3.

Figure 20-3:
The
Advanced
Search
dialog box.

5. **Tell PowerPoint what you're looking for.**

You can type text in any of the fields in the Advanced Search dialog box to narrow the search. You can look for files with a certain title, author, keyword, or subject stored with the file's summary information. Or you can look for files that contain a particular word by typing the word in the Containing Text field. The Advanced Search dialog box in Figure 20-3 is set up to look for files that have the word *arachnid* in the summary keyword field.

6. **Click OK to get back to the Search dialog box and then click OK again to start the search.**

PowerPoint searches your hard disk for files that match your criteria and then displays them in the Find File dialog box.

Did you notice that the Advanced Search dialog box has three index tabs across the top, labeled Location, Summary, and Timestamp? Click the Location tab to change the search location (drive, directory, and filename) or click the Timestamp tab to search for files that were created or last saved on a particular date.

You can type any text you want in the <u>C</u>ontaining Text field; it doesn't have to be a whole word.

The <u>K</u>eywords and S<u>u</u>bject field are of no use to you unless you religiously enter keywords and subjects for all PowerPoint files you create. Review Chapter 18 to learn how to add keywords and the like to your files.

Copying files

The Find File command enables you to make copies of your files. Follow these easy step-by-step instructions:

1. **Conjure up the <u>F</u>ile⇨<u>F</u>ind File command.**

2. **Choose the file that you want to copy.**

   To choose one file, just click it or press the up- and down-arrow keys to highlight it.

3. **Click the <u>C</u>ommands button to reveal the command menu and then click <u>C</u>opy.**

   Figure 20-4 shows the command menu, in case you're curious.

Figure 20-4: The command menu pops up when you click the Command button.

4. **When the Copy dialog box appears, tell PowerPoint where you want to copy the file (see Figure 20-5).**

   If you're a DOS junkie, you can simply type a complete directory path in the Path box. Otherwise, you can click the <u>D</u>irectories and Dri<u>v</u>es lists.

5. **Click OK.**

   Hold your breath while PowerPoint copies the files.

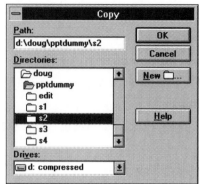

Figure 20-5:
The Copy
dialog box.

These tips help you when you're copying files:

✔ To copy a file to a floppy disk, just type **a:** or **b:** in the Path field or choose drive A or B from the Dri_ves_ list. Make sure that you have a formatted disk ready to stick in drive A or B. (If you're not sure how to format a disk, read the section "Formatting Floppy Disks" in Chapter 21.)

✔ To change the name of a file when you copy it, first pick the destination drive and directory and then type a new filename in the _P_ath field. The file is copied and uses the new name.

✔ If you try to copy a file to a directory that already has a file with the same name, Find File balks. All runners advance one base, and PowerPoint asks whether you're sure that you know what you're doing. Click No unless you're certain beyond a reasonable doubt that you want to overwrite the existing file.

✔ If you want to create a new directory to house the files, click the _N_ew Directory button.

Creating a new directory

It happens to me all the time: I'm working on a new presentation, and when I'm ready to save it, I decide that I want to create a new directory for it. One way to do that is to press Alt+Tab to move over to Program Manager, launch File Manager, create the new directory, exit from File Manager, and then press Alt+Tab to move back to PowerPoint and save the file in the new directory. Bother.

Mercifully, PowerPoint's Find File command enables you to create a new directory.

Here's the procedure:

1. **Activate the File⇨Find File command.**

2. **Choose the directory you want the new directory to live in.**

3. **Click the Commands button and choose the Copy command.**

4. **Click the New Directory button.**

   The Create Directory dialog box appears, as shown in Figure 20-6.

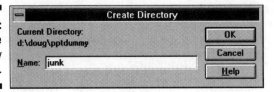

5. **Type the name of the directory you want to create.**

   In the example in Figure 20-6, I typed **junk**.

6. **Click OK.**

7. **When you return to the Copy dialog box, click Cancel.**

You can leave File Manager running if you have gobs and gobs of memory. But in the real world, few of us have enough memory to leave File Manager sitting there taking up precious memory while you try to get real work done.

Too bad they didn't include Create Directory as a choice on the Commands menu. Just remember that the New Directory button hides inside the Copy command and all will be well.

Deleting files

Don't need a file anymore? Free up the valuable disk space it occupies by using the Find File command's Delete option. Here's how you do it:

1. **Conjure up the File⇨Find File command.**

2. **Choose the file or files you want to delete by clicking them.**

3. **Think about it.**

   Do you really want to delete these files? What did they ever do to you?

4. Click the Commands button and then choose the Delete command.

PowerPoint warns you that what you are about to do is crazy and asks whether you really mean to do these files harm.

5. Click Yes.

If anyone questions you about it later, you can always claim temporary insanity.

Backing Up Your Files

When was the last time you changed the oil in your car, took your dog for a walk, or backed up the files on your hard disk? The neglect of any of these three tasks can have disastrous consequences. This isn't the time or place for a stern lecture about the importance of backing up, though, so I'll spare you the soapbox lecture.

One way to back up a file is to use PowerPoint's Save As command to save a copy of the file to a floppy disk. Or you can use the Find File command to select a bunch of files and then copy them to disk.

The best way to back up your files is to use an Official Backup Program. If you have DOS 6 or 6.2, you're lucky because you already own a decent backup program called Microsoft Backup. You should be able to find it somewhere buried in Program Manager, probably in a group named Microsoft Tools.

Keep in mind these hints about backing up your files:

- Remember what I said about this not being the time or place for a lecture? I lied. Back up your files every day. You never know when a stray asteroid will strike your city and possibly wipe out all human life and erase your files too! So don't put it off! Back up today!

- Always have plenty of disks on hand for backups.

- You don't have to back up every file on your hard disk every day. Just back up the files you changed that day. Microsoft Backup has a slick feature called *incremental backup* that does precisely that, and it does it automatically so that you don't even have to think about it.

- If you want to learn how to put Microsoft Backup to good use, check out Chapter 6 in *More Windows For Dummies* (IDG Books Worldwide), by Andy Rathbone.

Chapter 21

Using File Manager (Blech!)

● ●

In This Chapter

▶ Starting File Manager

▶ Finding files and directories

▶ Doing things to files and directories

▶ Formatting disks

● ●

*F*ile Manager is what separates normal people from computer nerds. Computer nerds love File Manager. They think that it's cool, and there's nothing they would rather do than point and click their way through dense tree-structured directories, electronic machete in hand. Hack! Hack!

Normal people like you and me dread File Manager. I turn to it only when I must and then with resentment and spite. The bad news is that I need File Manager all too often. I need it to do such routine file-management chores as copying files, creating directories, renaming and deleting files, and formatting disks. You can do some of these chores by using PowerPoint's Find File command, but for serious file management, you have little choice but to turn to File Manager.

This chapter covers File Manager with a Special Forces mentality. It shows you how to get in, get the job done, and get out quickly.

File Manager is not a part of PowerPoint, but it's available on every Windows system because it comes with Windows.

Starting File Manager

Follow this procedure to fire up File Manager:

1. Switch to Program Manager.

Press Alt+Tab repeatedly until Program Manager appears, or press Ctrl+Esc and double-click Program Manager in the Task List.

2. Find the File Manager icon (usually in the Main group).

Figure 21-1 shows what the File Manager icon looks like. If it's not on your screen, look for a Program Manager group icon named Main and double-click it. File Manager usually hangs out in this Main group.

File Manager

3. Double-click it.

File Manager springs to life. Hide your children. Don't let them look at Figure 21-2.

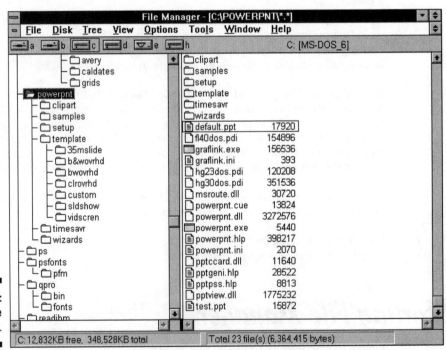

Figure 21-2:
File
Manager.

Some people set their computers up so that File Manager starts automatically whenever Windows fires up. If File Manager is already running, there's no need to start it again. Just press Ctrl+Esc, find File Manager in the resulting Task List, and double-click it.

When File Manager fires up, it may not take over your entire screen. If it doesn't, the first thing you should do is click the maximize button in the top right corner of the File Manager window.

Finding Files and Directories

The most basic File Manager chore is riffling through the directories on your disks to find and select files. This list summarizes the most important file-finding tasks:

Look at a different drive: To change File Manager's display to a different drive, click that drive's button.

Peer into a specific directory: To display the files that reside in a particular directory, click that directory's folder button.

Find directories that aren't shown: You can expand the directory tree so that all directories are shown by using the Tree⇨Expand All command. Depending on how many directories you have, you may also have to scroll the directory tree to find a directory.

Select files: To select a file, click it. To select several files, hold down the Ctrl key while you're clicking files. To select a block of files, click the first file you want to select and then hold down the Shift key and click the last file in the block. The two files you clicked plus all the files in between are selected.

Select all the files in a directory: Use the File⇨Select Files command, which pops up the dialog box shown in Figure 21-3. Click the Select button and then click Close. (When you click Select, the Cancel button changes to the Close button. That's why there's no Close button in Figure 21-3.)

Avoid the natural urge to double-click the drive buttons. This action opens up a separate window for the drive. If you keep doing this, pretty soon you have dozens of little drive windows cluttering up your screen. These little drives have a purpose, but only advanced File Manager junkies know how to use them.

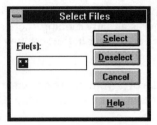

Figure 21-3:
The Select
Files dialog
box.

If you double-click a PowerPoint file, File Manager launches PowerPoint and opens the file. After you've selected a file, you can deselect it by clicking it again.

Doing Stuff to Files

File Manager comes fully equipped with all the file-management features that you need. With it, you can copy or move files, change a file's name, and delete files. Table 21-1 lists the menu commands and keyboard shortcuts you use to perform these routine file-handling chores.

Table 21-1	Routine File-Handling Chores	
Chore	*Menu Command*	*Shortcut*
Copy a file or files	File⇨Copy	F8
Move a file or files	File⇨Move	F7
Delete a file or files	File⇨Delete	Del
Undelete deleted files	File⇨Undelete	(None)
Rename a file	File⇨Rename	(None)
Create a directory	File⇨Create Directory	(None)

Copying and moving files

Copying a file means making a duplicate of it in another directory (perhaps on another drive) or in the same directory but with a different name. *Moving* a file is similar, but after the duplicate is made, the original file is deleted.

To move or copy files, follow these steps:

1. **Select the file or files you want to copy or move.**

2. **Drag the files to the directory you want them copied or moved to.**

   The hard part is knowing whether to hold down the Ctrl key or the Shift key while you drag the files. The four possibilities follow:

   Copy a file to a different directory on the same drive: Hold down the Ctrl key while you drag the files.

   Move a file to a different directory on the same drive: Don't hold down any key. Just drag the files.

   Copy a file to a different drive: Don't hold down any key. Just drag the files to one of the drive buttons.

   Move a file to a different drive: Hold down the Shift key while you drag the files to one of the drive buttons.

3. **If you're confronted with an annoying question about whether you really want to copy the files, answer Yes — unless you were just kidding.**

4. **If you're confronted with a scary question about overwriting an existing file, think about it before clicking Yes.**

Confused about when to hold down the Ctrl or Alt keys? So am I. The guy or gal who made up these rules is now selling hot dogs at the Kingdome.

You also can copy and move files by using the File⇨Copy or File⇨Move commands. This technique spares you the mental anguish of having to remember whether to use the Ctrl or Shift keys, but it replaces one form of punishment with another: You now have to remember how to type a DOS path (see Figure 21-4). You just can't win the File Manager game.

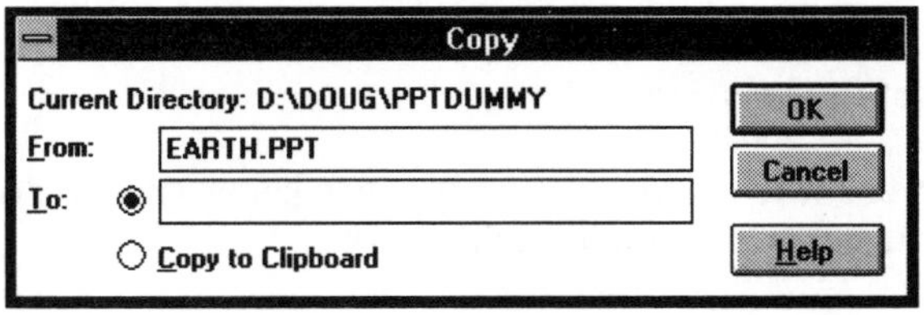

Figure 21-4:
The Copy
dialog box.

If you want to make a duplicate of a file in the same directory but using a different name, use the File⇨Copy command and type the new filename when the Copy dialog box appears.

Renaming files

To change the name of a file, follow these steps:

1. **Select the file you want to rename.**
2. **Use the File⇨Rename command.**
3. **Type the new name for the file.**
4. **Click OK.**

   That's all there is to it.

If you attempt to change a file's name to the name of some other file, File Manager complains bitterly. Don't be offended. File Manager is just trying to keep you out of trouble.

You can rename more than one file at a time, but only if you're a whiz with wild cards. If you're a mere mortal, rename files one at a time.

Deleting files

Deleting files is the only thing that's easy to do with File Manager. Follow this simple, two-step procedure:

1. **Select the file or files you want to delete.**

   See how easy this is?

2. **Press the Del key.**

   I told you that this was easy.

File Manager may ask whether you're sure that you know what you're doing. Feel your forehead and click Yes if it's not too hot.

Keep these tips in mind when you're deleting files:

✔ To delete a whole directory, click the directory folder icon to select it and press Del.

✔ If you like to do things the hard way, you can delete files by using the File⇨Delete command.

✔ If you delete a file by mistake, quickly run the File⇨Undelete command to get the file back. But don't delay. Every time you save another file to disk, you reduce the odds of getting your file back by undeleting it. (The Undelete command is available only if you're using DOS 6 or later.)

Formatting Floppy Disks

One common computer chore that often makes you turn to File Manager is formatting floppy disks. File Manager's Disk⇨Format Disk command is a welcome alternative to the bare-bones DOS FORMAT command.

To format a floppy disk, follow these steps:

1. **Buy some disks.**

   Yeah, you really do need them.

2. **Fire up File Manager.**

   Double-click the File Manager icon in Program Manager's Main group or press Ctrl+Esc to pop up the Task List and see whether File Manager is already running.

3. **Use the Disk⇨Format Disk command.**

   This step calls forth the friendly Format Disk dialog box, shown in Figure 21-5.

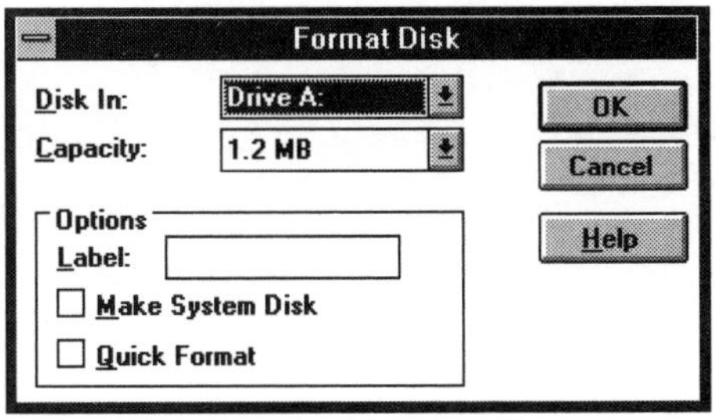

Figure 21-5: The Format Disk dialog box.

4. **If you have two disk drives, pick the one you want to use from the Disk In drop-down list.**

   The Disk In field is initially set to format disks in drive A. You have to change it if you want to format disks in drive B.

5. **Insert a blank floppy disk in the drive and press OK.**

6. **When File Manager asks whether you really mean it, click Yes.**

7. **Wait while File Manager formats the disk.**

8. **Do it again if you need to format more disks.**

   When File Manager finishes formatting the disk, it asks whether you want to format another disk. This feature makes it easy to format a batch of disks.

You can type a name for the disk in the Label field if you want, but little purpose is served. I usually ignore the label.

I hate formatting disks. I usually spend the extra buck or two to buy disks that are already formatted, so I hardly ever get to use this command. Sniff. When I buy disks, I always look for special offers, like *Free game on eleventh disk*. I've collected a couple of good ones in recent years, including a great submarine simulation and a couple of good card games. Any day now I expect to see OS/2 offered free with a box of disks.

Formatting a disk completely wipes out any files that you have stored on the disk. Unless you're formatting brand new disks right out of the box, always check the disk first to make sure that it doesn't contain any important files.

Part V
The Part of Tens

"There's been some concern, Roy, that, as Director of Finance, you've been spending a little too much time with our new graphics presentation package."

In this part...

PowerPoint is great at creating bulleted lists, so how fitting indeed that this book should end with a bevy of chapters that aren't much more than glorified bulleted lists. Each chapter in this part covers ten (more or less) things worth knowing about PowerPoint. Without further ado, here they are, direct from the home office in Fresno, California.

Chapter 22

Ten PowerPoint Commandments

*B*ut the hapless Windows user said, "Who am I to make this presentation? For I am not eloquent, but I am slow of speech and of tongue, and my charts runneth over." And Microsoft answered, "Fear not, for unto you this day is given a program, which is PowerPoint, and it shall make for you slides, which shall bring forth outlines and notes and yea, even handout pages."

— Presentations 1:1

And so it came to pass that these ten PowerPoint commandments were passed down from generation to generation. Obey these commandments and it shall go well with you, with your flip chart, and with your overhead projector.

I. Thou Shalt Frequently Savest Thy Work

Every two or three minutes, press Ctrl+S. It takes only a second to save your file, and you never know when an errant Scud may drop in your backyard.

II. Thou Shalt Storeth Each File in Its Proper Directory

Whenever you save a file, double-check the directory in which you're saving the file. It's all too easy to save the file in the wrong directory and then spend hours searching for the file later.

III. Thou Shalt Not Abuseth Thy Program's Formatting Features

Yes, PowerPoint enables you to set every word in a different font, use 92 different colors on a single slide, and fill every last pixel of empty space with clip art. If you want a ransom-note look, go ahead. Otherwise, keep it simple.

IV. Thou Shalt Not Stealeth Thy Neighbor's Clip Art

It's not yours. Your neighbor paid for it, which gives her or him the right to use it. If you want to use it, buy your own copy.

V. Thou Shalt Not Departeth from the Way of Thy Color Scheme; Neither Shalt Thou Departeth from the Pattern of Thine AutoLayout or the Appearance of Thy Template

Microsoft hired a crew of out-of-work artists to pick the colors for the color schemes, arrange things on the AutoLayouts, and design beautiful backgrounds for the templates. Humor them. They know what they're doing.

VI. Thou Shalt Not Fondle Thy POWERPNT.INI, GRAFLINK.INI, or Other INI File

These files are off-limits. If you break this commandment, you had better keep the next one.

VII. Remember Thy Computer Gurus, to Keep Them Happy

Throw them an occasional Twinkie or bag of Cheetos. Treat them like human beings, no matter how ridiculous that seems. You want them to be your friends.

VIII. Thou Shalt Backeth Up Thy Files Day by Day

Yes, every day. One of these days, you'll come to work only to discover a pile of rubble where your desk used to be. If you back up every day, you won't lose more than one day's work.

IX. Thou Shalt Fear No Evil, for Ctrl+Z Is Always with Thee

March boldly ahead. Not sure what that button does? Click it! If you don't like it, you can always press Ctrl+Z to undo it.

X. Thou Shalt Not Panic

You're the only one who knows that you're nervous. You'll do just fine. Imagine the audience naked if it helps.

Chapter 23
Ten Things That Often Go Wrong

*T*here are probably closer to 10,000 things that can go wrong, but these 10 are among the things that go wrong most often.

I Can't Find My File!

You spent hours polishing that presentation and now you can't find the file. You know that you saved it, but it's not there! The problem is probably one of two things: Either you saved the file in a directory other than the one you thought you did, or you used a different name to save it than you intended. The solution? Use the File⇨Find File command. See Chapter 20 for detailed procedures.

I've Run Out of Memory!

Many computers with only 4M of internal memory are running Windows these days. Although 4M may be enough to load up Windows and PowerPoint, it isn't long before you get messages about running short on memory. Short of purchasing more computer memory (which isn't a bad idea), avoid running more than one Windows program at a time. Also, try removing fonts that you don't need. The more fonts you have installed on your computer, the less memory you have free for other programs. (To remove fonts, fire up the Control Panel and click the Fonts icon. Choose the fonts you don't need and then click the Remove button.)

I've Run Out of Disk Space!

Nothing is more frustrating than creating a fancy PowerPoint presentation and then discovering that you're completely out of disk space. What to do? Press Alt+Tab to move over to Program Manager and then launch File Manager and rummage through your hard disk, looking for files you don't need. Delete enough files to free up a few megabytes and then press Alt+Tab to move back to PowerPoint and save your file. I did this just a few days ago; I had to delete a bunch of sound files I recorded from the movie *Young Frankenstein*. (It was either them or the Word for Windows document files for the first few chapters of this book. Not an easy decision.)

If your disk is full and you can't find more than a few files to delete, you may consider activating the DOS 6 disk-doubling program, DoubleSpace. Check out *More DOS For Dummies,* by Dan Gookin (IDG Books Worldwide), for information about using DoubleSpace.

PowerPoint Has Vanished!

You're working at your computer, minding your own business, when suddenly — Whoosh! — PowerPoint disappears. What happened? Most likely, you clicked some area outside the PowerPoint window or you pressed Alt+Tab or Alt+Esc, which whisks you away to another program. To get PowerPoint back, press Ctrl+Esc. A list of all the active programs pops up; double-click PowerPoint to return to PowerPoint.

PowerPoint can also vanish into thin air if you use a screen saver program. Try giving the mouse a nudge to see whether PowerPoint reappears.

I Accidentally Deleted a File!

Just learned how to delete files and couldn't stop yourself, eh? Relax. It happens to the best of us. Odds are that you can get the deleted file back, if you act fast enough. Conjure up File Manager and use the File⇨Undelete command or launch the Undelete program from the Microsoft Tools group. (Undelete is available only if you have DOS 6 or later.)

It Won't Let Me Edit That!

No matter how hard you click the mouse, PowerPoint won't let you edit that doohickey on the screen. What gives? The doohickey is probably a part of the Slide master. To edit it, use the View⇨Master⇨Slide Master command. This step displays the Slide master and enables you to edit it.

Something Seems to Be Missing!

You have just read the chapter about Equation Editor, but nothing happens when you try to use it. You, or whoever installed PowerPoint on your computer, probably decided not to install it. To correct this oversight, gather up your original installation disks and launch the PowerPoint Setup program from the Microsoft Office group. (This problem can happen with many optional components of PowerPoint, including Microsoft Chart, clip art, and templates.)

What Happened to My Clip Art?

You just purchased and installed an expensive clip art collection that has 500 stunning photographic-quality images from the 1994 USA Synchronized Swimming Championships, but you can't find them in the ClipArt Gallery. Where did they go? Nowhere. You just have to tell ClipArt Gallery about them. Fire up the Gallery by clicking the Insert Picture button or by double-clicking a clip art object. Then click the Options button. Then click Add and tell PowerPoint where the new picture files are located.

One of the Toolbars Is Missing!

You reach for the Bold button, but it's not there. In fact, the whole Formatting toolbar seems to be missing. What gives? Somehow the view got messed up. It happens all the time, so don't feel bad. Just look in the mirror and say to yourself, "It's not my fault that the toolbar disappeared. It happens even to experts like that nice Mr. Lowe, who wrote a whole book about PowerPoint. I shouldn't blame myself. After all, I'm good enough, I'm smart enough, and, doggone it, people like me."

Then use the View⇨Toolbars command to reactivate the missing toolbar.

All the Text Is the Same!

This problem happens in Outline view when you've clicked the Show Formatting button. Just click Show Formatting again to restore text formatting, such as font, point size, italics, and so on.

Chapter 24

Ten PowerPoint Shortcuts

*J*ust about anything you can do with PowerPoint you can do by hacking your way through the menus or clicking the correct toolbar button. But a few shortcuts are worth knowing about.

Shift+Click the View Buttons to Display Masters

You can use the View⇨Masters command to display the Slide, Notes Pages, Handout, or Outline masters. But an easier way is to hold down the Shift key while clicking the status bar buttons. The following table shows the buttons.

Button Combination	Master
▣	Slide Master
▤	Outline Master
▦	Handout Master
▣	Notes Pages Master

Right-Click Anywhere to Get a Quick Menu

You can right-click just about anything with the mouse button to get a quick menu of common things you can do to the object. Try it — it's kind of fun.

Ctrl+X, Ctrl+C, or Ctrl+V to Cut, Copy, or Paste

Just about all Windows applications respond to these keyboard shortcuts.

Shortcut	Action
Ctrl+X	Cuts the selection to the Clipboard.
Ctrl+C	Copies the selection to the Clipboard.
Ctrl+V	Inserts the contents of the Clipboard.

Note: Before you use Ctrl+X or Ctrl+C, select the object you want to cut or copy.

Ctrl+Z to Undo a Mistake

Oops! Didn't mean to double-click there! Don't panic. Press Ctrl+Z and whatever you did last is undone.

Ctrl+B or Ctrl+I for Bold or Italics

Like most Windows applications, PowerPoint accepts the following keyboard shortcuts for text formatting:

Shortcut	Action
Ctrl+B	Bold
Ctrl+I	Italic
Ctrl+U	Underline
Ctrl+spacebar	Return to normal format

Note: Before using these shortcuts, highlight the text that you want to format.

Ctrl+S to Save a File

Press Ctrl+S to save the current presentation to a file. The first time you save a new file, PowerPoint displays the Save As dialog box, in which you can assign a name to the file. Thereafter, Ctrl+S saves the file by using the same name.

Ctrl+G to Show the Guides

Need help aligning drawn objects? Press Ctrl+G to display the guides. You can then drag the guidelines around and snap objects to them.

Shift while Drawing to Constrain Objects

If you hold down the Shift key while drawing an object, the object is drawn as straight as an arrow. Circles will be circles, squares squares, and lines will stick to 45-degree angles.

Alt+Esc, Alt+Tab, or Ctrl+Esc to Switch to Another Program

This isn't really a PowerPoint shortcut, but a Windows one. To switch to another application, use one of these keyboard combinations:

Alt+Esc: Switches to the next program in line.

Alt+Tab: Displays the name of the next program in line. While holding down the Alt key, keep pressing Tab until the name of the program you want appears. Release both keys to switch to that program.

Ctrl+Esc: Pops up a list of all active programs. Double-click the one you want to switch to.

F1: The Panic Button

Stuck? Press F1 to activate PowerPoint's Help. With luck, you can find enough information to get you going. The help is *context-sensitive,* which means that it tries to figure out what you were doing when you pressed F1 and give you specific help for that task.

Chapter 25
Ten Tips for Creating Readable Slides

*T*his chapter gives you a few random tips and pointers that help you produce readable slides.

Try Reading the Slide from the Back of the Room

The number-one rule of creating readable slides is that everyone in the room should be able to read them. If you're not sure, there's one sure way to find out: try it. Put the slide in the projector, walk to the back of the room, and see whether you can read it. If you can't, you have to make an adjustment.

Five Bullets, Tops

Ever notice that David Letterman uses two slides to display each of his Top Ten lists? Dave's producers know that ten items is too many for one slide. Five is just right. Take a cue from Dave's show and limit yourself to no more than five bullet points per slide.

Avoid Small Text

If you can't read a slide from the back of the room, it's probably because the text is too small. The rule of thumb is that 24 points is the smallest you should go for slides, and 18 points for overheads. Twelve-point type may be perfectly readable in a word processing document, but it just doesn't cut it on an overhead or slide.

Avoid Excessive Verbiage Leading to Excessively Lengthy Text That Is Not Only Redundant but Also Repetitive and Reiterative

This heading could have been "Be Brief." Get the point?

Use Consistent Wording

Whenever possible, be consistent in the way you word your bulleted lists. Consider this list:

- Profits will be improved
- Expanding markets
- We must reduce the amount of overseas competition
- Production increase

Each sentence uses a different grammatical construction. The same points made with consistent wording have a more natural flow:

- Improved profits
- Expanded markets
- Reduced overseas competition
- Increased production

See what I mean?

Stick to the Color Scheme

With all the professionally chosen color schemes packed into PowerPoint, there's no reason to try to create your own. The color schemes combine colors that work well together. Why spoil the party?

Stick to the AutoLayouts When You Can

You can't, at least not always. But try to if you can. The AutoLayouts include various placeholder objects that are already lined up for best readability.

Keep the Background Simple

Don't splash a bunch of distracting clip art on the background unless it is essential. The purpose of the background is to provide a well-defined visual space for the slide's content. Avoid templates that have beach scenes in the background. For overheads, it's best to use light-colored backgrounds. Dark backgrounds work well with slides.

Use Only Two Levels of Bullets

Sure, it's tempting to develop your subpoints into sub-subpoints and sub-sub-subpoints, but no one can follow you. Don't make your slides more confusing than they need to be. If you need to make sub-sub-subpoints, you probably need a few more slides.

Keep Graphs Simple

Microsoft Graph can create elaborate graphs that even the best statisticians will marvel at. But the most effective graphs are pie charts with three or four slices and column charts with three or four columns.

If you remember only one rule when creating your presentation, remember this one: *Keep it simple, clean, and concise.*

Chapter 26

Ten New Features in PowerPoint 4

*I*f you're an experienced PowerPoint 3 user just upgrading to PowerPoint 4, you probably turned to this chapter first. It lists the ten most important new features in PowerPoint 4.

Consistency with Word for Windows and Excel

If you already know how to use either Word for Windows 6 or Excel 5, you already know how to do about a million things in PowerPoint. Wherever possible, PowerPoint has borrowed WinWord's or Excel's way of doing things.

Wizards

Silence! The Wizard of PowerPoint has every intention of granting your requests.

Wizards have been creeping into the new breed of Microsoft application programs. The new Word for Windows and Excel both have them, and the programming team that developed PowerPoint didn't want to be left out.

What, you ask, is a wizard? It's really nothing more than a glorified macro that assists you in some routine task. PowerPoint comes with two wizards: The Pick-a-Look wizard asks you some questions about how you want your presentation to look and then picks an appropriate template and sets up the Slide, Notes pages, Handouts, and Outline masters for you. Figure 26-1 shows the part where you tell it that you want your company name, the date, and the page number to appear at the bottom of each slide. The Pick-a-Look wizard may not be the best thing since sliced bread, but it is a genuine time-saver.

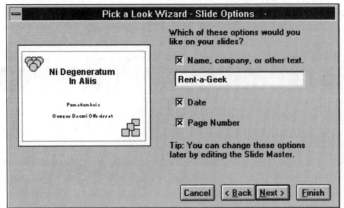

Figure 26-1:
The Pick-a-
Look wizard.

The other wizard that comes with PowerPoint is the AutoContent wizard, which is supposed to all but write your presentation for you. It amounts to a little more than a few sample presentations that provide a basic outline for various types of presentations. The sample outline guides you in creating your finished presentation (for example, *Insert a lawyer joke here* or *Insult the client now*).

Cue Cards

Cue cards are somewhat like wizards, but they don't do any work for you. Instead, they stand on the sidelines like a coach, telling you how to line up and where to click, and yelling at the referee whenever necessary.

Cue cards help you with such tasks as adding a logo to every slide, making the computer belch whenever a new slide appears, or changing the color scheme to something a little more hip. Figure 26-2 shows a part of the cue card that says Add a Logo or Text to Every Slide. The cue card hangs around the screen while you work so that you can follow its instructions. If you successfully complete the task, the traditional thing to do is to dump the ice bucket on the cue card's head.

Tip of the Day

Every time you start PowerPoint, you are greeted with a helpful tip, affection-ately known as the Tip of the Day. Figure 26-3 shows one of the more useful tips. After you've seen them all two or three times, you'll probably want to turn this feature off.

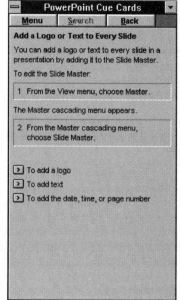

Figure 26-2:
The friendly
cue card
coaches
from the
sidelines.

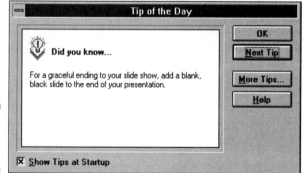

Figure 26-3:
The tip du
jour.

More Toolbars

PowerPoint includes seven different *toolbars,* which are collections of buttons that you can click to invoke commonly used functions. For maximum screen clutter, you can display all of them at once. Or you can just display the ones you use most often and call forth the others only when you need them.

Toolbars are the way things seem to be going with Windows programs; it's hard to find a program that doesn't include them. Like other Microsoft programs, PowerPoint enables you to customize its toolbars by adding or removing buttons to configure them any way you want.

If you forget what a button does, just let the mouse linger over it for a moment, and a bright yellow description of the button appears (called *balloon help*).

AutoLayouts

Whenever you add a new slide to a PowerPoint presentation, the New Slide dialog box shown in Figure 26-4 appears. From this dialog box, you can choose from 21 different layouts for the slide. These layouts provide placeholder objects for various types of objects, such as title text, body text, clip art, charts, and generic objects. All you have to do is click the placeholders and finish the slide.

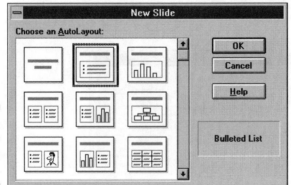

Figure 26-4:
The New
Slide dialog
box.

OLE 2

PowerPoint 4 uses Microsoft's new OLE 2 technology to scare the bejeebers out of drawings, graphs, equations, Word for Windows, and Excel. With OLE 2, you don't have to call up a separate window to edit an embedded object. Instead, you just double-click and watch as PowerPoint magically borrows some of the menu commands and toolbars from the program that owns the object. For example, double-click a chart and PowerPoint's menus and toolbars are temporarily replaced by Microsoft Chart's menus and toolbars. Very cool, but a little spooky.

Font Control

Mention the Font command in PowerPoint 3 to Microsoft employees and watch how quickly they look at their shoes. It was truly a discredit to the state of Washington. I would show you a picture, but I'm not that cruel. Suffice it to say that Microsoft has fixed the Font command so that it now works the way it should.

ClipArt Gallery

No more fumbling through a directory list to find clip art. The ClipArt Gallery, shown in Figure 26-5, shows you a thumbnail sketch of all the pictures in your clip art collection. Just double-click the one you want to insert.

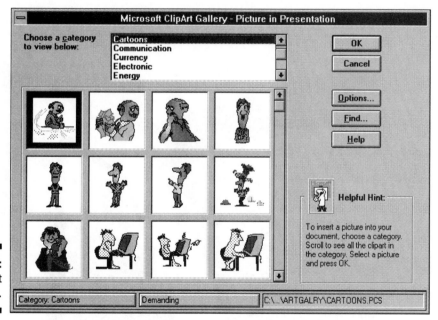

Figure 26-5:
The ClipArt
Gallery.

New Version of Microsoft Chart

The new version of Microsoft Chart included with PowerPoint is the same version of Chart that comes with Excel 5. It uses OLE 2 so that you don't have to work in a separate window to edit a chart. It includes several new chart types and makes it easier to add legends, labels, and other embellishments.

Organization Charts

PowerPoint now comes with a program that draws organization charts. Unfortunately, it doesn't use OLE 2, so you have to pop up a separate window to create the chart. It's not the most powerful organizational chart program in the world, but it's more than powerful enough to create the types of organizational charts you're likely to use on a slide or overhead.

Equation Editor

In the unlikely event you teach advanced hydrophysics at the local community college, you'll be delighted by the new, vastly improved Equation Editor. Otherwise, you'll say, "Huh?"

The 5th Wave   **By Rich Tennant**

"IF YOU THINK WE'VE HAD TOUGH AUDIENCES UP TO NOW, WAIT'LL YOU MEET THIS GUY."

Chapter 27

Ten Ways to Keep Your Audience Awake

*N*othing frightens a public speaker more than the prospect of the audience falling asleep during the speech. Here are some things you can do to prevent that from happening. (Yawn.)

Don't Forget Your Purpose

Too many presentations ramble on and on with no clear sense of purpose. The temptation is to throw in every clever quotation and every interesting fact you can muster that is even remotely related to the purpose of your presentation. The reason that this temptation is so big is that you most likely haven't identified what you hope to accomplish with your presentation. In other words, you haven't pinned down your *purpose*.

Don't confuse a presentation's title with its purpose. Suppose that you're asked to give a presentation to a prospective client on the advantages of your company's new, improved ChronoSimplastic Infindibulator. Your purpose in this presentation is not to convey information about the new Infindibulator, but to persuade the client to buy one of the $65 million beasties. The title of your presentation may be *Infindibulators for the '90s*, but the purpose is to "convince these saps to buy one, or maybe two."

Don't Become a Slave to Your Slides

PowerPoint makes such beautiful slides that the temptation is to let them be the show. That's a big mistake. *You* are the show, not the slides. The slides are merely visual aids, designed to make your presentation more effective, not to steal the show.

It's tempting to dim the lights, hide behind the lectern, and let your slides do the talking for you. Keep the slides in their place.

Don't Overwhelm Your Audience with Unnecessary Detail

On November 19, 1863, a crowd of 15,000 gathered in Gettysburg to hear Edward Everett, one of the nation's most eloquent orators, speak for two hours about the events that had transpired during the famous battle. When Everett finished, Abraham Lincoln rose to deliver a brief two-minute postscript that has since become the most famous speech in American history.

If PowerPoint had been around in 1863, Everett probably would have spoken for four hours. PowerPoint practically begs you to say too much. After you get cranking on that outline, the bullets just fly, one after the other. Pretty soon, you have 40 slides for a 20-minute presentation. That's about 35 more than you probably need. Try to shoot for one slide for every two to four minutes of your presentation.

Don't Neglect Your Opening

As they say, you get only one opportunity to make a first impression. Don't waste it by telling a joke that has nothing to do with your presentation, apologizing for your lack of preparation, or listing your credentials. Don't pussyfoot around; get right to the point.

The best openings are those that capture the audience's attention with a provocative statement, a rhetorical question, or a compelling story. A joke is OK, but only if it sets the stage for the subject of your presentation.

Be Relevant

The objective of any presentation is to lead your audience to say, "Me too." Unfortunately, far too many presentations leave the audience thinking, "So what?"

The key to being relevant is giving your audience what it needs, not what you think is interesting or important. The most persuasive presentations are the ones that present solutions to real problems rather than opinions about contrived problems.

Don't Forget the Altar Call

You've spent hours putting your presentation together. Don't forget to ask for the order. Invite your audience to respond and show them how. Make them an offer they can't refuse. Tell 'em your 800 number. Roll the pen across the table. Give the altar call. (The buses will wait.)

Practice, Practice, Practice

Somehow a rumor got started that Abraham Lincoln hastily wrote the Gettysburg Address on the train, just before pulling into Gettysburg. In truth, Lincoln agonized over every word of the address.

Practice, practice, practice. Work through the rough spots. Polish the opening and the altar call and all the awkward transitions in between. Practice in front of a mirror or with a tape recorder. Time yourself.

Don't Panic

Don't worry! Be happy! Even the most gifted public speakers are scared silly every time they step up to the podium. Whether you're speaking to one person or ten thousand, relax. In 20 minutes, it will all be over.

No matter how nervous you are, no one knows it except you. That is, unless you tell them. The number-one rule of panic avoidance is "Never apologize for your fears." Behind the podium, your knees may be knocking hard enough to bruise yourself. But no one else knows. After you swab down your armpits and wipe the drool off your chin, people will say, "Weren't you nervous? You seemed so calm!"

Expect the Unexpected

Expect things to go wrong because they will. The light bulb in the overhead projector will burn out. The microphone won't work. You'll drop your notes as you approach the podium. Who knows what else?

Above All Else, Don't Be Boring

An audience can overlook almost anything, but one thing they cannot overlook is being bored. Above all, you must never bore your audience.

This guideline doesn't mean that you have to tell jokes, jump up and down, or talk fast. Jokes, excessive jumping, and rapid speech can be as boring as formatting disks. If you obey the other commandments — if you have a clear-cut purpose and stick to it, avoid unnecessary detail, and address real needs — you'll never be boring. Just be yourself and have fun. If you have fun, so will your audience.

Appendix A
Installing PowerPoint

*T*hroughout this book, I've assumed that PowerPoint already lives on your computer. If you're not so lucky, this appendix guides you through the tedious process known as *installation,* a form of torture devised by sadistic programmers back in the early days of computing.

If you are faced with the prospect of installing PowerPoint on your computer, you have two choices:

- ✔ Do it yourself.
- ✔ Bribe your friendly neighborhood computer guru to do it for you.

A one-pound bag of M&Ms and a six-pack of Jolt Cola is usually sufficient to persuade a computer guru to do the installation for you. You can probably pull it off yourself, though. It's tedious, but not overly complicated.

System Requirements

To run PowerPoint, you need two things:

- ✔ A computer that runs Windows 3.1
- ✔ About 39M (megabytes) of free disk space

Yes, I said 39M of disk space. That's how much disk space PowerPoint consumes if you install all its options. (If you're tight on space, you can instruct PowerPoint to leave out some of its lesser used features, like import filters, fonts, or applets you don't plan on using.)

Installing PowerPoint

To install PowerPoint, follow these steps:

1. **Cancel all appointments.**

   Installing PowerPoint takes half an hour or so, but then you will want to fire it up and play with it awhile. I suggest that you set aside the better part of an afternoon to indulge yourself.

2. **Find the PowerPoint installation disks.**

   I assume that you have your own set of PowerPoint disks. If you are "borrowing" someone else's copy of PowerPoint, shame on you! That's stealing, it's against the law, and it just isn't nice. Put this book down right now and march straight over to your local computer store to buy your own copy of PowerPoint. You'll sleep much better tonight.

3. **Start your computer and Windows.**

   If your computer doesn't automatically launch right into Windows, type this line at the DOS prompt:

   > **C:\> win**

4. **Find Program Manager.**

   If Program Manager isn't displayed on-screen, press Crtl+Esc (hold down Ctrl and press Esc once) to pop up the Task List. Look through the list until you find Program Manager and then double-click it.

5. **Stick the PowerPoint Setup disk (disk 1) in the disk drive.**

   If you have just one floppy drive, it is called drive A. If you have two floppy drives, one atop the other, the one on top is usually drive A, and the one on the bottom is drive B. If you have two floppy drives side by side, the one on the left is usually drive A and the one on the right is drive B.

6. **Choose the File⇨Run command.**

   This step calls forth the Run dialog box in which you can run a DOS command. The command you want to run here is SETUP, on either the A or B drive, depending on in which drive you inserted Disk 1. For drive A, type the following line in the Command Line field:

   > **A:SETUP**

   For drive B, type this line:

   > **B:SETUP**

   No spaces and no period at the end. Just the letter A or B followed by a colon and the single word SETUP. Figure A-1 shows the Run dialog box with the correct command for the B drive.

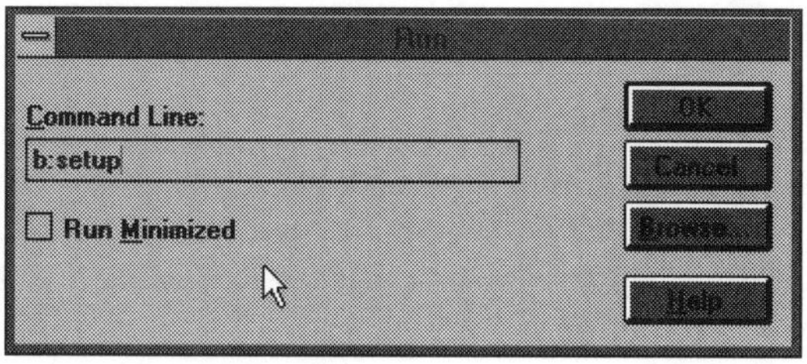

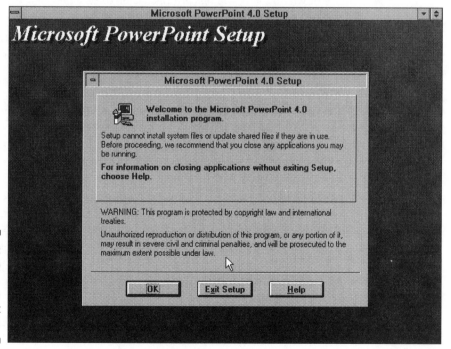

Figure A-1:
The Run
dialog box.

7. Press the Enter key.

You hear the floppy drive churn back and forth for an unbearably long time. Finally, just when you're about to give up, the Microsoft PowerPoint 4.0 Setup dialog box appears, as shown in Figure A-2. From this point on, just follow the instructions on-screen.

Figure A-2:
The Setup
dialog box.
Welcome to
PowerPoint
installation!

These pointers can help to get you through the day:

✔ Read and follow instructions carefully.

✔ Setup asks you for the path where you want to install PowerPoint. If you just press Enter here, PowerPoint is installed in a directory named POWERPNT on drive C. Change this setting only if you know what you're doing. Otherwise, simply press Enter.

✔ When asked to choose which type of installation to perform, pick Complete. This option installs everything, including the Ginsu knives, cheese shredder, and optional rotisserie attachment. It requires about 39M of disk space. Setup displays a list of components to be installed. If you don't have enough disk space available for all of them, you can omit certain components by unchecking them. For example, if you don't plan on lecturing about advanced hydrophysics, you may leave out the equation editor.

✔ When Setup says to swap disks, take the old disk out of the drive and place it face down on top of the discard pile. Then draw a new disk from the top of the kitty, insert it in the drive, and press Enter.

✔ When PowerPoint tells you its serial number, don't bother writing it down. You can see the serial number at any time by starting PowerPoint and choosing the Help⇨About PowerPoint command.

✔ Now is a good time to fill out the registration card.

✔ When Setup finishes, it restarts Windows. After Windows is up and running again, you can start using PowerPoint. Time to turn to Chapter 1.

✔ When you're done, don't forget to remove the last disk from the floppy drive. Gather up the spent installation disks and store them someplace safe. You never know when you may need them again.

✔ PowerPoint Setup leaves an icon representing itself in the Microsoft Office Program Manager group (shown in the margin). If you decide later that you want to remove part of PowerPoint you don't use or add something you left out, just double-click the PowerPoint Setup icon to launch the setup program.

"It's powerful enough for me."

Index

• *H* •

• *I* •

Here's a complete listing of IDG Books' ...For Dummies® titles

Title	Author	ISBN	Price
DATABASE			
Access 2 For Dummies®	by Scott Palmer	ISBN: 1-56884-090-X	$19.95 USA/$26.95 Canada
Access Programming For Dummies®	by Rob Krumm	ISBN: 1-56884-091-8	$19.95 USA/$26.95 Canada
Approach 3 For Windows® For Dummies®	by Doug Lowe	ISBN: 1-56884-233-3	$19.99 USA/$26.99 Canada
dBASE For DOS For Dummies®	by Scott Palmer & Michael Stabler	ISBN: 1-56884-188-4	$19.95 USA/$26.95 Canada
dBASE For Windows® For Dummies®	by Scott Palmer	ISBN: 1-56884-179-5	$19.95 USA/$26.95 Canada
dBASE 5 For Windows® Programming For Dummies®	by Ted Coombs & Jason Coombs	ISBN: 1-56884-215-5	$19.99 USA/$26.99 Canada
FoxPro 2.6 For Windows® For Dummies®	by John Kaufeld	ISBN: 1-56884-187-6	$19.95 USA/$26.95 Canada
Paradox 5 For Windows® For Dummies®	by John Kaufeld	ISBN: 1-56884-185-X	$19.95 USA/$26.95 Canada
DESKTOP PUBLISHING/ILLUSTRATION/GRAPHICS			
CorelDRAW! 5 For Dummies®	by Deke McClelland	ISBN: 1-56884-157-4	$19.95 USA/$26.95 Canada
CorelDRAW! For Dummies®	by Deke McClelland	ISBN: 1-56884-042-X	$19.95 USA/$26.95 Canada
Desktop Publishing & Design For Dummies®	by Roger C. Parker	ISBN: 1-56884-234-1	$19.99 USA/$26.99 Canada
Harvard Graphics 2 For Windows® For Dummies®	by Roger C. Parker	ISBN: 1-56884-092-6	$19.95 USA/$26.95 Canada
PageMaker 5 For Macs® For Dummies®	by Galen Gruman & Deke McClelland	ISBN: 1-56884-178-7	$19.95 USA/$26.95 Canada
PageMaker 5 For Windows® For Dummies®	by Deke McClelland & Galen Gruman	ISBN: 1-56884-160-4	$19.95 USA/$26.95 Canada
Photoshop 3 For Macs® For Dummies®	by Deke McClelland	ISBN: 1-56884-208-2	$19.99 USA/$26.99 Canada
QuarkXPress 3.3 For Dummies®	by Galen Gruman & Barbara Assadi	ISBN: 1-56884-217-1	$19.99 USA/$26.99 Canada
FINANCE/PERSONAL FINANCE/TEST TAKING REFERENCE			
Everyday Math For Dummies™	by Charles Seiter	ISBN: 1-56884-248-1	$14.99 USA/$22.99 Canada
Personal Finance For Dummies™ For Canadians	by Eric Tyson & Tony Martin	ISBN: 1-56884-378-X	$18.99 USA/$24.99 Canada
QuickBooks 3 For Dummies®	by Stephen L. Nelson	ISBN: 1-56884-227-9	$19.99 USA/$26.99 Canada
Quicken 8 For DOS For Dummies® 2nd Edition	by Stephen L. Nelson	ISBN: 1-56884-210-4	$19.95 USA/$26.95 Canada
Quicken 5 For Macs® For Dummies®	by Stephen L. Nelson	ISBN: 1-56884-211-2	$19.95 USA/$26.95 Canada
Quicken 4 For Windows® For Dummies® 2nd Edition	by Stephen L. Nelson	ISBN: 1-56884-209-0	$19.95 USA/$26.95 Canada
Taxes For Dummies,™ 1995 Edition	by Eric Tyson & David J. Silverman	ISBN: 1-56884-220-1	$14.99 USA/$20.99 Canada
The GMAT® For Dummies™	by Suzee Vlk, Series Editor	ISBN: 1-56884-376-3	$14.99 USA/$20.99 Canada
The GRE® For Dummies™	by Suzee Vlk, Series Editor	ISBN: 1-56884-375-5	$14.99 USA/$20.99 Canada
Time Management For Dummies™	by Jeffrey J. Mayer	ISBN: 1-56884-360-7	$16.99 USA/$22.99 Canada
TurboTax For Windows® For Dummies®	by Gail A. Helsel, CPA	ISBN: 1-56884-228-7	$19.99 USA/$26.99 Canada
GROUPWARE/INTEGRATED			
ClarisWorks For Macs® For Dummies®	by Frank Higgins	ISBN: 1-56884-363-1	$19.99 USA/$26.99 Canada
Lotus Notes For Dummies®	by Pat Freeland & Stephen Londergan	ISBN: 1-56884-212-0	$19.95 USA/$26.95 Canada
Microsoft® Office 4 For Windows® For Dummies®	by Roger C. Parker	ISBN: 1-56884-183-3	$19.95 USA/$26.95 Canada
Microsoft® Works 3 For Windows® For Dummies®	by David C. Kay	ISBN: 1-56884-214-7	$19.99 USA/$26.99 Canada
SmartSuite 3 For Dummies®	by Jan Weingarten & John Weingarten	ISBN: 1-56884-367-4	$19.99 USA/$26.99 Canada
INTERNET/COMMUNICATIONS/NETWORKING			
America Online® For Dummies® 2nd Edition	by John Kaufeld	ISBN: 1-56884-933-8	$19.99 USA/$26.99 Canada
CompuServe For Dummies® 2nd Edition	by Wallace Wang	ISBN: 1-56884-937-0	$19.99 USA/$26.99 Canada
Modems For Dummies® 2nd Edition	by Tina Rathbone	ISBN: 1-56884-223-6	$19.99 USA/$26.99 Canada
MORE Internet For Dummies®	by John R. Levine & Margaret Levine Young	ISBN: 1-56884-164-7	$19.95 USA/$26.95 Canada
MORE Modems & On-line Services For Dummies®	by Tina Rathbone	ISBN: 1-56884-365-8	$19.99 USA/$26.99 Canada
Mosaic For Dummies® Windows Edition	by David Angell & Brent Heslop	ISBN: 1-56884-242-2	$19.99 USA/$26.99 Canada
NetWare For Dummies® 2nd Edition	by Ed Tittel, Deni Connor & Earl Follis	ISBN: 1-56884-369-0	$19.99 USA/$26.99 Canada
Networking For Dummies®	by Doug Lowe	ISBN: 1-56884-079-9	$19.95 USA/$26.95 Canada
PROCOMM PLUS 2 For Windows® For Dummies®	by Wallace Wang	ISBN: 1-56884-219-8	$19.99 USA/$26.99 Canada
TCP/IP For Dummies®	by Marshall Wilensky & Candace Leiden	ISBN: 1-56884-241-4	$19.99 USA/$26.99 Canada

Title	Author	ISBN	Price
The Internet For Macs® For Dummies® 2nd Edition	by Charles Seiter	ISBN: 1-56884-371-2	$19.99 USA/$26.99 Canada
The Internet For Macs® For Dummies® Starter Kit	by Charles Seiter	ISBN: 1-56884-244-9	$29.99 USA/$39.99 Canada
The Internet For Macs® For Dummies® Starter Kit Bestseller Edition	by Charles Seiter	ISBN: 1-56884-245-7	$39.99 USA/$54.99 Canada
The Internet For Windows® For Dummies® Starter Kit	by John R. Levine & Margaret Levine Young	ISBN: 1-56884-237-6	$34.99 USA/$44.99 Canada
The Internet For Windows® For Dummies® Starter Kit, Bestseller Edition	by John R. Levine & Margaret Levine Young	ISBN: 1-56884-246-5	$39.99 USA/$54.99 Canada

MACINTOSH

Title	Author	ISBN	Price
Mac® Programming For Dummies®	by Dan Parks Sydow	ISBN: 1-56884-173-6	$19.95 USA/$26.95 Canada
Macintosh® System 7.5 For Dummies®	by Bob LeVitus	ISBN: 1-56884-197-3	$19.95 USA/$26.95 Canada
MORE Macs® For Dummies®	by David Pogue	ISBN: 1-56884-087-X	$19.95 USA/$26.95 Canada
PageMaker 5 For Macs® For Dummies®	by Galen Gruman & Deke McClelland	ISBN: 1-56884-178-7	$19.95 USA/$26.95 Canada
QuarkXPress 3.3 For Dummies®	by Galen Gruman & Barbara Assadi	ISBN: 1-56884-217-1	$19.99 USA/$26.99 Canada
Upgrading and Fixing Macs® For Dummies®	by Kearney Rietmann & Frank Higgins	ISBN: 1-56884-189-2	$19.95 USA/$26.95 Canada

MULTIMEDIA

Title	Author	ISBN	Price
Multimedia & CD-ROMs For Dummies® 2nd Edition	by Andy Rathbone	ISBN: 1-56884-907-9	$19.99 USA/$26.99 Canada
Multimedia & CD-ROMs For Dummies® Interactive Multimedia Value Pack, 2nd Edition	by Andy Rathbone	ISBN: 1-56884-909-5	$29.99 USA/$39.99 Canada

OPERATING SYSTEMS:

DOS

Title	Author	ISBN	Price
MORE DOS For Dummies®	by Dan Gookin	ISBN: 1-56884-046-2	$19.95 USA/$26.95 Canada
OS/2® Warp For Dummies® 2nd Edition	by Andy Rathbone	ISBN: 1-56884-205-8	$19.99 USA/$26.99 Canada

UNIX

Title	Author	ISBN	Price
MORE UNIX® For Dummies®	by John R. Levine & Margaret Levine Young	ISBN: 1-56884-361-5	$19.99 USA/$26.99 Canada
UNIX® For Dummies®	by John R. Levine & Margaret Levine Young	ISBN: 1-878058-58-4	$19.95 USA/$26.95 Canada

WINDOWS

Title	Author	ISBN	Price
MORE Windows® For Dummies® 2nd Edition	by Andy Rathbone	ISBN: 1-56884-048-9	$19.95 USA/$26.95 Canada
Windows® 95 For Dummies®	by Andy Rathbone	ISBN: 1-56884-240-6	$19.99 USA/$26.99 Canada

PCS/HARDWARE

Title	Author	ISBN	Price
Illustrated Computer Dictionary For Dummies® 2nd Edition	by Dan Gookin & Wallace Wang	ISBN: 1-56884-218-X	$12.95 USA/$16.95 Canada
Upgrading and Fixing PCs For Dummies® 2nd Edition	by Andy Rathbone	ISBN: 1-56884-903-6	$19.99 USA/$26.99 Canada

PRESENTATION/AUTOCAD

Title	Author	ISBN	Price
AutoCAD For Dummies®	by Bud Smith	ISBN: 1-56884-191-4	$19.95 USA/$26.95 Canada
PowerPoint 4 For Windows® For Dummies®	by Doug Lowe	ISBN: 1-56884-161-2	$16.99 USA/$22.99 Canada

PROGRAMMING

Title	Author	ISBN	Price
Borland C++ For Dummies®	by Michael Hyman	ISBN: 1-56884-162-0	$19.95 USA/$26.95 Canada
C For Dummies® Volume 1	by Dan Gookin	ISBN: 1-878058-78-9	$19.95 USA/$26.95 Canada
C++ For Dummies®	by Stephen R. Davis	ISBN: 1-56884-163-9	$19.95 USA/$26.95 Canada
Delphi Programming For Dummies®	by Neil Rubenking	ISBN: 1-56884-200-7	$19.99 USA/$26.99 Canada
Mac® Programming For Dummies®	by Dan Parks Sydow	ISBN: 1-56884-173-6	$19.95 USA/$26.95 Canada
PowerBuilder 4 Programming For Dummies®	by Ted Coombs & Jason Coombs	ISBN: 1-56884-325-9	$19.99 USA/$26.99 Canada
QBasic Programming For Dummies®	by Douglas Hergert	ISBN: 1-56884-093-4	$19.95 USA/$26.95 Canada
Visual Basic 3 For Dummies®	by Wallace Wang	ISBN: 1-56884-076-4	$19.95 USA/$26.95 Canada
Visual Basic "X" For Dummies®	by Wallace Wang	ISBN: 1-56884-230-9	$19.99 USA/$26.99 Canada
Visual C++ 2 For Dummies®	by Michael Hyman & Bob Arnson	ISBN: 1-56884-328-3	$19.99 USA/$26.99 Canada
Windows® 95 Programming For Dummies®	by S. Randy Davis	ISBN: 1-56884-327-5	$19.99 USA/$26.99 Canada

SPREADSHEET

Title	Author	ISBN	Price
1-2-3 For Dummies®	by Greg Harvey	ISBN: 1-878058-60-6	$16.95 USA/$22.95 Canada
1-2-3 For Windows® 5 For Dummies® 2nd Edition	by John Walkenbach	ISBN: 1-56884-216-3	$16.95 USA/$22.95 Canada
Excel 5 For Macs® For Dummies®	by Greg Harvey	ISBN: 1-56884-186-8	$19.95 USA/$26.95 Canada
Excel For Dummies® 2nd Edition	by Greg Harvey	ISBN: 1-56884-050-0	$16.95 USA/$22.95 Canada
MORE 1-2-3 For DOS For Dummies®	by John Weingarten	ISBN: 1-56884-224-4	$19.99 USA/$26.99 Canada
MORE Excel 5 For Windows® For Dummies®	by Greg Harvey	ISBN: 1-56884-207-4	$19.95 USA/$26.95 Canada
Quattro Pro 6 For Windows® For Dummies®	by John Walkenbach	ISBN: 1-56884-174-4	$19.95 USA/$26.95 Canada
Quattro Pro For DOS For Dummies®	by John Walkenbach	ISBN: 1-56884-023-3	$16.95 USA/$22.95 Canada

UTILITIES

Title	Author	ISBN	Price
Norton Utilities 8 For Dummies®	by Beth Slick	ISBN: 1-56884-166-3	$19.95 USA/$26.95 Canada

VCRS/CAMCORDERS

Title	Author	ISBN	Price
VCRs & Camcorders For Dummies™	by Gordon McComb & Andy Rathbone	ISBN: 1-56884-229-5	$14.99 USA/$20.99 Canada

WORD PROCESSING

Title	Author	ISBN	Price
Ami Pro For Dummies®	by Jim Meade	ISBN: 1-56884-049-7	$19.95 USA/$26.95 Canada
MORE Word For Windows® 6 For Dummies®	by Doug Lowe	ISBN: 1-56884-165-5	$19.95 USA/$26.95 Canada
MORE WordPerfect® 6 For Windows® For Dummies®	by Margaret Levine Young & David C. Kay	ISBN: 1-56884-206-6	$19.95 USA/$26.95 Canada
MORE WordPerfect® 6 For DOS For Dummies®	by Wallace Wang, edited by Dan Gookin	ISBN: 1-56884-047-0	$19.95 USA/$26.95 Canada
Word 6 For Macs® For Dummies®	by Dan Gookin	ISBN: 1-56884-190-6	$19.95 USA/$26.95 Canada
Word For Windows® 6 For Dummies®	by Dan Gookin	ISBN: 1-56884-075-6	$16.95 USA/$22.95 Canada
Word For Windows® For Dummies®	by Dan Gookin & Ray Werner	ISBN: 1-878058-86-X	$16.95 USA/$22.95 Canada
WordPerfect® 6 For DOS For Dummies®	by Dan Gookin	ISBN: 1-878058-77-0	$16.95 USA/$22.95 Canada
WordPerfect® 6.1 For Windows® For Dummies® 2nd Edition	by Margaret Levine Young & David Kay	ISBN: 1-56884-243-0	$16.95 USA/$22.95 Canada
WordPerfect® For Dummies®	by Dan Gookin	ISBN: 1-878058-52-5	$16.95 USA/$22.95 Canada

Fun, Fast, & Cheap!™

10/31/95

NEW!

The Internet For Macs® For Dummies® Quick Reference
by Charles Seiter

ISBN: 1-56884-967-2
$9.99 USA/$12.99 Canada

NEW!

Windows® 95 For Dummies® Quick Reference
by Greg Harvey

ISBN: 1-56884-964-8
$9.99 USA/$12.99 Canada

SUPER STAR

Photoshop 3 For Macs® For Dummies® Quick Reference
by Deke McClelland

ISBN: 1-56884-968-0
$9.99 USA/$12.99 Canada

SUPER STAR

WordPerfect® For DOS For Dummies® Quick Reference
by Greg Harvey

ISBN: 1-56884-009-8
$8.95 USA/$12.95 Canada

Title	Author	ISBN	Price
DATABASE			
Access 2 For Dummies® Quick Reference	by Stuart J. Stuple	ISBN: 1-56884-167-1	$8.95 USA/$11.95 Canada
dBASE 5 For DOS For Dummies® Quick Reference	by Barrie Sosinsky	ISBN: 1-56884-954-0	$9.99 USA/$12.99 Canada
dBASE 5 For Windows® For Dummies® Quick Reference	by Stuart J. Stuple	ISBN: 1-56884-953-2	$9.99 USA/$12.99 Canada
Paradox 5 For Windows® For Dummies® Quick Reference	by Scott Palmer	ISBN: 1-56884-960-5	$9.99 USA/$12.99 Canada
DESKTOP PUBLISHING/ILLUSTRATION/GRAPHICS			
CorelDRAW! 5 For Dummies® Quick Reference	by Raymond E. Werner	ISBN: 1-56884-952-4	$9.99 USA/$12.99 Canada
Harvard Graphics For Windows® For Dummies® Quick Reference	by Raymond E. Werner	ISBN: 1-56884-962-1	$9.99 USA/$12.99 Canada
Photoshop 3 For Macs® For Dummies® Quick Reference	by Deke McClelland	ISBN: 1-56884-968-0	$9.99 USA/$12.99 Canada
FINANCE/PERSONAL FINANCE			
Quicken 4 For Windows® For Dummies® Quick Reference	by Stephen L. Nelson	ISBN: 1-56884-950-8	$9.95 USA/$12.95 Canada
GROUPWARE/INTEGRATED			
Microsoft® Office 4 For Windows® For Dummies® Quick Reference	by Doug Lowe	ISBN: 1-56884-958-3	$9.99 USA/$12.99 Canada
Microsoft® Works 3 For Windows® For Dummies® Quick Reference	by Michael Partington	ISBN: 1-56884-959-1	$9.99 USA/$12.99 Canada
INTERNET/COMMUNICATIONS/NETWORKING			
The Internet For Dummies® Quick Reference	by John R. Levine & Margaret Levine Young	ISBN: 1-56884-168-X	$8.95 USA/$11.95 Canada
MACINTOSH			
Macintosh® System 7.5 For Dummies® Quick Reference	by Stuart J. Stuple	ISBN: 1-56884-956-7	$9.99 USA/$12.99 Canada
OPERATING SYSTEMS:			
DOS			
DOS For Dummies® Quick Reference	by Greg Harvey	ISBN: 1-56884-007-1	$8.95 USA/$11.95 Canada
UNIX			
UNIX® For Dummies® Quick Reference	by John R. Levine & Margaret Levine Young	ISBN: 1-56884-094-2	$8.95 USA/$11.95 Canada
WINDOWS			
Windows® 3.1 For Dummies® Quick Reference, 2nd Edition	by Greg Harvey	ISBN: 1-56884-951-6	$8.95 USA/$11.95 Canada
PCs/HARDWARE			
Memory Management For Dummies® Quick Reference	by Doug Lowe	ISBN: 1-56884-362-3	$9.99 USA/$12.99 Canada
PRESENTATION/AUTOCAD			
AutoCAD For Dummies® Quick Reference	by Ellen Finkelstein	ISBN: 1-56884-198-1	$9.95 USA/$12.95 Canada
SPREADSHEET			
1-2-3 For Dummies® Quick Reference	by John Walkenbach	ISBN: 1-56884-027-6	$8.95 USA/$11.95 Canada
1-2-3 For Windows® 5 For Dummies® Quick Reference	by John Walkenbach	ISBN: 1-56884-957-5	$9.95 USA/$12.95 Canada
Excel For Windows® For Dummies® Quick Reference, 2nd Edition	by John Walkenbach	ISBN: 1-56884-096-9	$8.95 USA/$11.95 Canada
Quattro Pro 6 For Windows® For Dummies® Quick Reference	by Stuart J. Stuple	ISBN: 1-56884-172-8	$9.95 USA/$12.95 Canada
WORD PROCESSING			
Word For Windows® 6 For Dummies® Quick Reference	by George Lynch	ISBN: 1-56884-095-0	$8.95 USA/$11.95 Canada
Word For Windows® For Dummies® Quick Reference	by George Lynch	ISBN: 1-56884-029-2	$8.95 USA/$11.95 Canada
WordPerfect® 6.1 For Windows® For Dummies® Quick Reference, 2nd Edition	by Greg Harvey	ISBN: 1-56884-966-4	$9.99 USA/$12.99/Canada

Microsoft and Windows are registered trademarks of Microsoft Corporation. Mac and Macintosh are registered trademarks of Apple Computer. UNIX is a registered trademark of AT&T. WordPerfect is a registered trademark of Novell. The "...For Dummies Book Series" logo, the IDG Books Worldwide logos, Dummies Press, The Fun & Easy Way, and Fun, Fast, & Cheap! are trademarks, and ---- For Dummies and ... For Dummies are registered trademarks under exclusive license to IDG Books Worldwide, Inc., from International Data Group, Inc.

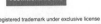

"A lot easier to use than the book Excel gives you!"

Lisa Schmeckpeper, New Berlin, WI, on PC World Excel 5 For Windows Handbook

Official Hayes Modem Communications Companion
by Caroline M. Halliday

ISBN: 1-56884-072-1
$29.95 USA/$39.95 Canada
Includes software.

1,001 Komputer Answers from Kim Komando
by Kim Komando

ISBN: 1-56884-460-3
$29.99 USA/$39.99 Canada
Includes software.

BESTSELLER!

PC World DOS 6 Handbook, 2nd Edition
by John Socha, Clint Hicks, & Devra Hall

ISBN: 1-878058-79-7
$34.95 USA/$44.95 Canada
Includes software.

PC World Word For Windows® 6 Handbook
by Brent Heslop & David Angell

ISBN: 1-56884-054-3
$34.95 USA/$44.95 Canada
Includes software.

BESTSELLER!

PC World Microsoft® Access 2 Bible, 2nd Edition
by Cary N. Prague & Michael R. Irwin

ISBN: 1-56884-086-1
$39.95 USA/$52.95 Canada
Includes software.

PC World Excel 5 For Windows® Handbook, 2nd Edition
by John Walkenbach & Dave Maguiness

ISBN: 1-56884-056-X
$34.95 USA/$44.95 Canada
Includes software.

PC World WordPerfect® 6 Handbook
by Greg Harvey

ISBN: 1-878058-80-0
$34.95 USA/$44.95 Canada
Includes software.

QuarkXPress For Windows® Designer Handbook
by Barbara Assadi & Galen Gruman

ISBN: 1-878058-45-2
$29.95 USA/$39.95 Canada

NATIONAL BESTSELLER!

Official XTree Companion, 3rd Edition
by Beth Slick

ISBN: 1-878058-57-6
$19.95 USA/$26.95 Canada

NATIONAL BESTSELLER!

PC World DOS 6 Command Reference and Problem Solver
by John Socha & Devra Hall

ISBN: 1-56884-055-1
$24.95 USA/$32.95 Canada

SUPER STAR

Client/Server Strategies™: A Survival Guide for Corporate Reengineers
by David Vaskevitch

ISBN: 1-56884-064-0
$29.95 USA/$39.95 Canada

"PC World Word For Windows 6 Handbook is very easy to follow with lots of 'hands on' examples. The 'Task at a Glance' is very helpful!"

Jacqueline Martens, Tacoma, WA

"Thanks for publishing this book! It's the best money I've spent this year!"

Robert D. Templeton, Ft. Worth, TX, on MORE Windows 3.1 SECRETS

10/31/95

Macworld® Mac® & Power Mac SECRETS,™ 2nd Edition
by David Pogue & Joseph Schorr

HOT!

This is the definitive Mac reference for those who want to become power users! Includes three disks with 9MB of software!

ISBN: 1-56884-175-2
$39.95 USA/$54.95 Canada

Includes 3 disks chock full of software.

NEWBRIDGE BOOK CLUB SELECTION

WINNERS 1994-95 TECHNICAL PUBLICATIONS AND ART COMPETITIONS OF THE SOCIETY FOR TECHNICAL COMMUNICATION

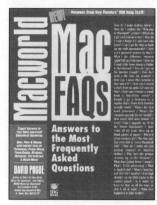

Macworld® Mac® FAQs™
by David Pogue

HOT!

Written by the hottest Macintosh author around, David Pogue, *Macworld Mac FAQs* gives users the ultimate Mac reference. Hundreds of Mac questions and answers side-by-side, right at your fingertips, and organized into six easy-to-reference sections with lots of sidebars and diagrams.

ISBN: 1-56884-480-8
$19.99 USA/$26.99 Canada

Macworld® System 7.5 Bible, 3rd Edition
by Lon Poole

ISBN: 1-56884-098-5
$29.95 USA/$39.95 Canada

NATIONAL BESTSELLER!

Macworld® ClarisWorks 3.0 Companion, 3rd Edition
by Steven A. Schwartz

ISBN: 1-56884-481-6
$24.99 USA/$34.99 Canada

NATIONAL BESTSELLER!

Macworld® Complete Mac® Handbook Plus Interactive CD, 3rd Edition
by Jim Heid

ISBN: 1-56884-192-2
$39.95 USA/$54.95 Canada

Includes an interactive CD-ROM.

NEWBRIDGE BOOK CLUB SELECTION

BMUG SPRING 1995 CHOICE PRODUCT

Macworld® Ultimate Mac® CD-ROM
by Jim Heid

ISBN: 1-56884-477-8
$19.99 USA/$26.99 Canada

CD-ROM includes version 2.0 of QuickTime, and over 65 MB of the best shareware, freeware, fonts, sounds, and more!

Macworld® Networking Bible, 2nd Edition
by Dave Kosiur & Joel M. Snyder

ISBN: 1-56884-194-9
$29.95 USA/$39.95 Canada

Macworld® Photoshop 3 Bible, 2nd Edition
by Deke McClelland

ISBN: 1-56884-158-2
$39.95 USA/$54.95 Canada

Includes stunning CD-ROM with add-ons, digitized photos and more.

WINNERS 1994-95 TECHNICAL PUBLICATIONS AND ART COMPETITIONS OF THE SOCIETY FOR TECHNICAL COMMUNICATION

NEW!

Macworld® Photoshop 2.5 Bible
by Deke McClelland

ISBN: 1-56884-022-5
$29.95 USA/$39.95 Canada

NATIONAL BESTSELLER!

Macworld® FreeHand 4 Bible
by Deke McClelland

ISBN: 1-56884-170-1
$29.95 USA/$39.95 Canada

Macworld® Illustrator 5.0/5.5 Bible
by Ted Alspach

ISBN: 1-56884-097-7
$39.95 USA/$54.95 Canada

Includes CD-ROM with QuickTime tutorials.

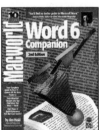

Order Center: **(800) 762-2974** *(8 a.m.–6 p.m., EST, weekdays)*

Quantity	ISBN	Title	Price	Total

Shipping & Handling Charges

	Description	First book	Each additional book	Total
Domestic	Normal	$4.50	$1.50	$
	Two Day Air	$8.50	$2.50	$
	Overnight	$18.00	$3.00	$
International	Surface	$8.00	$8.00	$
	Airmail	$16.00	$16.00	$
	DHL Air	$17.00	$17.00	$

*For large quantities call for shipping & handling charges.
**Prices are subject to change without notice.

Ship to:

Name _____

Company _____

Address _____

City/State/Zip _____

Daytime Phone _____

Payment: ☐ Check to IDG Books Worldwide (US Funds Only)

      ☐ VISA   ☐ MasterCard   ☐ American Express

Card # _____ Expires _____

Signature _____

Subtotal _____

CA residents add
applicable sales tax _____

IN, MA, and MD
residents add
5% sales tax _____

IL residents add
6.25% sales tax _____

RI residents add
7% sales tax _____

TX residents add
8.25% sales tax _____

Shipping _____

Total _____

Please send this order form to:
IDG Books Worldwide, Inc.
7260 Shadeland Station, Suite 100
Indianapolis, IN 46256

Allow up to 3 weeks for delivery.
Thank you!

IDG BOOKS WORLDWIDE REGISTRATION CARD

RETURN THIS REGISTRATION CARD FOR FREE CATALOG

Title of this book: **PowerPoint 4 For Windows For Dummies**

My overall rating of this book: ❏ Very good [1] ❏ Good [2] ❏ Satisfactory [3] ❏ Fair [4] ❏ Poor [5]

How I first heard about this book:

❏ Found in bookstore; name: [6]

❏ Advertisement: [8]

❏ Word of mouth; heard about book from friend, co-worker, etc.: [10]

❏ Book review: [7]

❏ Catalog: [9]

❏ Other: [11]

What I liked most about this book:

What I would change, add, delete, etc., in future editions of this book:

Other comments:

Number of computer books I purchase in a year: ❏ 1 [12] ❏ 2-5 [13] ❏ 6-10 [14] ❏ More than 10 [15]

I would characterize my computer skills as: ❏ Beginner [16] ❏ Intermediate [17] ❏ Advanced [18] ❏ Professional [19]

I use ❏ DOS [20] ❏ Windows [21] ❏ OS/2 [22] ❏ Unix [23] ❏ Macintosh [24] ❏ Other: [25]_____
(please specify)

I would be interested in new books on the following subjects:
(please check all that apply, and use the spaces provided to identify specific software)

❏ Word processing: [26]

❏ Data bases: [28]

❏ File Utilities: [30]

❏ Networking: [32]

❏ Other: [34]

❏ Spreadsheets: [27]

❏ Desktop publishing: [29]

❏ Money management: [31]

❏ Programming languages: [33]

I use a PC at (please check all that apply): ❏ home [35] ❏ work [36] ❏ school [37] ❏ other: [38] _____

The disks I prefer to use are ❏ 5.25 [39] ❏ 3.5 [40] ❏ other: [41]_____

I have a CD ROM: ❏ yes [42] ❏ no [43]

I plan to buy or upgrade computer hardware this year: ❏ yes [44] ❏ no [45]

I plan to buy or upgrade computer software this year: ❏ yes [46] ❏ no [47]

Name: _____ Business title: [48] _____ Type of Business: [49] _____

Address (❏ home [50] ❏ work [51]/Company name: _____)

Street/Suite# _____

City [52]/State [53]/Zipcode [54]: _____ Country [55] _____

❏ **I liked this book!** You may quote me by name in future
IDG Books Worldwide promotional materials.

My daytime phone number is _____

IDG BOOKS

THE WORLD OF
COMPUTER
KNOWLEDGE